Communication and the Human Condition

W. Barnett Pearce

Southern Illinois University Press
Carbondale and Edwardsville

92 91 90 89   4 3 2 1

Library of Congress Cataloging-in-Publication Data

Pearce, W. Barnett.
    Communication and the human condition.

    Bibliography: p.
    Includes index.
    1. Communication—Social aspects. I. Title.
HM258.P4 1989   302.2   88-30565
ISBN 0-8093-1411-8
ISBN 0-8093-1412-6 (pbk.)

for
Nur Intan Murtadza
among other things, my favorite pianist

Contents

Illustrations   ix

Acknowledgments   xi

Introduction   xiii

I. The Communication Perspective

    1. The Discovery of Communication   3

    2. Coordination   32

    3. Coherence and Mystery   67

II. Forms of Communication and Ways of Being Human

    4. "Forms" and "Ways"   91

    5. Monocultural Communication   96

    6. Ethnocentric Communication   118

    7. Modernity   134

    8. Neotraditional Communication, Wails, and Relativism   156

    9. Cosmopolitan Communication   167

    10. The Practicality of Cosmopolitan Communication   196

Bibliography   207

Index   215

Illustrations

Figures

1–1. The "communication perspective"   24
2–1. Coordination problems in high places   33
2–2. The process of coordination in communication   38
2–3. Four aspects of logical force   40
2–4. Rules for the game "Coordination"   41
2–5. A practice that reconstructs resources   46
2–6. A stable hierarchy   47
2–7. Abstract model of a strange loop   47
2–8. The alcoholic's strange loop   48
2–9. The prisoner's dilemma   64
5–1. Relationships among the resources of primitive society   104
6–1. Relationships among resources in traditional society   125
7–1. The apparent structure of modern society   140
7–2. The strange loop of modernity   145
7–3. The actual structure of modernity   150
9–1. Interaction between the new Christian right and secular humanists 176

Plates

5–1. Baby talk   100
6–1. A Cardinal instructs a scholar   130
7–1. The pursuit of knowledge   139
7–2. A disillusionment with modernistic communication   149
9–1. Who's observing whom   179

Acknowledgments

My friend and colleague, Vernon E. Cronen, has been my intellectual companion for fifteen years, during which we have argued against each other, stood with each other against common foes, nurtured successive generations of students, comforted each other in our paradigm shifts and watched each other's hair turn gray. Virtually every page of this book contains ideas we have hammered out between us. I find it impossible to reconstruct whose was the originating impulse, whose the restraining hand, and whose the secondary and tertiary "reframing." Although it is customary to absolve one's colleagues for mistakes, I shall not continue the custom. He is responsible for *some* of the mistakes of judgment in these pages, just as he is responsible for much of the "good stuff." He is vindicated only because I am the storyteller this time.

Many students contributed to the development of these ideas. Those who enrolled in COMM 312 at the University of Massachusetts, Amherst, were in many ways the inspiration (and sometimes the dis-inspiration) for these ideas. They were the audience whose reaction told me how various materials "played" and sometimes the source of specific information and phrases. Because of them, the book is considerably shorter than it otherwise would have been.

Five students contributed especially much. Robert J. Branham, now associate professor of rhetoric and communication at Bates College, was my primary intellectual companion when working out the ideas on "mystery." Kyung-wha Kang, who now lectures at Yonsei University and works for the Korean Broadcasting Service, was my partner in developing the basic conceptual moves that differentiate the "forms of communication." Michele Gielis, then a double major in communication and anthropology, assisted me in accessing and understanding a great deal of ethnographic data that enriched the discussion of various ways of being human. Victoria Chen improved the manuscript with her close reading and triumphant discoveries of nonstandard punctuation and spelling. She also helped me into the current literature on "representation," which informs the latter chapters. Deb Johnson helped in the final stages of preparing the manuscript and sharpened my thinking about "irony" as a part of cosmopolitan communication.

Stephen Littlejohn, professor at Humboldt State University, was the source of the greatest encouragement for perservering through the lonely days of preparing the manuscript and of the sharpest, most helpful/painful criticisms of particular passages. He and Sally Freeman, associate dean of the College of Arts and Sciences at the University of Massachusetts, were also the primary models for what I know of "cosmopolitan communication."

In 1977 I received a Faculty Growth Grant for Teaching from the University of Massachusetts, which enabled me to devote a full summer to the acquisition of materials for the first offering of COMM 312. For that, I am deeply grateful.

Finally, staff members of the Department of Communication were particularly nurturing. They were unresentful of my distraction when I was trying to work something out and my impatience to see it in clear type, and they made me feel that this project was in part their own. In particular, Debra Madigan was protective of my time spent working on the manuscript and resourceful in converting what passes for my penmanship into coherent English.

Introduction

People often talk past each other. Even when their conversation appears coherent and well coordinated, they may subsequently give vastly different accounts of what they were talking about and what each said.

College professors have to develop a certain callousness: when they read their students' exams or their colleagues' review of their work, they may not recognize what they thought they had said in lectures or publications. This is a general phenomenon, of course. Politicians are daily surprised by newspaper accounts of their doings, and when group gossip finishes, the events of the day are likely much more interesting than when they happened.

These situations surround us all, and it is possible to simply disregard them or to take them as a normal part of the business of being human. But much of my professional life (and perhaps more of my personal life than I would be comfortable admitting) has been shaped by my unwillingness or inability to ignore instances of "poor" communication. Not only can I not remain oblivious to them, my own "moral order" makes me feel compelled to "improve" them.

My feeling of obligation to improve communication stems less from an altruistic desire to help others than from my impatience with unnecessary error and my selfish desire to live in a world not filled with unnecessary perils. I find little esthetic pleasure in lengthy quarrels that could be settled by an explanation to each of what the other means. (Perhaps this is why I was so quickly attracted to the American Pragmatists— although had I read Wittgenstein earlier, I might well have become thoroughly enmeshed in his project.) I enjoy good argument and am offended by its counterfeit: acrimonious quarrels in which "nonartistic proofs" such as intimidation and the ability to bluster are empowered. I want to live in a world in which the normal business of life (sewers, traffic safety, banking, the supply of goods and services) is done well and without unnecessary hassle, and in which I can realistically envision peace and prosperity for myself and my family. When I hear world leaders engaging in discourse that has all the subtlety and sophistication of two boys on a schoolyard using each other as foils against which to prove their budding manhood, I am distressed. The world is sufficiently interesting that excitement does not have to be generated artificially by unnecessary human conflict; it is sufficiently complicated that my time need not be occupied by the tangles of misunderstandings objectified in the institutions in which I work and play; and it is sufficiently dangerous that the perils of war need not be added to those of famine, flood, disease, and pestilence.

However motivated, the desire to improve communication does not necessarily carry with it a notion of how to go about it. In a more naïve stage of life, I tried to "improve" communication by explaining to the persons involved how they had misunderstood each other. In a number of painful lessons, I learned that self-appointed interpreters of the differences among what others said, what they meant, and what they were heard to have said are seldom thanked for their services. Further, I learned that conflicts are seldom "resolved" even if the participants can be brought to the happy state of reciprocal understanding. Two women may understand perfectly each other's feelings toward the same man, and this may intensify rather than reduce their conflict. Finally, I learned that poor communication is self-sustaining, and for many of the participants, the conflict itself is more important than the ostensible "object."

Assume that two persons (or groups or nations) have conflicting claims about the ownership of a parcel of land, and have different notions of how such conflicts should be resolved. They state their own claim according to the "script" they envision for "conflict management." Because these scripts differ, each litigant is offended by the *manner* in which the other presents the claim, as well as by the *content* of the claim. As a result, each seeks to oppose not only the other's claim, but the manner of and the right of the other one to make it. At this point, the parcel of land—the ostensible object of the conflict—is superfluous; were the land to disappear in an earthquake, the conflict could continue without interruption. The principals can sustain their conflict based entirely on their perceptions of the perfidy or stupidity of the other, or the moral inadequacy of the other's script for conducting a conflict.

Patterns of communication like these are sometimes dangerous and usually unproductive but always inelegant. When asked I sometimes describe my work as dealing with "conflict management"; ways of describing and intervening in patterns of communication like these.

Conflict management is a useful fiction because it makes my interlocutors think they know what I mean and it opens the way for further talk that gets at my real interests. The more accurate response—that I am interested in the coevolutionary relationship between forms of communication and ways of being human, with particular attention to the communicative requisites of contemporary society—is a guaranteed conversation-stopper. But conflict management as generally understood is a fiction. It is usually taken to refer to an array of techniques that, if skillfully employed, can terminate "conflicts" and restore interpersonal relationships to a nonconflictful state. To the contrary, I have come to believe that conflict inevitably and inexorably arises from fundamental tensions in the human condition, and that these tensions can be coped with in a variety of forms, but never "solved." By conflict management I mean the form of communication in which we engage with our fellows.

Despite its grandiose title, *Communication and the Human Condition* explicates a simple observation: there are qualitatively different forms of communication, each of which affords a particular array of opportunities and problems. I first remember making this observation when confronted by adult guardians of the cookie jar (which, at that stage of my development, was the repository of the most desired treasures I knew to covet). I found that polite requests were more successful than demands or whines in getting a cookie, and that they led to more satisfactory relationships with the guardians. In retrospect, it seems that most of my professional life has been spent in an attempt to articulate this childish observation. In the more mature version, it consists in a more adequate taxonomy of communication forms, a more scientific analysis of what makes these forms occur, a more accurate description of what each form facilitates and what it impedes, and an account of how these forms of communication shape and are shaped by the structure of social life. The quest has led from the cookie jar to an attempt to understand the human condition in many of its varied forms.

(The "cookie jar" anecdote tells more about the culture of my family than about the role of politeness in human affairs; not all families follow the same rules of meaning and action. My point has to do with differentiable forms of communication, however, which simultaneously "fit" the social contexts in which they occur and create those contexts.)

In the adult world, the stakes are higher than access to the cookie jar, and amicable relationships among nations and persons more important than personal preference. The annual expenditure of billions of dollars for weapons while programs to feed the hungry, heal the sick, educate the young, protect the environment, and explore the universe are underfunded is shameful. Cogent arguments of great persuasiveness are frequently advanced showing that, given the present situation, military expenditures must be given first priority. It is not my purpose to rebut these arguments; rather, I cite them as *prima facie* proof of the shamefulness of "the present situation."

Note that my judgment of "shameful" applies to the context in which persons act, not (necessarily) to the actors themselves. If "the present situation" is such that weapons are more important than food or disaster relief, then the situation—not just the morals of the individuals involved in it—is seriously at fault. The historical pattern of relationships among nations constitutes a form of communication that facilitates xenophobia, jingoism, superpatriotism, and war; it impedes international understanding, cooperation, and the evolution of civility. The "present situation" embodies a moral order in which altruistic acts are disempowered, whereas suspicion, trickery, and deceit are "winning moves."

Any self-respecting civilization would find preferable forms of communication. Surely there are alternatives to the same old episodes of hot and cold wars resulting from the performance of scripts based on the notion of "peace through strength" coupled with the practice of defining "others" as "enemies" and of engaging in "strategic" thinking based on the assumption that "enemies" will make whatever mischief of which they are capable. Our civilization celebrates its creativity and technological prowess, but this creativity has not yet been extended to patterns of communication among nations or individuals. Modern men and women are probably more like their primitive forebears in their interpersonal relationships than in any other way.

How can we bear this shame?

My first book (Rossiter and Pearce, 1975) attempted to differentiate forms of communication. In retrospect, it clearly was limited by the social milieu in which it was written and was conceptually far too naïve.

My second book (Pearce and Cronen, 1980) explicated the discovery that persons live *in* communication rather than somehow standing outside it and "using" communication for other purposes. This discovery makes the process of identifying forms of communication simultaneously more difficult and more important. It is more difficult because the shape of things is harder to discern from inside than from outside, and the attempt to talk about forms of communication quickly becomes reflexively convoluted. In what form of discourse, one might inquire, may forms of discourse be described? Are forms of communication equal in their ability to describe forms of communication, or—as seems more likely—are some forms of communication inherently restrictive in their ability to detect and describe other communication forms?

The process of describing forms of communication is made more important because the discovery that we live *in* communication transmutes communication from a secondary to a primary role in human life. Rather than a means by which "internal" states are expressed and "objective" facts represented, communication is that process by which "persons," "institutions," and "facts" are constructed. Instead of a process that *should* be odorless, colorless, tasteless, and with neither redundancy nor distortion, the characteristics of communication are seen as endemic to human nature. In addition to the determinants of attitude change or the components of rhetorical flourishes, communication theory, I came to believe, must deal with what it means to live a life, the shape of social institutions and cultural traditions, the pragmatics of social action, and the poetics of social order. My third book (Narula and Pearce, 1986) documented the forms of communication between the development bureaucracy and the inhabitants of two communities in India. We found that their form of communication unintentionally created a problem that retarded development, and that "more" communication (of the same type) would only make the problem worse.

Communication and the Human Condition continues my concern for forms of communication. However, my treatment of this topic was shaped by the mundane fact that, not being independently wealthy or having a financial patron, I have to work for a living.

My job, then and now, is that of a professor in an American state university. This job imposes a peculiar set of constraints and opportunities, most of which stem from the assignment to confront diverse sets of students and, by some mysterious process, to "educate" them. Given this responsibility, professors either reconcile themselves to explaining the "same" material to each successive class, or they find/write textbooks that will do it for them. The content of my "yellowed lecture notes" did not impress me sufficiently for me to spend my energies polishing the delivery of my lectures, and I was not satisfied with any of the books that might serve as "texts." As a result, I began improvising lectures, then writing them down; reviewing literature and writing summaries; taking problematics and writing essays, and so forth. In 1977 I began offering a new course at the University of Massachusetts: COMM 312: Communication and the Human Condition. The reading materials that I provided for my students were a diverse lot, ranging from diagrams of intellectual history, ethnographies, analyses of contemporary events, essays in the philosophy of science, poems, photographs of artistic or cultural artifacts, and worse.

All of this was an attempt to come to grips with a series of learnings about communication that was sustained (semester-long), coherent (comprehensible to undergraduates), and permanent (so I would neither have to hold it "in my head" nor repeat it in lectures to each new class). At each point during the last decade, the process of writing required me to make more clear what I needed to say, and—by functioning as a text—freed me to push on, letting each new learning lead to the next.

Anyone who writes and gives lectures for a living must have some faint sense of a storyteller, and it is my opinion that this story is ready to be told as a whole rather than as a jumble of pieces, and to a larger audience than to my students in COMM 312.

Starting with the premise that we live *in* communication, this book claims that persons who live in various cultures and historical epochs do not "merely" communicate differently, but experience different ways of being human *because* they communicate differently. At this point, I try to outflank Marx in much the same way that he claimed to have turned Hegel on his head: rather than arguing whether "infrastructure" determines "superstructure" or vice versa, I claim that both are a part of a coevolutionary process whose ontological substance consists in the aggregate of (often mundane) communicative actions. The driving force of history—it seems to me incontestable—is the way that persons speak, listen, posture, strike, ignore—and the like—among themselves. This includes, of course, the hand that rocks the cradle as well as the finger on the button that starts World War III; it includes patterns of honesty and politeness as well as agreements about the distribution of wealth and power; and it includes praying congregations as well as marching armies, spending consumers and unionized workers. Finally, the story attempts to describe and evaluate several "forms" of communication.

In saying that the story is ready to be told as a whole, I mean that it is a complete story, not that it is "finished." I suspect that our descendents will think of us as "primitives": we barely comprehend the powers of our minds and have what our descendents will consider to be only the most murky concepts of the social institutions in which we live. The best that we can hope for is their respect, like that accorded the valor of individual members of defeated armies. This book will be judged a success if it consolidates some "gains" made in the discovery of communication and in explorations of its nature, and if it serves as a basis for further advances.

All stories, I suspect, are told *to* particular audiences. I have three overlapping audiences in mind. The first is the rapidly growing number of persons who do formal study of communication in college classrooms. For them, *Communication and the Human Condition* is a nontechnical statement of "the coordinated management of meaning" (Pearce and Cronen, 1980) and an extension of it.

The second audience is broader, including the eclectic, intellectually alive public that already participates in contemporary discussion on the meaning and quality of life, the nature and destiny of humankind, and the proper evaluation of particular forms of social institutions. "Communication" is already an important word for this group; it will become even more central and be used in a more sophisticated manner.

Much of this group's concern about communication has been prompted by technology. New technologies of communication have empowered communicators to do more, faster, at greater distances, and with less effort than ever before, and they have greedily been put into play by those who would speak, write, listen, eavesdrop, monitor, organize, inform, persuade, educate, or entertain. These amplified powers have raised with new intensity some old questions. When an advocate approaches an audience, who is persuaded, and for what reasons? What are the available means of persuasion, and what consequences adhere to their use? When the truth is not sufficient to persuade, what else—if anything—is legitimate? Should certain forms or processes of communication be regulated in order to protect the current social order, and if so, by whom? How can an educated audience discern among truth, rhetorical tricks, and the biases of language or media? What is the role of communication in decision-making and its connections to logic, to power, to reality, and to truth? Is communication a prerequisite of the state, the church, or the political party, or is it a "right" for all humankind? If a "right," does it adhere to each individual or to society as a collectivity?

These are not new questions. Most can be traced at least as far back as the fourth century B.C. when the Greeks made "rhetoric" one of their civilization's special interests. However, the events of this century—from demagogues like Goebbels and McCarthy, debates about the New International Information and Communication Order, and concern about what effects derive from children's consumption of vast quantities of ostensibly entertainment programs—confirm that these questions continue to outstrip the answers we have for them.

In addition, new questions have presented themselves. Does the current structure of international communication perpetuate the economic exploitation of the Third World by its former colonizers? Does capitalist ownership of the dominant forms of communication media sustain a particular ideology? If so, what are the alternatives? What are the implications of living in an information-saturated environment for society, for personalities, for personal relationships? In what ways will the new communication technologies affect ways of doing business, government, and education? What are the biases of electronic media, and do these biases facilitate or impede democratic processes? What forms of religion, philosophy, and business are possible and desirable in an environment of mass communication, interactive telecommunications, and data-based computer networks? Will increased ease of transportation and communication erode cultural differences, producing a monoculture based on fast foods, disposable clothing, and transient relationships? Although these questions seem to outweigh their answers, a sophisticated understanding of communication seems to be more central than had been thought.

The third audience includes those with a professional interest in communication. This is a surprisingly large and diverse group of persons. Historically, communication theory is culturally Western. However, the worldwide spread of "modernity" carried with it sufficient strands of westernization that now there are communication professionals in every nation.

Communication is difficult to study. The problem is reflexivity: one cannot study or talk about or observe communication without engaging in communication. This feature of communication has been perceived by savants of all cultures, and treated in ways consistent with their own intellectual and institutional heritage, but seldom as an academic discipline, as a curriculum available to a broad spectrum of the populace, or as communication theory. For example, Cheng (1980) showed how the cultural milieu of China oriented persons away from a "theory" of communication, and how such a theory—had one somehow been developed—would have denied its own nature as a "theory."

The turbulent times of the "classical" period in Greece provided an exception. The first discipline of communication arose as a combination of three factors. First, political upheaval did away with traditional standards for thought and action; there was no consensual criterion for adjudicating among different opinions or contested claims (e.g., for ownership of property). Not only the content of beliefs but the institutions for verifying them were put at issue. Second, communication—in this case public oral argument—was taken seriously, institutionalized as the means of conducting public business. Communication as the means of government accompanied the democratization of the Greek cities: instead of the decree of tyrants, oral argument was used to persuade a jury about the praise or blame merited by a politician and the guilt or innocence of those accused of crimes. Third, an intellectual pattern for what knowledge should look like was proposed by the venerable triad of Socrates, Plato, and Aristotle, and—for good or ill—knowledge of communication was cast in that mold. Socrates and Plato believed that knowledge must be of "general" or "real" things, not merely of "particulars" or "accidents." Knowledge, thus, must be eternal, immutable, and ahistorical.

The discipline known as "rhetoric" emerged from this milieu. Social and political instability helped new ideas, including rhetoric, to gain a hearing. The institutionalization of talk as the means of politics coupled intellectual interests with practical necessity, spawning a new breed of professionals (Sophists) who offered instruction in public speaking. And, at the price of squashing many of the insights of the Sophists, the prevailing philosophical schools legitimated the study of persuasion as a part of the Western intellectual enterprise. With the usual ironies and meanderings, this tradition of rhetoric extends from the fourth century B.C. to the present.

The rhetorical tradition was reborn three times in the United States in the twentieth century. The first rebirth occurred when Charles Woolbert applied the research methods of behavioral psychology to the rhetorical agenda posed by Aristotle. This initiated what became known as the Midwestern School of Speech. In the 1920s, Herbert Wichelns and others initiated the Cornell School of Rhetoric by combining history and current events with the formal study of classical rhetorical treatises. The Cornell and Midwestern schools, in a loose and often bitterly confrontational alliance, established a professional organization in 1914, now known as the Speech Communication Association. The third rebirth derived from interdisciplinary studies and activities that named "communication" their common thread. The essays of John Dewey and George Herbert Mead might have become the dominant frame for this movement, but did not. Instead, a largely unaffiliated group of Communication Research Institutes or Centers (CRIs or CRCs) were developed. They drew, in differing proportions, from the political/sociological work of Paul Lazarsfield, Harold Lasswell, Wilbur Schramm, Bernard Berelson, Carl Hovland, and Elihu Katz; the cybernetic theories of Norbert Wiener and the information theories of Claude Shannon; the studies of communication patterns in business organizations by Charles Redding; and the General Semantics of Alfred Korzybski and S. I. Hayakawa. The CRCs at Stanford, Illinois, and Columbia, and the research projects at Yale created a climate for the formation in 1950 of the National Society for the Study of Communication, which changed its name in 1960 to the International Communication Association.

Outside the United States, both intellectual and political events led to the development of the profession. Primarily centered in the Frankfurt School in Germany and the Birmingham School of Cultural Studies in England, the evolution of critical theory found itself focusing on the processes of communication. Also in England, analytical philosophy turned its attention to understanding "what we mean by what we say," or, as in the title of J. L. Austin's classic book, *How to Do Things with Words*. In the Third World, the sudden emergence of over a hundred "new" nations, most of which were politically shaky, economically disadvantaged, and well aware of a history of colonial exploitation, created two agendas that involved communication. The first was the task of economic and political development, a process in which communication was thought to play an important instrumental role; the second was the discovery that asymmetrical patterns of international communication perpetuated the world wide pattern of exploitation of the new nations.

As a result, "development communication" became a large state-sponsored profession. Most new nations instituted communication policies designed to further the interests of the government vis-à-vis former colonizers. International associations were formed to facilitate communication among Third World states (e.g., the Asian News Network). Various information and documentation centers were established (e.g., the Asian Mass Communication and Information Centre in Singapore). An impassioned debate began in UNESCO and in the International Association for Mass Communication Research about the establishment of a New International Information and Communication Order.

The diversity of communication professionals is thus one of the most salient characteristics of this segment of our audience. Their diversity can be expressed by using the central organizing themes of part I: coherence, coordination, and mystery.

Coherence alludes to those who tell the stories by which our culture interprets itself and the world around us. Novelists, editorialists, publishers, television producers, development agents, politicians, advertisers, teachers, actors, reporters, and grandparents are all storytellers.

Coordination identifies those who facilitate interaction among persons. Judges, coaches, public relations directors, trainers, ombudsmen, personnel directors, mediators, police officers, and parents are all involved in setting patterns for coordination— or for intervening when these patterns do not work.

Mystery connotes those whose work reminds us that there is more to life than the mere facts of daily existence. Artists, poets, priests, prophets, ministers, historians, philosophers, science fiction writers, fantasists, and children are all reminders of mystery.

I write with a sense of urgency. There are jeremiads all around warning us of catastrophe if we do not solve a whole series of problems that seem insolvable: ecological pollution, political oppression, economic imbalance, genetic tampering, threats to public health, the population explosion, and escalating militarism. Perhaps these problems can be solved by a new technology here, a vaccine there, and a political reform elsewhere, and I commend those whose energies are aimed in these directions. However, I suspect that these problems will not so much be solved as bypassed by a new socio-politico-economic order. It is not at all certain that the emergence of such an order would be an improvement. A worldwide epidemic would reduce the population problem (for a while) and bypass others; an international economic depression might bypass escalating militarism and the effects of recombinant DNA research. But neither of these is a "solution" and neither is particularly desirable.

The best that can happen is a major step forward in our understanding of ourselves that will reconstruct social institutions as well as informal ways of treating each other. Moral orders evolve (or at least change) just as do physical orders. There was a time when war was considered good sport for kings and when society was thought to require such a sporting monarch. Through a process of increasing social sensitivity, in part fostered by technological innovations, these ideas now seem unfashionable and dangerous. What practices, now taken for granted, should join these as outmoded remnants of a less enlightened age? The patterns of relationships embedded in contemporary society are obviously in flux. What is the shape of the forms of communication that will emerge as better suited to the material and social conditions of postmodern society?

I believe that the "materials" for a major evolutionary step in patterns of social relationships are now available; it requires only (!) to assemble them, assess their significance, and implement them as viable programs. This social development is the "communication revolution," where communication is not understood simply as ways of getting messages from one place to another or even as a set of techniques for increasing our understanding of each other, but as the process by which reality itself and with it particular ways of being human are co-constructed in all those events where we interact with each other. As Jürgen Habermas argued in *Legitimation Crisis,* "if the form of life reflected in such system-conforming rewards as money, free time, and security can no longer be convincingly legitimated, the 'pursuit of happiness' might one day mean something different—for example, not accumulating material objects of which one disposes privately, but bringing about social relations in which mutuality predominates and satisfaction does not mean the triumph of one over the repressed needs of the other" (McCarthy, 1979, p. xxiv).

I.
The Communication Perspective

1.
The "Discovery" of Communication

Future historians who record what is being said and done today will find it difficult to avoid giving a prominent place to our preoccupation with communication
Richard McKeon, *Communication, Truth and Society*

It seems a bit presumptuous to speak of the "discovery" of communication. Human beings have always communicated, and have always known that they were communicating. However, the extent to which our contemporaries talk about communication is unprecedented, as is the amount of importance they attribute to it.

There is considerable talk of a "communication revolution" borne by successive waves of technological innovations each of which alters the capacity for society to inform, amuse, and persuade itself. Some analysts greet this revolution ecstatically; the musings of others are tinged with a disquieting sense that something is being done to us that we do not fully understand and of which we may not approve. "The realm of communications . . . has undergone . . . a series of revolutions . . . already more than a century old, the end of which is yet beyond our vision or prevision" (Matson and Montagu, 1967, p. 1).

More importantly, there is a revolutionary discovery that communication is, and always has been, far more central to whatever it means to be a human being than had ever before been supposed. Prior to this century, no major analysis of international relations explained inequitable standards of life or power as the result of a particular pattern of communication between nations, but this is a common theme today. No major analysis of the form of government focused on the media and channels of communication, but this is a common orientation today. No interpretation of the pathologies of individuals or families cited patterns of communication as the causes of problems or the means of their solution, but this is a unifying concept in half a dozen disciplines today. Philosophers in all cultures and in all ages have wrestled with apparently insolvable problems of ethics, esthetics, and cosmology, but only in this century did many of them become convinced that these were problems of language rather than of the nature of reality itself. Some social scientists claim that "the world" exists in communication; that the apparently stable event/objects of the social world—from economic systems to personality traits to "dinner with friends"—are collectively constructed in patterns of conversations; and that the "solution" to (some? most? all?) problems consists in changing the conversations we have about them.

The title of this book brazenly links "communication" with "the human condition." Although such a connection has precedent, it remains at the intellectual avant-garde. The human condition deals with "mysteries": fundamental, existential questions of life, meaning, and human destiny. Scholarly conversations about these topics have not usually included communication theorists. Priests and prophets have been listened to for discourse about God and the good. Social scientists have spoken often about the means of accomplishing politicians' goals and sometimes well about the way current institutions broker power and mask oppression. Politicians of every sort are prepared to show how their vision of the national interest is involved in a wide range of policy choices. What have communication theorists to add to these conversations?

Pairing "the human condition" with "communication" seems asymmetrical. The former seems to overbalance the latter, something like "Mosquitoes and the Meaning of Life" or "Sammy's Used Umbrella Stand and the Origin of the Universe." The new voice that communication theorists bring to venerable questions presupposes a radically new concept of what communication is like, what work it does, and how it works. Traditional notions of communication see it as a tool, undoubtedly useful but still only an instrument by which persons accomplish other, more important purposes, such as instructing, amusing, or insulting others. Some believe that communication(s) is a name for an industry specializing in the transmission of messages—and needs to be regulated. Others think of it as a part of relationships between persons where "problems" occur with distressing frequency, or something that "breaks down" with frustrating consequences, or a commodity of which it would be nice if we had "more."

A more sophisticated understanding of communication has evolved in this century. It makes its pairing with "the human condition" appropriate. This understanding has followed (rather than led) an increased interest in communication resulting from three interrelated factors: new communication technologies; an appreciation of the economic and political significance of communication; and developments in humanistic and scientific thinking about communication.

New Communication Technologies

From "wireless" to videotext, developments in the technological capacity to produce, record, transmit, and transform messages is the most visible occasion for the discovery of communication. Books, radio, television, computers, satellite "dish" antennas, talk shows, street demonstrations, commercials, and political campaigns are cultural artifacts continuously reminding us that we communicate continuously, and that our technological capacity to communicate expands continuously. Quite simply put, ordinary citizens of a contemporary industrial society can do things that were not only impossible but unthinkable even for the elites of most of the civilizations that have existed on this planet. Further, we can contemplate with some assurance that persons in each succeeding generation will be able to communicate faster, farther away, and with less distortion than those in previous generations, and with less effort.

The rate of technological development has reached such a point that even gifted imaginations are hard pressed to keep up with the vanguard of research and development institutes. For example, literally hundreds of science fiction stories about the first person to land on the moon were published before it happened in 1969. Many were quite accurate in their descriptions of the mechanics of space flight and about the experience of astronauts in lunar gravity and an airless environment. Writing in the eighteenth century, Jules Verne even guessed that the first journey to the moon would be made by Americans (he thought them natural mechanics) and would leave from Florida. (Somehow I am relieved to note that he did not refer to the Kennedy Space Flight Center by name!) However, *none* of those stories anticipated that the first human footstep on the moon would be watched "live" on television by hundreds of millions of persons all over the earth!

The most recent (fifteenth) edition of the *Encyclopaedia Britannica* contains a supplement in which "communications" is listed alongside other things one might want to know about the nations of the world, such as major cities, economies, education, population, religion, and the like. The communications entry includes statistics for various nations' newspaper circulation, radio stations, ratio of receivers to population, and so forth.

The first edition of the encyclopedia, published in 1768–1771, contained no such list. The editors of that edition would probably have been astonished at the idea of giving "communication" such prominence. Somewhat defensively, the editors of the fifteenth edition (vol. 3, p. 45) wrote: "Although Aristotle discussed dramatic and literary communication in his *Poetics* and *Rhetoric*, explicit definitions and theories of communication were not proposed until after the twentieth-century advances in science and technology that gave rise to the mass communications media." The editors of the *Britannica* were wrong: by the start of the twentieth century, a long and sometimes distinguished tradition of "explicit definitions and theories of communication" had been proposed. However, the *Britannica*'s hyperbole accurately expresses the twentieth-century communication theorists' belief that they were starting something new. Not creation ex nihilo, surely, but certainly a renaissance.

There is a shrill tone of excitement in the voices of those who contemplate the effects of communication technology. In *The Communications Revolution* (1982), Frederick Williams (p. 11) claimed: "We are changing. Not just in our institutions, the automobiles we buy, nor the fashions we wear, but in how we behave as human beings. . . .The contemporary explosion in communications technologies—computers, satellites, tape, disc, microprocessors, and new telephone and radio services—are perceptively changing the nature of our human environment."

Yoneji Masuda, in *The Information Society as Post-Industrial Society* (1981), speculated about the shape of society in the twenty-first century. It will be unique in human history, he suggested, because it will be "invisible" (p. 156), based on information rather than material artifacts such as the huge skyscrapers and superhighways of the twentieth century. Envisioning a "computopia," Masuda claimed that communication technology is the most important development in ten thousand years.

In *The Coming Information Age* (1982), Wilson Dizard imagined a society of unprecedented creativity aided by communication technology. He recalled the dictum of the great American inventor Thomas A. Edison, who said that "genius" is composed of 99 percent perspiration and 1 percent inspiration. This ratio of effort to creative product is sufficiently daunting to dull the genius of all but the most inspired or the most disciplined. But what, Dizard asks, if the ratio could be changed? Information networks linking home computers to data bases and computational resources would enable creativity with less perspiration. Dizard believes a nation that exploits its communication technology will be filled with the inventive equivalents of Edisons and Einsteins!

Economics and Politics

Communication has become "big business," and where money goes, interest follows. The communication revolution has not only increased individuals' capacity to generate and transmit messages, it has changed the institutions of society and the roles to which ambitious young persons aspire.

This effect is most clearly seen by comparison. The industrial revolution did more than simply produce an array of machines where none had existed before; it created a whole new relationship between wealth and land. Previously, a given area of the earth's surface had a fixed potential for producing wealth, and the only way to increase income was to conquer, buy, or annex new territory. With industrialization, however, the degree of technological sophistication determined how much wealth could be produced, and relatively small areas became more prosperous than less developed, larger areas. Profound social changes followed: new professions; new crimes; new visions of hope and of despair.

In the same way, the communication revolution has profoundly affected the visions, vices, and vocations of contemporary society. "Information" has unique properties that require the development of new ethical and legal principles. For example, we have long had the doctrine of "fighting words." In American law, specific words are considered equivalent to a physical assault. Now we have to decide whether unauthorized access to data files stored in a computer constitutes theft, trespass, or an exercise of one's rights to acquire information. Should the government sell lists of names and addresses to direct-mail advertising and solicitation agencies? Do individuals have the "right" of privacy, or may one branch of government give its information to another? Is duplication of a videotape or computer program stealing, violation of copyright, or just an illegal but not immoral feature of the new society like jaywalking or parking without putting money in a meter?

Some of the most technologically advanced countries spend more of their gross national product on information than on commodities or services. These are called "information societies," and their economies require a large cadre of persons with skills that were nonexistent a century ago: word processors; data managers; group facilitators; statistical analysts; opinion pollsters; continuity editors; camera operators; video editors; teleprompter repair crews; and others.

Executives pay exorbitant fees for consultants to come into their offices and perform "communication audits" or train them in communication skills. Many persons in business feel that they and their company cannot compete unless they have instantaneous access to many forms of data. Perhaps they are right: the *Wall Street Journal* portrays the information it provides, and the timeliness of that information, as essential for junior executives who want to be promoted.

Children in the United States spend more time watching television than they do in school, reading, and talking with others. Some wonder if so much television is a good environment for children. Millions of persons in virtually every nation watch American television programing. Some decry the "cultural imperialism" that results when U.S. television programs constitute much of the learning environment for children of other countries; others see in it a great financial opportunity; still others as a divisive force that separates the cultural elite (those who own television sets and video cassette players) from the masses (who do not).

By an act of capitalist metamorphosis, the faces and minds of these audiences change into "markets." The television "industry" serves its clients, not its audience. Its primary function is to manufacture a specific commodity: the attention of an estimated number of viewers in its audience for a specified period of time. It generates this commodity by collusion. It offers programing tailored to the audience's viewing habits, and the public allows itself to become habituated to watching television. This commodity can be retailed, wholesaled, or auctioned to advertisers just as any other commodity can be sold to consumers or collectors.

Even the production of communication technology has become a big business. American Telephone and Telegraph (AT&T) and International Business Machines (IBM) are industrial giants by any criterion.

The market for communication technology continually increases. Banks in France give away home computer terminals so that their depositors can communicate directly with the bank's computers without having to appear physically before a teller. The bankers feel that their apparent generosity is economically effective because it takes them out of the "bricks and glass" business and allows them to concentrate on communication. Whole towns in Japan have been wired with multiway communication technology, enabling any person or group of persons to interact with each other. Less sophisticated equipment available in the United States permits anyone with a terminal, a modem, and a telephone to be, in a real sense, at the center of culture. Whole new industries are being developed that service such networks with data, hardware and software, specialty publications, support groups, and so on.

Even less affluent countries such as Indonesia and India have invested hundreds of millions of dollars in communication technology. The government of India has put communication satellites in orbit and is currently in the process of extending television coverage beyond urban centers. Persons in isolated villages who know little or nothing about other villages a hundred miles away have a Hollywood perspective on the United States and watched video coverage of the weeks of rioting in Seoul on the eve of the 1987 presidential elections. Surely this makes the villagers more cosmopolitan, but what kind of an image does it give them of the world and of their place in it?

Academics and Communication

In this century, many lines of research independently discovered that they are really dealing with communication. Phillipe Le Corbeiller (1966, p. 9) mused: "Some words are characteristic of an epoch, summing up an intellectual climate. 'Enlightenment,' 'romanticism,' 'progress,' 'evolution,' 'democracy'—each of these brings to mind a period of several decades during which almost every kind of intellectual activity concerned itself with a new password. In the last two decades *communication* has been such a password."

With commendable energy, Stephen Littlejohn (1982, p. 253) accepted the task of surveying the academic disciplines from which have come major contributions to human communication theory. In addition to communication itself, he identified philosophy, psychology, sociology, and anthropology as the source of major insights into the process of communication. However, he confessed that even such a comprehensive list was inadequate. The story of the academic discovery of communication, he said, remains incomplete if it does not acknowledge the contributions of mathematics and engineering, English, literature, media criticism, general semantics, general system theory, psychiatry, and management.

Even Littlejohn's longer list does not exhaust the possibilities. Passionate arguments could be made that "communication" has most productively surfaced in linguistics, computer science, economics, history, political economy, or critical theory.

In the general public, discovery of communication occurred primarily because of the ubiquity and influence of the new communication technologies. This effect was felt in some of the most common of modern experiences: as students began to use computers, "erasable bond" paper was made obsolete (to the eternal gratitude of those of us who grade papers for a living). Persons in the remote corners of our civilization became able to be contemporaries of their cousins in urban centers, sharing fashions and slang transmitted by radio, television, and film. Mobile young adults found that they were still in touch with their parents, and could be in touch with their spouses, even though thousands of miles separated their homes. "Commuter marriages" are but one index of these changes.

In business and government, communication was discovered because it seemed a means of wealth and power. Conceptually, this was a lateral move, encompassing communication as one more substance or process by which the same old games are played. Of course, the unique characteristics of communication brought certain concerns into play, such as ownership of bandwidths for radio or television broadcasts and the protection of copyright over material transmitted in a form that could be intercepted by recording devices. But these are variations on a theme, conceptually equivalent to the changes in an agricultural economy in which tobacco is replaced by coffee as the "cash crop."

The discovery of communication by the intellectual community is far more radical, with far greater significance for our collective understanding of ourselves and our place in the world. The story is a familiar one, repeated a dozen times in various intellectual traditions.

The common element in the Western tradition was some form of "foundationalism" (Rorty, 1979). Knowledge was assumed to be "about" something external to the knower. The arguments about what comprised a sufficient and compelling foundation differed considerably, from Platonic "forms" to Cartesian "*cogito*" to Baconian "observations." However, the intellectual "move" was the same. To paraphrase Archimedes, "give me a foundation, and I will deduce/infer/generalize the world!"

In this tradition, communication was considered an odorless, colorless, tasteless vehicle of thought and expression. It was a tool that persons used to describe their thought, the substance within which they framed their logic, and the vehicle for naming, counting, and categorizing their observations. That is, this is the way communication *should* work and *in principle* could work. Granted, various thinkers got caught up in their metaphors and others ran afoul of the snares of language, but these were "mistakes" caused by carelessness or malice; they served as cautionary tales for others.

Of course, all through Western history, there have been those who questioned the strategy of foundationalism; some even challenged the dependability of communication as a reliable tool of representing truth. However, these critics were seldom very influential and even now, when it seems that they were right all along, it was not the power of their arguments that convinced the "foundationalists."

The intellectual history of the twentieth century, in discipline after discipline, may fairly be summarized as the decline and fall of foundationalism. In mathematics, physics, logic, philosophy, psychology, literary criticism, art, and more, those who most powerfully pursued their search for the foundation repeatedly found that it eluded them. Further, profoundly disturbing "proofs" were generated that this illusiveness was not only frequent; it was *necessary*. For example, Kurt Gödel offered mathematical proof that no symbolic system can be both consistent and complete (Nagel and Newman, 1958). Quantum physicists found that the indeterminacy of observations in the smallest, most elemental elements of nature is not due to the "mistakes" or even limitations of the observer, but are representations of the state of nature (Gribbon, 1984).

The argument has shifted. Instead of convincing demonstrations of the unsatisfactoriness of what *others* claimed as the foundation on which knowledge is built, those using the most powerful means of inquiry found that what they themselves had relied upon as "foundational" did not exist. This discovery set the problematic for the contemporary era: if there is no ahistorical, immutable, objectively knowable "foundation" for determining what is good, true, and beautiful, then how can we make justifiable knowledge claims, political policies, and esthetic judgments? Does the decline of "objectivity" or "foundationalism" inevitably throw us into ethical nihilism, political subjectivism, and philosophical relativism? Is the phrase "different strokes for different folks" the only alternative to policies of "my country right or wrong" or ethics based on the principles "me first; mine second; and you last"?

This is a crucial issue, and the efforts of those in various disciplines to cope with it make for fascinating reading. I believe that these struggles reflect a radical redefinition of the role of communication in the human condition. To varying extents, of course, communication has become "visible" as the process by which inquiry, thought, and even academic disciplines themselves are constituted. In the past, matters of style and patterns of communication were taken as reflections of idiosyncrasy or simply ignored unless they caused problems. Now academic disciplines examine the patterns of who talks to whom about what (in conventions or in the citations of scholarly publications), that which is taken for granted in the conversations and arguments among researchers, and the effects of the institutionalized rhetoric of inquiry and reports. Scholars in some disciplines believe that "reality" itself is located only within language. Others believe that reality has an objective existence but that those who would know it are inextricably mired in communication practices that have their own structure. Either way, communication has been "discovered."

The following sections attempt to accomplish two purposes simultaneously. First, they give a brief survey of some of the major lines of scientific and humanistic inquiry to document the claim that there is a convergent "discovery" of communication among those who otherwise think of themselves as doing quite different work. My selection of literatures to include and what to say about them are guided by my second purpose, that of laying the groundwork for a reconstruction of how communication works. In my judgment, we are still far from realizing the full implications of the discovery of communication. Our attempts to reform our understanding of how communication works have been insufficiently radical.

Starting around 1950, a group of intelligent and energetic scholars attempted to devise a model of communication that would enable them to come to grips with what they sensed was a richer concept of how communication works. Their frustration showed in the titles of articles published in the 1960s: "On Defining Communication: Another Stab" (Miller, 1966) and "On Defining Communication: Still Another View" (Gerbner, 1966). In 1970 Frank E. X. Dance proposed a moratorium on these attempts. Let communication be something described by a "family" of definitions and models, he suggested, from which particular researchers could draw those that best served their needs.

Dance's suggestion was well received, virtually ending a period of struggle with this piece of the puzzle. And there is an honorable precedent for the procedure of maintaining multiple, incompatible models for the same phenomena: the treatment of light in physics. Light is modeled both as a particle and as a wave, and it makes sense to keep both models, for each represents something about the property of light that the other does not. Perhaps communication should be treated in the same way.

The analogy limps, of course. Both wave and particle models of light lead to precise, operationally defined predictions about what can be observed as a property of light. Models of communication do not. With the partial exception of Shannon and Weaver's (1949) mathematical model, communication models are heuristic devices or theoretical strategies used to legitimate the modeler's interests.

As of this writing, it is fair to say that the "discovery" of communication resembles the experience of a tall person who discovers a low doorway while walking about in a darkened room. The fact of the existence of something there is painfully obvious, but its meaning and shape remain to be ascertained. There is now a general consensus that we have collectively passed a watershed of some sort in our understanding of communication, but there is no consensus about just what the new idea of how communication works is or in what vocabulary it should be expressed.

In what follows, I intend to give just enough information about the various lines of work to document their part in the discovery of communication and to provide the "raw materials" for a reconstruction of the concept of communication elaborated in subsequent chapters. I hope to show that a reasonable response to the issues raised in the several discoveries of communication requires a profound revolution in the way we think about ourselves and the world around us. It is this, far more than the expanding economic and technological aspects of communication, that constitutes the most important aspect of the "communication revolution" in the twentieth century.

For present purposes, three statements summarize the insights produced by academic studies of communication with which communication theorists must cope: (1) we live *in* communication; (2) communication is more complex than we had imagined; and (3) communication is more a way of thinking than an artifact to be produced or transmitted.

Taken together, these insights "promote" communication to a more prominent place within the social pecking order than it has had since the sophists of the fifth century B.C. in the Greek city-states. However, such upward mobility is not without its costs. Not only is "communication" disturbing as an intellectual yuppie, bringing an unfamiliar set of interests to the cultural agenda, but the reasons why "communication" has prospered stem from a profound crisis of confidence in the more established intellectual traditions. Both the new agenda and the crises of confidence are necessary to understand why so many scholars in so many disciplines suddenly started talking about communication.

We Live in Communication

The traditional concept of communication holds that "we" exist in a material world, and we use communication to express our "inner" purposes, attitudes, or feelings, and to describe the events and objects of the external world. Communication works well to the extent that it accurately expresses (or, when used by a cad, strategically distorts) inner feelings or external reality, and when it produces understanding (or deliberate misunderstanding) between the speaker and the audience(s) addressed.

The alternative view is that "we" consist of a cluster of social conversations, and that these patterns of communication constitute the world as we know it. In this view, communication is a *primary* social process, the material substance of those things whose reality we often take for granted, such as our "selves," motives, relationships, what we would otherwise describe as "facts," and so forth. The forms of communication in which we participate either liberate or enslave us; they facilitate or subvert human values. The characteristics of the material universe and the properties of mind are sufficiently different that any number of stories may be told that "adequately" account for the facts. (I put "adequately" in quotation marks to indicate that the criterion to be met, just as the story designed to meet it, is socially constructed.)

This second view radically differs from traditional notions of reality and of epistemology as well as of communication. If it is accepted, it has profound implications for what it means to live a life, for social theory, for ethics and values, and for social institutions. As such, it should be accepted only with great caution. Below are brief accounts of how some persons came to adopt such a counter-intuitive position.

Scientific Revolutions

In both physical and social sciences, Thomas Kuhn's (1970) *The Structure of Scientific Revolutions* set the stage for a new concern with communication. Flying in the face of the orthodox view of science, Kuhn's studies of the changes from one theory to another located scientists within "paradigms" consisting of ways of thinking and acting through which they looked at "the world," rather than in some "objective" place from which they constructed theories and observed facts.

The public myth of science claimed that scientists' basic concepts were incontrovertibly grounded on the objective events and objects of the physical world. As Sir Isaac Newton claimed, they did not "make" (in Latin, *fingo*) hypotheses; rather, they observed the world and described the relationships among variables. Progress occurred in a series of incremental "advances" as they were able to account for ever more of the variance in those relationships.

This myth was perpetuated by the work of a certain kind of philosophy of science. Given the unquestioned success of the "scientific method," some thinkers set themselves to the task of articulating the philosophic underpinnings of what scientists described themselves as doing. The result was the philosophy of "positivism" or "operationalism" (Rapoport, 1953), which sacrificed everything of value and significance to the single criterion of replicable observability.

However, those who observed how scientists actually behave, rather than how they describe themselves, arrived at a very different account. Briefly, they showed that scientists were better at *doing* science than in *describing* it. For example, Grene (1974) noted that Newton's descriptions of his methods were enormously influential, but although he was a first-rate scientist, he was a third-rate philosopher of science. Despite his protestations to the contrary, he did "make" hypotheses.

Burtt (1927) noted that scientists who claimed only to observe the phenomena of nature in fact presumed a metaphysic that included, among other things, highly specific and nonobservational concepts such as "space," "time," and "mass." In the twentieth century, just these concepts came into controversy, showing that the smug "realism" of nineteenth-century scientists was simply the familiar conceit of those who mistake the horizons of their paradigm for the boundaries of the world. In contemporary language, this critique of the public myth of science is expressed in the dictum that all observations are "theory-laden." It is not that one sees only what one expects to see, but that one's expectations inevitably, inalterably affect what one sees.

The means by which new ideas are achieved has always posed a problem for accounts of the scientific method. The orthodox solution has been to differentiate a "context of verification" in which every idea, however derived, can be operationally defined and empirically studied in a rational manner, from a "context of discovery," in which hypotheses are produced in a manner not subject to rational reconstruction. The separation of these contexts suggests that scientists may engage in irrational processes in arriving at a hypothesis as long as they subsequently subject it to the rigor of rational verification procedures.

The solution seems inelegant. It results in what Kaplan (1964) called "reconstructed logic" in which—by golly!—the irrational processes of discovery are shown to have been rational all along. By the time a scientific report is published, what might have been an intuition on a bus, in a shower, or while dreaming has become the inexorable conclusion of a rational process. Another problem with the "discovery/verification" dichotomy is that the sequence is wrong. Koestler (1964) showed that scientists work far more by intuition, guess, preconceived hunches, and esthetic preferences than they—or their publics—are allowed to know. Further, imaginative reconstruction often follows rather than precedes verification.

Kuhn (1970) put this all together in an explanation of how scientific knowledge changes. Paradigms are "scientific achievements" that provide a model and a community for scientific work. Paradigms include assumptions that define what problems are worth working on, procedures described in sufficient detail that various persons recognize each other as working within the same community, and achievements sufficiently unprecedented to attract an enduring group of adherents from competing modes of scientific activity. "Paradigms gain their status because they are more successful than their competitors in solving a few problems that the group of practitioners has come to recognize as acute" (p. 23).

Within paradigms, "normal science" occurs. This is a sophisticated form of puzzle-solving within a shared (and usually unquestioned) frame. One of the primary functions of a paradigm is to define a world. Inasmuch as no paradigm is or can be both internally consistent and complete, the careful elaboration of the paradigm identifies problems of a particular sort. These problems are assumed to be solvable by the ingenious use of the methods specified in the paradigm. The passionate conduct of scientific research may be seen as an attempt to scrutinize some aspect of nature through the lens of a particular paradigm and, when some pockets of disorder are detected, to refine the observational techniques or to extend the theories so as to better understand and precisely describe the world.

In the history of science, the conduct of normal science produces "anomalies," or "the recognition that nature has somehow violated the paradigm-induced expectations that govern normal science" (pp. 52–53). The accumulation of anomalies produces a "crisis" for the paradigm: in short, the puzzle looks insolvable given the assumptions, definitions, and methods of the "old paradigm." Defections occur; the faithful are troubled; and—sometimes, ultimately—"discoveries" are made that lead to the emergence of a new paradigm, and the process continues.

Perhaps the most controversial of Kuhn's claims is that the transition from one paradigm to another is revolutionary. Not "a cumulative process, one achieved by an articulation or extension of the old paradigm . . . . Instead, the new paradigm, or a sufficient hint to permit later articulation, emerges all at once, sometimes in the middle of the night, in the mind of a man [*sic*] deeply immersed in crisis" (pp. 84, 89–90).

The controversy about the suddenness of the arrival of new paradigms is irrelevant for present purposes. The significance of Kuhn's work derives from his ability to show that even the human enterprise that most successfully claims to be in touch with external reality is in fact constituted by processes of communication. Paradigms exist in patterns of conversations among graduate students and their advisors, conversations between those who submit articles for publication in scientific journals and the reviewers/editors who decide what to publish, conversations within the mind of those who assess what their colleagues would say about their latest idea or data, and conversations between scientists and the governmental agencies that call upon them for advice or offer research grants to those who excel in fitting into whatever paradigm is dominant at the time.

Kuhn's analysis strikes at the heart of the authority of science as a social institution. It claims that the consensuality of scientists is the result of their shared deep enmeshment in a particular set of conversations in which they have trained themselves to respond to each other and to the world in a similar fashion, not because their story necessarily "fits" the world better than some other. Further, it implies that the rationality of science derives from the paradigmatic statement of what the puzzle is, and that the choice among paradigms is disturbingly nonrational. If two paradigms specify different puzzles to be solved, and perhaps different criteria for determining what counts as a solution, then on what basis is one paradigm to be chosen rather than another?

Again, we need not be concerned at the moment with the philosophical issue of rationality; I want to use Kuhn's argument to illumine the extent to which all of us— even those scientists who would protest the suggestion most vehemently—live in a network of communication. The point is most clearly seen, of course, in instances of paradigm shift:

> When paradigms change, the world itself changes with them. Led by a new paradigm, scientists adopt new instruments and look in new places. Even more important, during revolutions scientists see new and different things when looking with familiar instruments in places they have looked before. It is rather as if the professional community had been suddenly transported to another planet where familiar objects are seen in a different light and are joined by unfamiliar ones as well. Of course, nothing of quite that sort does occur: there is no geographical transplantation; outside the laboratory everyday affairs usually continue as before. Nevertheless, paradigm changes do cause scientists to see the world of their research-engagement differently. In so far as their only recourse to that world is

through what they see and do, we may want to say that after a revolution scientists are responding to a different world [Kuhn, 1970, p. 111].

Perception

When we wake in the morning and look around, the events and objects around us appear to present themselves to us as pictures, sounds, smells, and the like. Studies of the process of perception, however, have shown that what we actually perceive is very remote from that which engages our senses, and that which engages our senses is quite different from the "things-in-themselves" that constitute the world we think we perceive.

Look out your window. You may think you perceive a tree, but you do not. The event/object you are now perceiving presents itself to you not as a "tree" but as a pattern of light waves/particles and perhaps minute traces of chemicals in the air. Freshman philosophy classes argue whether the "tree" actually exists, but here I want to make a much more serious claim: that the *sensations* you receive are dissimilar from the *object* you perceive. Trees are made of wood but you see light; trees are solid or liquid but you smell gases.

In the same manner, there is a discontinuity between the excitation of neurons in your eyes and nose and the concept "tree." At some point in the process, everything you have ever seen, touched, tasted, smelled, or heard has existed in the form of neurochemical impulses traveling along your nervous system in ways structured by the physical properties of your nervous system—not by the alleged characteristics of the tree outside your window.

The point here is not to deny the *existence* of external reality but to demonstrate that any *knowledge* of it derives from characteristics of our perceptual processes. Speculate a moment: What would the world look like if the receptors in our eyes included not only rods and cones but a third type that responded to electricity or magnetism? We could see a magnetic field; watch the buildup of energy prior to a lightning bolt; and probably would avoid areas of our cities where microwave transmissions create fields of energy. What would the world taste like if the energy required to transmit a signal from one synapse to another was less than it is? We might be able to discriminate tastes that now seem the same, making gourmets of us all. As these speculations show, the human construction of "reality" is in a sense arbitrary, resulting from the peculiar characteristics of our nervous systems. Perhaps our nervous systems—and thus the world in which we live—differ in these ways from the Neanderthals who preceded us, and perhaps our remote descendents will differ from us, and thus perceive a different world.

These facts about the process of perception are by now well known. However, few have dared to think through their significance for the human condition. Humberto Maturana, a Chilean biologist, is an exception. Maturana describes the nervous system as "operationally closed." The world that humans construct, filled with "love," "honor," "democracy," and "status," is discontinuous from the raw sensations that we get from the external world. Further, things exist *for us* as they are brought forth in a process of naming. "Human beings can talk about things because they generate the things they talk about by talking about them" (Maturana, 1978, p. 56). Finally, this process is a social one in which various "operationally closed" systems perturb each other until they achieve some coordinated way of responding to each other and the world around them. (Maturana calls this the "consensual domain"; I prefer "coordination.")

This view of perception leads directly to questions of metaphysics and politics. For example, Maturana denies the existence of a universe. Rather, he insists, there is a *multi*verse comprised of all the stories yet told (and yet to be told) that make it coherent. All the stories in this multiverse are *valid*. This does not imply that they are all "true," but shows that it is not particularly useful to contrast one story with another by claiming that one is "false." Inasmuch as all stories are constructed in a discontinuous process from their encounter with external reality, one can argue that some stories are better than others, but not that some are "true" and others "false."

Extending Maturana's analysis, Peter Lang and Martin Little (in a personal communication) argue that many social problems occur when the stories told by some members of an organization are invalidated. Lang and Little are consultants who create contexts in which all persons' views can be taken as valid. This process usually requires a fundamental shift in the "dominant" stories of any organization.

In this way, the study of perception—how we know about a tree—moves inexorably to a radical metaphysics and a political concern with patterns of conversation and the stories that persons tell.

Philosophy and Criticism

In the twentieth century, philosophy has abandoned what has been its traditional concerns: to describe the ultimate nature of reality and to account rationally for human knowledge. Instead, it has made a succession of "turns" and wound up dealing with human communication. In the same period, literary and cultural criticism has evolved in such a way that it shares many concerns and much vocabulary with modern philosophy. There are scores of strands in these developments, and the following is a highly selective, very simple summary.

The Linguistic Turn

Philosophers have traditionally used language to think about things "beyond" language, such as "truth," "beauty," and "goodness." However, they have developed a bit of well-earned myopia, and now focus on language itself.

The "linguistic turn" results from a suspension of the belief in "cognitive transparency," the assumption that language is a transparent tool allowing philosophers to think and write about the world without distortion. Many philosophers now believe that the "problems" with which they deal—"truth," "beauty," and "goodness"—themselves exist *in* language and "may be solved (or dissolved) either by reforming language, or by understanding more about the language we presently use" (Rorty, 1967, p. 3).

Needless to say, the linguistic turn is highly controversial. Some hail it as "the most important philosophical discovery of our time, and, indeed, of the ages." Its opponents see it as "a sign of the sickness of our souls, a revolt against reason itself, and a self-deceptive attempt (in Russell's phrase) to procure by theft what one has failed to gain by honest toil" (ibid.).

For our purposes, the "linguistic turn" may or may not solve the problems of philosophy, but it is an additional aspect of the discovery of communication. At the very least, philosophers such as Ludwig Wittgenstein have demonstrated that our "forms of life" are composed of clusters of "language-games" in which meaning derives from social rules (see Janik and Toulmin, 1973).

The Interpretive Turn

At the beginning of the twentieth century, many responded to J. B. Watson's call for "behaviorism" in the study of humankind. Unimpressed with the results of research based on introspection, he argued that the careful observation of how persons actually behave could produce lawlike generalizations. In deliberate parallel to Newtonian physics, such laws could be used to describe, predict, explain, and understand human behavior.

The anomalies produced by this paradigm seemed to require the reintroduction of "actor's meanings" into any account of social life. One unintended result of the theoretical shifts was a profound reconceptualization of the meaning of "explanation." For the behavioralists, explanation and prediction were differentiated only temporally: prediction was the statement of a lawlike relationship *before* an instance of it was observed; explanation was the same statement *after* it was observed (Homans, 1967). The new "interpretive" researchers found themselves giving accounts of actors' meanings, citing reasons and causes, reconstructing frames and logics of meaning and action—in short, either engaging in communication with the ostensible "subjects" in their research or describing the research activity as one in which the grounds for improved communication could take place (Fay, 1975). Whole subdisciplines developed, showing the various means of unintended communication between researcher and subjects in experimental settings (Rosenthal, 1976) and exploring the open-ended stories that can be constructed from any given research setting (Gergen, 1982).

As behavorists "turned" toward interpretation, they found that there were many persons already there. In the United States, the work of Alfred Schutz, William James, John Dewey, and George Herbert Mead initiated several lines of inquiry that attempted to offer interpretations of social action. One way of characterizing the interpretive turn is to pose some simple questions. You observe a person whose left eyelid closes, then opens. What more would you need to know to determine whether this is a wink or a blink? If a wink, what more would you need to know to determine whether it is conspiratorial, jocose, or flirtatious?

Structuralism

Ferdinand de Saussure proposed a separation between *langua* ("language") and *parole* ("speech"). Following his lead, Chomsky (1986) disregarded the vagaries of linguistic performance in favor of an analysis of "competence," defined as that which all native speakers know that enable them to identify all and only grammatical sentences. Lévi-Strauss (1964, p. 12) made much the same move with myths. His mythological analysis, he claims, does not show "how men [*sic*] think in myths, but how myths operate in men's [*sic*] minds without their being aware of the fact." This is a seductive way of thinking. It acknowledges the importance of communication, but disregards the (often imperfect, apparently chaotic) particular instances of communication in favor of the (underlying, immutable, perfect) structure that lies "behind" it. The seductiveness results from a grafting of the avant-garde (communication) with the traditional (what Rorty [1979] called the "spectator theory of knowledge").

In pre-Socratic Greece, there was an intense debate about the form of knowledge about the world. Heraclitus argued in favor of change as that which knowledge should illumine, while Parmenides claimed that knowledge must be about immutable, ahistorical, changeless things. Parmenides won. Ever since, there has been a powerful sentiment in the West that permanence, perfectness, and ahistoricity are the necessary attributes of knowledge. Structuralism enabled these attributes to be brought to the study of communication.

Poststructuralism

There are two telling critiques of structuralism, either of which seems sufficient. First, the Parmenidean notion of knowledge has become increasingly suspect. For example, Rorty (1979) summarized the challenges to the view that knowledge is "the mirror of nature," concluding that knowledge is in fact participation in a series of conversations.

The second critique of structuralism is empirical, and challenges the assumption that there is, ultimately, only one language in which knowledge can be expressed. MacDonell (1986, p. 7) cites the "basic inequality of class" and "the imposed inequalities of race, gender, and religion" as a challenge to the structural claim, which she renders as saying, "we are all the same: we all speak the same language and share the same knowledge, and have always done so." In fact, there are many languages within each society, some of which are privileged because those who use them find ways of exercising power.

One group of poststructuralists call themselves "textualists" and view their work as interpreting texts. Although members of this group include and are heavily influenced by literary critics, they are not limited to literature, because they view all forms of social action as textual. For example, Ricoeur (1981) wrote a celebrated essay in which he showed that texts are like "meaningful action," and vice versa.

Textual criticism is not without its assumptions and purposes. Literary critics assume that "all stories and accounts, no matter how much their style might protest innocence, contain a mythic level—that is, they have a job to do, a perspective to promote, a kind of world to affirm or deny. Seemingly neutral accounts of activities deliver, by dint of their grammatical and rhetorical structures, implicit political arguments, either legitimations for entrenched authority or polemical critiques which seek to demystify or disestablish existing structures of power and domination" (MacDonell, 1986, p. 7). The purpose of criticism is to dispell the illusion of rhetorical innocence, in the process refocusing attention on the act of communication itself, not the events or objects allegedly talked about in the text.

The Social Construction of Reality

Western intellectual history has tended to use communication as if it were an odorless, colorless, tasteless vehicle of thought and expression. In formal debate, scholarly essays, and polemical speeches, scholars looked past communication to talk about metaphysics, ethics, politics, religion, and the like. Intellectual developments in this century, however, have convincingly demonstrated that communication is not so benign an instrument. These developments focused attention on communication itself as the substance of "paradigms," the structure of philosophic problems, and the "real" content of apparently "innocent" essays about morality, economics, politics, and so forth.

There is an excitement about all of this. Critics like Shapiro (1984) relish the ability to expose the pretention of innocence in multilayered texts. Philosophers like

Wittgenstein say that venerable philosophical problems require therapy rather than solutions, and that this therapy consists of demonstrations of the language games philosophers play. Scientists have a better understanding of their relationship to their predecessors and to those in other paradigms.

For present purposes, we need not be concerned with the questions of whether paradigms change suddenly or incrementally, or whether all of the problems of philosophy exist only in language, or whether there are invariant structures behind the multiple layers of textuality in social life. Regardless of the answers to these questions, communication has been "discovered." The process and form of communication is the object of investigation where before it was thought of only as a transparent tool used to express or describe "other things."

Among other things, the discovery of communication implies that what academics do, despite their protestations of "objectivity" or "expertise," is not different in kind from what ordinary persons do in their daily lives. Neighbors arguing about the line between their property couch their arguments within a paradigm, and their argument is likely to be resolved more quickly if they share the same paradigm. Shoppers waiting at a checkout line in a grocery store respond to those around them in ways reflecting the discontinuity between percept and concept. Talk between parents and children constitutes multilayered texts. Even though the talk may seem to be about baseball or dating or household chores, the discourse contains legitimations of certain kinds of authority, the maintenance of certain social institutions, and a particular definition of what it means to live a life of honor and dignity.

The phrase "the social construction of reality" has been used to name the discovery of communication in the apparently mundane aspects of social life. Berger and Luckmann (1966, p. 15) noted that "theorizers" (like myself, I guess) tend "to exaggerate the importance of theoretical thought in society and history." This "intellectualistic misapprehension" should be corrected by focusing on "what people 'know' as 'reality' in their everyday, non- or pre-theoretical lives" because this commonsense knowledge "constitutes the fabric of meanings without which no society could exist." Further, they note that this kind of knowledge is first and primarily constructed in face-to-face interaction in which there is "a continuous interchange of my expressivity and his. I see him smile, then react to my frown by stopping the smile, then smiling again as I smile, and so on. Every expression of mine is oriented toward him, and vice versa, and this continuous reciprocity of expressive acts is simultaneously available to both of us" (p. 29).

The notion of the social construction of reality poses the same challenge to ordinary social activity as the "linguistic turn" poses to philosophy: instead of communication being "about" something else, it is constitutive of the experience itself.

Consider the apparently tangible events and objects of the social world: dinners with friends, personalities, emotions, purposes, universities, ships, kings, and sealing wax. In the life history of any individual, most of these are "found things." They preexist the individual, and we learn what to call them, how to do them, and what to think about them at a point in our own history when we cannot cite an alternative or remark upon their arbitrariness. A baby experiences a sensation and its parents offer a label and a story for it: "Does it hurt? Poor thing, let Daddy kiss it and make it well." Older humans have the same experience: recruits in the military are offered a comprehensive definition of the world with accompanying rules for meaning and action, just as are first graders, employees, and defendants.

But we are all playing the game of the emperor's new clothes, and sometimes the pretense slips. The rate of change may be sufficiently great as to produce new things (jet lag, cultural relativity), which our children will treat as "found things" but which to us are obviously socially constructed. Cross-cultural travel may bring us into sufficiently close contact with other ways to doing mourning, achieving honor, loving justice, and living humbly that we begin to see our own culture as one among many. Sometimes the social amnesia of culture fails, and we see the sordid (or glorious) fingerprints of human agency on the substance of the events and objects that comprise the world. At a more sophisticated level of development, we may learn that what was labeled "hurt" was really something else; that "patriotism," "religious faith," and "cynicism" often masquerade for pretty shoddy motives. Persons on the margins of two societies, members of an oppressed or minority group, and those who suffer stigmatic or traumatic life transitions are particularly enabled to see the processes of social structuration that may forever remain transparent to deeply enmeshed members of the majority whose lives are never disrupted by the rude shocks of history.

The events and objects of the social world are not what they appear. They are not external, "found" things. Rather, they are the product of social action whose continued existence depends on their reconstruction in patterns of communication.

Communication: More Complex Than We Had Thought

In the early 1950s, the writings of Wilbur Schramm were very important in giving direction to the new field of mass communication. In one of his books (Schramm, 1954), he published an essay entitled "How Communication Works." The second edition of that book, *The Process and Effects of Mass Communication*, was published in 1971. Rewritten for the occasion, Schramm's essay reflected the results of two decades of research. The later essay is longer, far broader in intellectual scope, and contains this summarizing statement: "we now know that communication is not nearly so simple a thing as we once thought it was" (Schramm, 1971, p. 6).

In retrospect, the simplicity of earlier notions of how communication works is astonishing. The usually unarticulated theory of communication in Western culture focused on an alleged "transfer" of meaning from one mind to another by means of some medium. In this "post office" model, George Miller (1986, p. 37) said, communication is erroneously thought to be "accomplished by wrapping an idea in words and sending it off to the other person, who unwraps the words and discovers the idea." Many problems with this notion became obvious as soon as good minds turned their attention to it. Miller commented on its inability to account for the communication of emotions. "Ordinarily there is little correspondence between a speaker's feelings and the feelings of different hearers: his jealousy embarrasses her, amuses you, and angers me. It may be possible to plant an idea of a chair in someone's mind by saying 'chair,' but planting a feeling or sympathy by saying 'sympathy' is not a reasonable expectation. For the communication of feelings and emotions, some different explanation is required" (ibid.).

The faults of the post office model of communication are more easily identified than improved upon. Those who have "discovered" communication—that is, who agree that the work it does is far more central to the human condition than previous generations had imagined—do not very much agree about how it works. My own reconstruction of how communication works focuses on three terms: coordination, coherence, and mystery.

Coordination names those practices in which persons attempt to call into being conjoint enactments of their visions of the good, the desirable, and the expedient, and to prevent conjoint enactments of what they envision as bad, ugly, and obstructive. It specifically does not presume that those who "coordinate" their actions "understand" each other or "agree" about what they are doing. Further, it does not presume that what is constructed resembles in any significant way the "intentions" of the communicators.

As a way of describing how communication works, coordination stands in marked contrast to the several varieties of "functionalism." Functionalists start with the observation that the social order exists, and that persons live, move, and have their being in it. From this, functionalists infer that the events and objects of the social world are a response to some "need" and have some "function."

Functionalism takes the social order as a made thing and marvels at its complexity and intricate patterns of relationships, but coordination focuses attention on the process by which the events and objects of the social world are made. This process is seen as highly imperfect and fallible; the events and objects of the social world are often (usually? always?) the nonsummative product of a conjoint process in which "outcomes" often are counterproductive and do not resemble the intentions of those who participate in them.

Consider the social event of a heated argument, complete with name-calling and high blood pressure. Two persons with whom I worked became all-too-predictable in constructing this social event. The interesting thing about it was that they both claimed that they did not like to fight with each other and that they did everything they could to avoid fights, but still fights continued.

Several of us took this as an opportunity for research. First, we convinced ourselves that the "fighters" were telling the truth about not wanting to fight. We noticed that they sought out their friends, asking for advice and help. They deliberately employed various strategies that these friends suggested for avoiding fights. They often went out of their way to avoid being with the other person as a way of evading a fight. These strategies, although sincere, were only partially effective: the fights continued.

We next observed the fights more closely. We found that these persons fought only about a certain range of topics, and then only with each other. They did not fight with other persons about these topics or with each other about other topics. Quite sensibly, we concluded that the unavoidable fights occurred because of something having to do with the combination of their relationship with each other and with specific topics.

We did a series of interviews. First, we asked what it felt like to be in these fights. They did not like it and felt out of control. Despite their best attempts to avoid a fight, they would feel *compelled* to act in ways that they knew would lead to a fight. "When he said what he did," each reported, "I had no choice. I *had* to respond as I did." "What did you think he would do next?" "Oh, I knew that we were getting into it again, but there was nothing else I could do."

We interviewed a large number of other persons, and found that virtually all could tell us about a similar experience, where a combination of their relationship with some other person and a topic produced what we came to call an "unwanted, repetitive pattern" or URP. Although the content of the URPs may be highly specific to the individual or the relationship, the experience seems quite common: you are in a highly predictable situation where you feel that you *must* say or do something even though you know it will set off an unpleasant, undesirable pattern of interaction (Cronen, Pearce, and Snavely, 1979).

The peculiar nature of URPs illuminates the fallible nature of the process by which the events and objects of the social order are constructed. More desirable events are also the conjoint products of a nonsummative process, the nature of which is described in some length in chapter 2.

Coherence refers to the process by which we tell ourselves (and others) stories in order to interpret the world around us and our place in it. It specifically does not assume that these stories are an accurate description of ourselves or of the world.

Coherence stands in opposition to any claim that there is an irreducible "foundation" for our interpretation of the world. From the perspective of coherence, it is dangerous and misleading to say that one interpretation of the world is "right" and another is "wrong."

Human beings do not have a choice about whether to tell stories to make the world coherent; part of what it means to be a human being is to be a storyteller. But the stories told are *underdetermined* by the facts of life; whatever set of stories has been told, an additional story can be constructed that meets the "facts" sufficiently well to make them coherent. In this sense, the stories by which we make the world coherent are infinite in number and variety. (I am thinking of humankind as a collectivity extending far into the past and the future, of course. Individual humans are much more limited in their story-making ability.)

The existence of multiple stories for the same "facts" makes the process of being human inherently problematic. The human condition is that of being simultaneously, variably enmeshed in multiple social realities, each with its own logic of meaning and action.

Let "social realities" refer to a set of social *practices* together with the other persons required to enact them and the *stories* that make them coherent. In this sense, the U.S. Marine Corps comprises a social reality, with distinctive practices including uniforms, an intricate kinship system in which some members are saluted and others are not, and honorific titles are used for some and not others. Marines tell stories that make "duty" and "courage" synonymous with "obedience." This social reality differs in many ways from that of a university in which there are fewer uniforms, a different kinship system, and the stories make "innovativeness" and "competence" the desired virtues. Each social reality includes certain stories, and for successful performance in that social reality, one must be sufficiently "enmeshed" in those stories so that one can take them seriously, follow them assiduously, and act sincerely.

But consider now a Marine who goes to the university. This person is simultaneously enmeshed in two social realities whose logics of meaning and action conflict at some important points. How does he (or she) act? Which "logic" predominates? To what extent can the logics of meaning and action be combined? Are there insurmountable conflicts between them?

Well, that is the issue. All human beings construct stories that make their world coherent, but not all stories are alike, not all stories work as well as others, and stories often contradict each other.

I observed a session in which a family therapist met with a family whose daughter was diagnosed as having anorexia nervosa, an eating disorder in which she was not receiving sufficient nourishment. Anorexia is a life-threatening condition, but what interested me (and the therapist) was the story that the family was telling about it.

As told by the father, the story was straightforward. The family was fine, but the daughter had a problem. This problem was an illness for which she could seek remedies but about which she carried no other responsibility. It was something that had happened to her, and of course was a topic of great concern to all family members, each of whom was trying to be as helpful as possible.

Like all stories, this one contains a "logic of meaning and action," which prescribes who should be praised or blamed for what, what kinds of reactions should follow what events, and what various things mean. In this case, no one was "at fault." The family was the place where the problem had occurred but was not part of the problem, and there was little that anyone could do except be kind and encourage the daughter to seek help. Anorexia was treated as a "found thing" (not a "made" one) that had intruded into the family.

Therapists know lots of things about anorexia, one of which is that if one of the children is "cured" of it another of them is likely to develop it. Is it contagious? Is it hereditary? Or is it a terrible, unwanted product of the conjoint construction of the social "object" called "family"?

The therapists who let me watch them work were using the assumption that anorexia is part of the social construction of reality. This does not deny that it is real—far from it; persons die from it—but makes the radical move of suggesting that because we live *in* communication, attention to those patterns of communication themselves is the best way to affect our lives.

These therapists tried to get the family to tell a different story about anorexia, one with a very different logic of meaning and action (not necessarily one they believed was "true"). In this story, the anorexia was treated as a means to accomplish a goal; rather than something that happened to her, it was a "problem" that she presented to the family in order to get the family to act in a certain way. As she approached the age when she might be expected to leave home, it was suggested that she subconsciously worried about what her departure would mean to the family. By becoming "sick," she gave the family a focus that kept it together. The therapists noted that the family was close, supportive, and loving. Further, they suggested that the daughter's concern was a real one; when a member of the family leaves, the family has to adjust somehow. Offering her "sickness" to the family was a loving, responsible gift, enabling it to bond together in anticipation of her moving out on her own. However, the gift was becoming too costly, and threatening her own health. Some time soon—but only she would know just when—it would be necessary for her to let someone else in the family take over the burden of keeping it together. In the interval, the family should continue to show her support; she should eat as much as she needed; and the others should simply wait for her to decide that the family ties were sufficiently robust that she did not need to assume such a terrible burden.

The story suggested by the therapists has quite a different logic of meaning and action. It defines her lack of appetite as purposive rather than caused by disease. It depicts the daughter as in control of the problem rather than helpless in the face of it. And it defines the family as a system of which anorexia is a part rather than simply a place where this dread disease struck. At the very least, this new story enables some forms of action that the first precluded.

Mystery is the recognition that the human condition is more than any of the particular stories that make it coherent or any of the particular patterns of coordination that construct the events and objects of the social order. It is a reminder that no matter how deeply enmeshed one might be in a particular range of stories, there are other stories in which one might find one's interpretation of the world. It is a way of looking around the edges of the event/objects of any particular social reality to see that they bear the marks of human agency, and that they might have been constructed very differently. Mystery is the essence of that "cosmopolitan" attitude that views one's own life and that of local society as a manifestation or part of something greater; it is a reminder of what is "beyond" the immediate, present moment.

Mystery stands in opposition to those who would attempt to impose an overrestrictive "rationality" on the stories and the coordinated patterns of action in which we live. For example, Habermas' (1979) theory of communication starts with the assumption that persons understand each other, and then works to determine what must have already, always been the case for such an understanding to be possible. But what if we live in a multiverse of stories? What if we interpret very differently the patterns of coordinated activities in which we engage? What if our best attempts to produce particular event/objects in the social world go astray, resulting in URPs and worse? Mystery is at once a reminder of the fallibility of the process of the social construction of reality, and of our emancipation from any particular set of stories and practices.

Communication: A Perspective, Not a Thing

The discovery of communication consists more in a new way of thinking about the human condition than in a new awareness of a particular form of human action. "Communication does not signify a problem newly discovered in our time, but a fashion of thinking and a method of analyzing which we apply in the statement of all fundamental problems" (McKeon, 1957, p. 89).

Commonsense notions of communication often refer to it as one thing among others that human beings do. That is, sometimes human beings sleep, sometimes they eat, and sometimes they communicate. Although this seems reasonable enough, it is not a sufficiently rich way to think about communication. The problem comes from constructing any viable definition of communication that excludes sleeping, eating, and other forms of activity. Sleeping while in a class is a communicative event, and the manner, place, and companions with whom one eats comprises a rich communicative system. So rather than defining communication as a subset of human activity, I propose that we view all forms of human activity from a "communication perspective" (just as we might view it from political or religious perspectives).

The communication perspective sees all forms of human activity as a recurring, reflexive process in which resources are expressed in practices and in which practices (re)construct resources (see Figure 1–1). In this sense, "practices" consist in actions such as building a bridge, playing bridge, and seeking to bridge misunderstandings; "resources" comprise the stories, images, symbols, and institutions that persons use to make their world meaningful.

The communication perspective portrays an inherent tension between what are sometimes separated as "actions" and "meanings." In fact, I chose to use the terms "resources" and "practices" to avoid having continually to explain that there can be no action without meaning and no meaning without action.

The dynamic of the process of communication derives from the fact that human beings live simultaneously on two levels and must work to make the two "fit" each other.

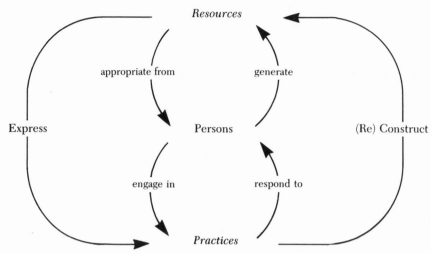

Figure 1–1. The "communication perspective."

The "fit" is never a perfect match, but it is almost always "close enough" for coherence, coordination, and mystery.

On one plane, human beings are physical entities just like rocks and trees. When hit by a truck, human bodies fly in a ballistic trajectory no different from any other object of the same size and density. The gravitational attraction between two love-crazed teenagers at twenty paces is not an erg greater than that between two trees of the same mass. When simple mechanical things go wrong with human beings, they die.

But on another plane, human beings live lives of moral significance in worlds of honor, dignity, and value. There never have been persons, at any time or place, who have lived only on the plane of brute physical existence. When a human is hit by a truck, the consequence is never simply a matter of ballistics: Was the victim "foolish" to have stepped in front of the truck? Was the driver "negligent"? Was it really an accident or a cleverly disguised homicide? When persons die, it is never simply a matter of mechanical malfunction: it may be a tragedy, a relief, or a crime. When they are born, it is never simply a biological event.

The notion of "expressing" resources in practices assumes that humans are active simply by virtue of being alive. It assumes further that humans do not act capriciously, outside the contexts of their culture, personal relationships, social roles, and autobiographies. "Projective" psychological tests have shown that personal histories, symbolic connections, and deeply felt values are *most* clearly revealed when it seems that we are acting spontaneously and without purpose. The communication perspective directs attention to the resources that shape and guide practices, often in subtle ways. Resources and practices are coevolutionary; each is the "cause" and each the "effect" of the other. I sometimes indicate this ongoing reciprocal process by using a parenthesis: practices (re)construct resources. Apparently stable patterns of social life are dynamically renewed, more like an eddy in a fast-moving stream than rigidly structured like a rock. From a communication perspective, both change and permanence in political and economic systems are achieved by the (re)construction of resources in practice, and both are equally interesting. The term "(re)constructs" thus identifies the impact that practices have on resources whether it changes or reaffirms the existing set of resources.

Some Applications of the Communication Perspective

Any aspect of human activity can be looked at as a process of communication in which resources are expressed and (re)constructed in practices. This includes those activities traditionally understood as communication: speaking, writing, television, and film. However, these practices are no more and no less fit subjects for communication analysis than any other kind of human activity.

As McKeon said, the communication perspective is a way of thinking, not a class of things about which to think. The "discovery" of communication is that the communication perspective is surprisingly useful. Specifically, this perspective enables us to see *as* communication some aspects of human activity that otherwise would seem irrelevant to communication analysis, and it enables us to see *in* communication processes some aspects of the human condition that are not so apparent from other perspectives.

In this section, some activities not usually thought of as communication—architecture, clothing, sidewalks—as well as some more traditional topics are examined from the communication perspective.

Architecture

In the United States, most houses have a semipublic lawn between the street and the doorway; in Korea, most houses have a wall adjacent to the street enclosing a very private lawn or courtyard between the street and the house. Whatever their historical or functional reasons, these design characteristics may be looked at from a communication perspective as *expressing* a particular concept of the relationship between the private and the public, and *(re)constructing* patterns of thought and action. Those who have lived all of their lives in one of these architectural patterns are likely to have internalized these concepts, finding them "natural" and those expressed in the other culture as "strange." Further, individual "personalities" are judged in terms of the way they "draw from" these resources. In suburban United States, a walled house such as is appropriate in Korea would quickly define the owner as "antisocial"; in urban Korea, an American suburban house and lawn would seem out of place and would suggest that the owner is socially naïve.

The architecture of churches may be seen as making theology visible, and thus is a form of communication. Cathedrals have often been noted as expressing the theology of the period of time when they were built. In the contemporary period, church styles vary tremendously, from Gothic to glass cathedrals, "drive-in" churches in which the faithful need not leave their car, and "electronic" churches in which it all happens on television in one's home. From a communication perspective, what does this express about the current state of theology? What form of religious life does it construct?

Clothing

Clothing styles may be usefully analyzed from a communication perspective. In the feudal period in Europe, vocation and socio-economic status could quickly and accurately be determined from the material and style of clothing. In addition to its protective function, clothing served as a communicative code for those who could "read" it. If you lived in, say, fifteenth-century Dubrovnik, you would make a "statement" every time you got dressed. This statement would amount to a "self-disclosure" about your income, occupation, relationship (if any) to the aristocracy, and so forth. In the modern period, the code is more complex and individualistic, but no less real. "Considered as a whole, the system of American clothing amounts to a very complex scheme of cultural categories and the relations between them, a veritable map—it does not exaggerate to say—of the cultural universe" (Sahlins, 1976, p. 179).

Some find aspects of this contemporary code distressing. One response has been to adopt "unisex" styles of hair and clothing. If the meaning of unisex style were put into discourse (that is, into a different code), it might go something like this. Unisex-attired young persons have become aware of dysfunctional gender distinctions in our society and wish to reduce them, and so are trying to dress in a manner that does *not* force them to say "I am male" or "I am female" every time they put on their clothes. Given the current code, there really is no way to dress and appear in public without making a vast array of statements about your gender, your perception of yourself, and of the social occasions for which you are prepared. The unisex style is an attempt to create a more flexible code.

But note how robust these resources are. Even if you want to avoid participation in this gender-sensitive code—for example, by adopting a unisex style of dress—you will still be perceived in terms of that code. Perhaps you will be perceived as a person who is not comfortable with your own gender identity; perhaps just as an ignorant dresser; or maybe as making a gender statement. The one thing that you cannot do in contemporary American society is appear clothed in public and be mute about gender.

Sidewalks

From a communication perspective, the existence and placement of sidewalks may be seen as part of the "resources" of a society. They set some parts of the physical world off from others by defining where it is and is not legitimate to walk. Further, they clearly separate areas where pedestrians can walk safely from those in which automobiles are free to move. As such, they shape certain practices. These practices, in turn, become part of the resources of society, (re)constructing the "stories" that persons tell to explain themselves to themselves and to others.

If you have been avoiding someone for weeks, but suddenly notice that he or she is approaching you on a sidewalk, what can you do? To strike out across the street or the lawn is an *obvious* attempt to avoid that person, but the sidewalk permits you no more graceful maneuver. The sidewalk has structured the kind of practices available to you, and whatever practice occurs—an argument otherwise avoided; a reconciliation; a juicy bit of gossip— will become a part of your resources.

Sidewalks in various places differ in size and in degree of crowdedness. In some midwestern towns in the United States sidewalks are broad and uncluttered. As many as three or four adults may walk side by side, and in these cities the "stroll" becomes a form of social practice in which business is discussed, plans are made, or simple pleasures at being together are enjoyed. In Bangkok, broad sidewalks are a major site for itinerant businesses. Early each morning, vendors stake out locations where they set up a hawker's stall, and cook and sell food, or offer services such as shining shoes or mending clothing. The sidewalks are never *quite* blocked so that a pedestrian cannot get through, but nearly so. A group of persons walking together must travel in single file, and they are in the midst of a shouting, noisy crowd, which makes conversation impossible. In the old part of Delhi, however, there are no sidewalks. Pedestrians travel by dodging bicycles, rickshaws, or automobiles. These practices (or the absence of them) become part of a society's resources, including what it means to "go for a walk" or to be jostled by another walker.

The role of sidewalks was graphically presented in a television documentary about the Titsany, a stone-age tribe found living in a remote part of the Philippines. One of the members of that society decided to accompany the anthropologists as they left the forest and returned to civilization. As you may expect, civilization presented many problems to this man: he did not have the "resources" to interpret many of the "practices" of which he was a part.

In one scene, he was shown walking beside a highway, obviously frightened and trying not to show it. He flinched every time a car passed. His civilized companions were not worried: they knew that they were on a sidewalk where cars were not permitted and thus were (relatively) safe. But consider the experience of the "uncivilized" person who could not "see" the sidewalk because he had no "resources" for it: a huge object roared toward him at high speed, missing by only a few feet, and then was followed by another. To him, the walk with his strange new friends must have seemed a combination of bravado and foolishness.

Reticence

"Reticence" is a term denoting a pattern of behavior in which persons avoid speaking if they can, and if they must speak, they do so with signs of discomfort. They are often nervous, speak too quietly, say less than they should, and often are not as eloquent as the situation demands. Roughly synonymous terms include "stage fright," "speech fright," "communication apprehension," and "shyness."

As a *process* of communication, reticence occurs in all cultures. Some research projects have compared the occurrence of reticence in several cultures, concluding that these behaviors are common everywhere. From the communication perspective, however, statistics describing the extent to which reticence *occurs* in several cultures are only tantalizing. The more appropriate question is that of what reticence *means* in these cultures. What resources are expressed and (re)constructed by reticence?

In the United States, reticence is perceived as a "problem" to be solved; a pathological condition that leads to undesirable consequences. There is a sizable body of data showing that, all else being equal, reticent persons are perceived as socially unattractive and less competent in the performance of various tasks. Some American universities offer programs whose purpose is to identify and "help" reticent students overcome their problem.

I know of no such program at universities in the Republic of Korea. Further, although Koreans may be just as reticent as their American counterparts, reticence is not—or at least not always—perceived as a problem, a symptom of personal unattractiveness, or an indication of diminished capability.

College students in the United States and in the Republic of Korea described a young woman on a series of scales measuring "task attractiveness" and "social attractiveness" (Kang and Pearce, 1984). The presentation of the young woman was manipulated so that half of each cultural group saw her as reticent, the other half as not reticent.

Both Americans and Koreans described the reticent woman as less attractive as a collaborator on a task. However, they differed in the way they perceived the "social attractiveness" of the woman. The Americans described the reticent woman as *less* socially attractive; the Koreans described her as slightly *more* attractive.

A closer analysis of the Korean group's responses clarifies the situation. All subjects were asked to write a short essay describing the woman. The Koreans consistently described the nonreticent woman as progressive but "insincere." The most frequent comment was that this person will have many acquaintances but no close friends. Many thought that she had a poor self-concept, and needed the approval of others for support. They suspected that she would work effectively only if closely monitored by others. The descriptions of the reticent woman were not nearly so consistent; in fact, they broke down into two patterns. About half of the Korean subjects perceived the reticent woman as quietly strong, perhaps hard to get to know but then becoming a good and trustworthy friend. However, the other half perceived her as having been scarred by some social injury or obsessively concerned about something to the extent that she could not interact easily with others.

From the communication perspective, we suspect that these differences in the meaning of reticence express and (re)construct differences in the cultures of the United States and of Korea. It is easy to advance a hypothesis about the significance of reticence in these cultures.

Rationalism is a major influence on patterns of social and task interaction in the United States, but in the Republic of Korea it competes with another influence. "Progressive" young Koreans have internalized much of the values and behavior patterns of the United States (as presented in television, movies, and the example of the numerous U.S. military personnel stationed in the country); whereas "traditional" young Koreans are primarily influenced by the legacy of Confucianism. Rationalistic and Confucian traditions generate very different rules for meaning and action. The Confucian perspective is that of a "fixed world of fixed duties, roles, and possibilities: not a process, but a state; and the individual is but a flash among the facets. There is no concept, or even sense, of either will or mind as a creative force. And when the Westerner exhibits these, the sage Oriental simply gazes, baffled, yet with the consoling sense of watching only a devil at work whose time will surely be short, and of himself, meanwhile, as securely rooted in all that is externally true in man, society, the universe, and the ultimate secret of being" (Campbell, 1964, p. 6).

The most important value in a Confucian society is harmony, and this is to be achieved when everyone exemplifies the virtues appropriate for their social roles. Verbal assertiveness, the conflict of differing opinions, and the moral duty to express how one feels about particular issues threaten harmony. On the contrary, verbal reticence in formal situations is perceived as the appropriate means of expressing and (re)constructing social harmony.

The resources drawn upon in the United States, on the other hand, include a deep confidence in rationalism. Rationalism is the belief that the "universe works the way a man's mind works when he thinks logically and objectively: that therefore man can ultimately understand everything in his experience as he understands, for instance, a simple arithmetical or mechanical problem" (Brinton, 1963, p. 83).

The duty of the state, in this view, is less that of achieving harmony than that of providing a context in which the conflict of opposing opinions can occur. The state should prohibit obstacles to the freedom of inquiry, learning, and communication. Some argue that the state should teach citizens how to communicate effectively and provide them with access to the means of communication. In this context, reticence is always viewed negatively; it connotes a person's failure to contribute to the collective search for truth.

Whatever its rate of occurrence, the *meaning* of reticence differs in rationalist and Confucian societies, and these differences illustrate the process by which societies and forms of communication (re)construct each other. As the stories of Confucianism (or rationalism) are repeated from generation to generation, they legitimate reticent (or nonreticent) behaviors. Those who act appropriately are praised, and those who do not are shunned, reproved, or "trained" to do "better." As this process continues through repeated iterations, practices (re)construct the stories they originally expressed—with increasing clarity and moral force.

Communication in National Development

Since India gained its independence from Britain in 1947, the central government has made a concerted effort to bring economic prosperity and social justice to its people. A series of five-year plans has guided massive programs of fiscal investment and human effort. The collective term for these activities is "development."

The results of forty years of development programs present a curious enigma. On the one hand, it can truly be said that India has never been in better economic shape. It has become an *exporter* of food rather than dependent on foods produced elsewhere. Villages have amenities that are new to them; there is a larger group of prosperous middle-class citizens and traditional patterns of exploitation have been changed by vigorous intervention by the government. On the other hand, there is pervasive discontent about the way development has proceeded. The masses feel that the government has been inefficient and corrupt, and those who work in the development program feel disempowered and blame the masses for being greedy and too dependent on the government.

Government planners have become increasingly sophisticated about the requisites for development. They have realized that even the immense resources of a national government are insufficient to achieve development. For national goals to be met, the people must participate in digging wells, supporting the laws, investing capital for agricultural machinery, and so forth. To elicit this participation, the government has engaged in a great deal of communication with the masses, designed to create in them a dissatisfaction with existing conditions, an awareness of alternatives, and a knowledge of what can be done to improve their way of life.

This communication program has been very successful. Indians in urban areas and in many of the villages have become dissatisfied with conditions that exist in their communities. However, instead of setting about to change them, their participation in national development seems limited to complaining to the government about these conditions and demanding that the government do something about them. Among development theorists and functionaries, this pattern is known as "passive participation." It denotes a condition in which persons *support* the development effort but are willing to participate in it only as critics or recipients of the efforts of others.

Narula and Pearce (1986) attempted to discover the reason for this pattern of discontent and passive participation. An initially attractive hypothesis was that the government's communication program was a failure. Ironically, we concluded that quite the contrary was the case: the patterns of pervasive discontent and passive participation turned out to be the result of very *successful* communication between the government and the people. However, the process of communication between the government and the people included more than either realized and the whole formed an unintended pattern. The seemingly paradoxical conclusion was that if the government tried to solve the problem by engaging in "more" or "more effective" communication, it was likely to make the problem worse rather than eliminate it. Doing "more of the same" would only add energy to the existing pattern. Improvement requires an intervention that changes the pattern itself.

In the development effort, the government set itself to engage in three kinds of activities: direct action, legislation, and communication. As government officials saw it, communication included the transmission of messages by All Indian Radio, films, television, wall posters, village-level workers, and so forth. Legislation included laws that, for example, broke up tracts of land owned by wealthy elites in villages, setting as much as half of the land aside for public ownership, and made certain practices of lending money—and collecting debts—illegal. Direct action took the form of building roads to connect previously isolated villages, providing transportation to nearby towns for health services and jobs, and so on.

The problem here is not that direct action and legislation were not needed; but rather that they were not thought of as communication. There is a very clear message delivered when the government sends law enforcement officials to isolated villages and tells them that the central government has decided that their traditional economic practices are exploitive and hence are illegal. A clear message is given when the government builds an all-weather hard-topped road from the state capital to a previously isolated village. Just as much as radio or television programs, legislation and direct government action express and (re)construct a set of beliefs about the role between the masses and the government. In this instance, these messages contradicted each other.

In what the government thought of as its communication activities, the message was "development is a national priority in which everyone has to participate actively." In its legislative and direct action programs, which government officials did *not* think of as a form of communication, the message was "development is a project that requires the expertise and resources of the government and we will do what we think is best for you." The latter message, of course, is a prescription for passive participation. The combination of messages provided the context for confusion and frustration.

Government officials thought that they were saying clearly "we need your active participation," but they heard the masses saying "all right, go ahead and do development for us, but do it faster, you are not succeeding rapidly enough." The harder the government tried to say "*you* must be actively involved," the more it got the response "we *are* actively involved; we are telling you what you should do for us." No wonder that government officials were discontented and felt disempowered!

The masses clearly heard the government say "you are not knowledgeable enough to decide what development projects should be done; you are exploited and limited in what you can do, so we must do it for you." Every time the masses tried to advise the government about what needed to be done, or what government projects were not working, the government scolded them for not doing enough. No wonder the masses have learned to be dependent on the central government for development!

Although the communication perspective does not suggest a clear-cut solution to the problem of development in India, it does explain an otherwise enigmatic result of forty years of development work. This explanation, in turn, empowers acts that may restructure the pattern sufficiently to improve the situation (see Narula and Pearce, 1986, chapter 8).

Summary

The "discovery" of communication must be a part of any comprehensive story of the twentieth century. Once keen intellects focused on communication itself, instead of using communication as a too familiar tool with which to describe and express other things, the deficiencies of commonsense notions of communication became quite obvious. However, it has been surprisingly difficult to construct a satisfactory alternative notion of how communication works and of what work it does.

The crucial insight, I believe, is a shift from thinking of communication as a subset of human activity to a conceptualization of it as a way of thinking about any given form of human activity. By displaying the way resources are expressed in and (re)constructed by practices, this "communication perspective" illuminates the way all forms of human activity participate in a continuous, reflexive process of the creation and maintenance of social realities.

The way communication works is grounded in three universal aspects of the human condition: persons interpret their environment and their experience; they interact with their fellows; and they remind themselves that there is more to life than the immediate moment. I call these, respectively, coherence, coordination, and mystery. These are not "options" in which persons may or may not engage, or variables that may be present to some extent; rather, they are constitutive aspects of what it means to be human. All human beings—everywhere and always—communicate by coordinating, achieving coherence, and experiencing mystery. Chapters 2 and 3 describe these processes in detail.

Although everyone achieves coherence, coordination, and mystery, not everyone achieves it in the same way. There are important differences among forms of communication, and these forms of communication comprise distinctive ways of being human. Chapters 4–9 describe these forms of communication and ways of being human.

2.
Coordination

In whatever culture we live and whatever our role in it, we must negotiate among a variety of events and objects. These include the normal activities of life (work, play, sleep) and the social contexts in which they occur (families, friendships, business, governments). This book is one such object, as is the network of interlocking economic and social relationships in which you read it: at "home," in a "library," on a "vacation," at "work."

The discovery of communication brings with it a radical rethinking of the nature of these events and objects. The traditional way of coming to grips with them (which I called "foundationalism" in chapter 1) assumes that these events and objects exist objectively and tangibly; that knowledge consists of more or less accurate descriptions of them; and that we "respond" to them or "cause" them to move/change by our actions. In short, it treats the events and objects of the world as things that we *find*.

The alternative view shows the events and objects of the world as the products of human agency. Rather than "found things" existing independently in an objective world, events and objects *as we know them* are constructed by the continuing dialectic of interpretation and action. Given this perspective, the events and objects among which we must fashion our lives are more matters of human responsibility but less under human control than they appear in foundationalism. Further, they are better understood through an analysis of the process by which they are produced than by lists of their attributes.

This view inverts the traditional assumption of the relationship between event/ objects and communication. Rather than treating wars, economic depressions, and political systems as objective events within which or about which we might communicate, it takes them as instances *of* communication, seeing them as complex products of an inherently imperfect process of conjoint interpretation and action. It is more productive to inquire why patterns of communication so often take the form we call "war" than to treat war as a found thing the probability of which is increased or decreased by specified amounts of communication.

Coordination refers to that process by which persons collaborate in an attempt to bring into being their visions of what is necessary, noble, and good, and to preclude the

Figure 2–1. Coordination problems in high places.
By Tom Toles, published in the Buffalo News.

enactment of what they fear, hate, or despise. The events and objects of the social world should be viewed as situated, conjoint accomplishments of an inherently imperfect process of coordination.

The games of chess and poker are social objects, collaboratively accomplished by the players. Figure 2–1 uses the problematic nature of this process to satirize international relationships, personified by Secretary General Gorbachev of the Soviet Union and President Reagan of the United States. It also shows some of the ways in which the process of coordination can go wrong. Each player is trying to bring into being his vision of his game, but each is frustrated by the acts of the other. Each tries to interpret what the other says in terms of the game he wants to play. (In large measure, the rest of this chapter attempts to provide a vocabulary and a set of concepts in which what is funny and tragic in this cartoon can be explained.)

As this example shows, the events/objects of the social world are not always successfully constructed. Sometimes we fail to produce a social event/object that any of the collaborators recognizes, and we walk away muttering, "What was *that?*" This does not happen very often, however, because human beings seem "overqualified" in interpreting the patterns of social action in which they participate. When all else fails (and sometimes well before that point), we can always explain what is happening by saying that the persons with whom we are collaborating are mad, bad, or sick.

More frequently, we successfully collaborate in reproducing a "safe" pattern of action. Although it falls far short of what it could be, at least it is not disastrous. Our lives, in the process of living them, seem ambiguous, unpredictable, even dangerous. But when they are over, they appear more like all others than unique: "All we find in the end is such a series of standard metamorphoses as men and women have undergone in every quarter of the world, in all recorded centuries, and under every odd guise of civilization" (Campbell, 1949, p. 13). However, every once in a while, we do something truly bizarre. "From the beginning," Joseph Campbell (1959, p. 3) noted, human history has been a story "of the pouring of blazing visions into the minds of seers and the efforts of earthly communities to incarnate unearthly covenants."

Toward a Poetics of Communication

Those who have studied the way human beings actually talk have made some important observations. "Real talk," transcribed from conversations in courts, cafeterias, and corner grocery stores, is ungrammatical, awkward, incomplete, and inelegant. Not only less than Shakespearean, it is unworthy of an amateur playwrite.

At the grammatical level, persons usually do not speak in complete sentences or follow formal patterns of logic. Their talk is filled with "ums" and "uhs" and run-on sentences and, you know, things like that. At the interactional level, their turn-taking is not neat. They interrupt each other, talk over each other, stop and start in the middle of sentences. And at the level of moral order, talkers are not always respectful of each other, they do not always listen carefully and make sure that they understand each other before agreeing or disagreeing, and they do not always acknowledge their own ideological commitments or personal biases. How shall we come to grips, in the social world, with event/objects that are ungrammatical, illogical, and sometimes downright nasty?

A Baptist minister (Harold Crowell), a Unitarian minister (Bob Wheatley), and a Jewish rabbi (Frank Waldorf) got together to talk about how religious groups should respond to homosexuality. (This sounds like the beginning of a bad joke, doesn't it!) Their discussion occurred on a talk show hosted by David Finnegan in Boston, and was broadcast in November 1985.

The following exchange occurred in the middle of the show.

Finnegan: "Is there any kind of sexual practice that you would consider to be wrong, any kind?"

Audience (male): "Celibacy."
(audience laughs)

Finnegan: (laughs) "Celibacy! There's a gentleman with a sense of humor obviously. Ok, independent of that unusual state, is there any kind of sexual practice that you would consider to be wrong? Some of you would say that's not enough, that we know that there are people who enjoy pain and torture, and the rest of it. So it's written I'd say. The point is that do we get any kind of practice that we would say 'that ain't right; nobody's gonna buy it.' Anybody here want to take that one?. . . Go ahead."

Audience one (male): "Anything that someone does to another person against their will; I'd say it's wrong."

Audience two (male): "But that's not sexual."

Audience one: "Any sexual thing that someone does to another person against their will is wrong. But if it's done between two consenting adults, then that's up to those two people."

Finnegan: "Do you mean that religiously though?"

Audience one: "Religiously or sexually, or morally, on any level."

Finnegan: "Alright, let me throw it back to you, Rev. Wheatley, do you agree with that?"

Wheatley: "Yes, I do. I can't understand how Fundamentalist Christians cannot accept the simple rule of life that Jesus himself proclaimed, 'a new commandment I've given to you that you love one another,' and yet I hear myself being condemned; I hear myself being . . .

[Crowell: "Jesus was speaking to his disciples."]

I hear myself being judged when I know that the Scripture that says judge not that you be not judged, and I don't understand how these Scriptures can be twisted into . . .

[Crowell: "You took that one out of context!"]

such a distortion of the love that Jesus was the author of."

Finnegan: "Rabbi Waldorf, can I get you involved with this? Let me ask you a question. Do you agree with that definition that we have just heard here that anything that two consenting adults want to do is not morally . . . there's no immoral practice between consenting people?"

Waldorf (nodding): "Exploitation of people is the one area that I think . . . and certainly uneven power arrangement. Sometimes the consent is not clear as it ought to be. If one person has more power than the other. And so getting really good consent is sometimes difficult. Certainly adults and children, another area where immorality would apply. Could I ask a question?" (points toward Crowell)

Finnegan: "Oh, I don't see why not, sure . . ."

Waldorf: "Why do you spend so much energy condemning *a* section of the community? Why is it so important . . ."

Crowell: "I don't. I was asked to come on the show to discuss this issue. Frankly, I don't like to discuss this issue at all."

Wheatley: "But your literature is full of condemnation of homosexuality. You use it as a money raising gimmick . . ."

(Audience reaction, clapping)

Crowell: "No, no, our literature is filled with facts . . ."

Wheatley: "I have . . . I have . . . I have read pages from Jerry Falwell's literature that

[Crowell: "I read all of them."]

(audience laughs)

says . . . I've just seen it, I've just read it; it came out of his office; it says. . ."

Crowell: "Homosexuality, let me tell you something, Dave, the San Jose *Mercury News* reported that a person is ten times more likely to contract a disease from a gay person than from a straight person (audience reaction). The National Bureau of Disease, the National Center for Disease Control in Atlanta . . .

Audience (female): "Oh . . . (shakes her head and squeals in exasperation)

Audience (male): "So you condemn me?"

[Crowell: Well, I won't shake your hand!]

(hostile audience reaction) . . . The National Center for Disease Control says San Francisco has a venereal disease rate, it's not two times greater than the national average but *twenty-two* times greater than the national average."

Audience (male): "When the ratio . . . "

Finnegan: "What does that got to do . . . "

Audience (female): "He makes it very hard for me to respect what he's saying although I would like to very much, as well as the gentleman over there, because sometimes you throw out facts *as* facts; they are not truly facts, like the one about the psychologist saying homosexuals are mentally ill."

Crowell: "Your *own* press, the gay press (audience reaction) in Boston, New York, Washington, and San Francisco. I've got . . ."

[Finnegan: "Why does that make any difference . . . "]

friends that monitor that for me. Your own press deals with the fact that you've got such a problem, drunkenness, drug abuse, and venereal disease (audience reaction) in your own camp, and *your* papers deal with it all the time. It's *true*." (Audience [female] gasps and theatrically shakes her head in exasperation.)

Finnegan: "I really don't think, honestly, let me say this to you, because I do want to conduct the discussion here, but we are clearly getting into name-calling it seems to me . . . "

How shall we understand this discourse? Bear with me while I tell two stories.

A large, irregular, featureless, unknown object suddenly appeared on the lawn in the middle of a college campus. Representatives from each of the academic disciplines in turn brought the tools of their trade to bear on the object, but none of the measurements, chemical analyses, and so on, gave any clue to the nature or origin of the object. Finally, a clinical psychologist passed by and said, "Hi. What's your name?" "Ralph," the object replied.

This story is told by Abraham Kaplan in his book *The Conduct of Inquiry* (1964). It makes the point that one must ask the right question to get the right answer. Does "How is it made?"—the poetic question—do better than "To what does it refer?" or "What effect does it cause?" Perhaps so.

For years, scientists were puzzled by the carved stone faces that stare out across the great empty sweeps of the South Pacific from Easter Island. Who carved them? From where did they come? Some had suggested that they were the work of alien visitors; others a lost prehistoric civilization. After centuries of speculation, Thor Heyerdahl asked the "poetic" question. Instead of taking the megaliths as "found things" and trying to figure out their origin, he turned to the natives and asked them if they could build one. "Sure," they replied, and for a small fee set out to do so. In less than ten working days, Heyerdahl witnessed the transformation of a featureless stone into the newest Easter Island head—and took pictures of the process by which it was made.

What might well be called the Heyerdahl solution is a shift in focus from that which has been *made* to the process of *making* it. It is a shift from "pragmatics" (an examination of that which is "done") to "poesis" (how it is made). The concept of coordination makes the same shift in the analysis of communication.

Rather than asking "What is referred to by what is said?" (the old "foundationalist" question) or "What is done by what is said?" (the newer philosophy of language question), it focuses on the manner in which the events and objects of social reality are constructed. The Greek word *poesis* means "to make." To say that the events and objects of social reality are produced by coordination is to say that they are "poetic" and we all are poets.

This happy conclusion, alas, does not mean that we are all *good* poets, or that the poetry of social reality is without its risks. The primary reason for attending to the process by which the event/objects of social reality are created is that the process is inherently imperfect.

The social object produced by the two ministers and the rabbi might best be labeled "diatribe." There is no "natural law" that makes diatribe necessary every time this threesome talks about homosexuality; whatever happens is the result of their collaborative efforts to bring into being their own vision of what is good. That being the case, why did the "discussion" evolve into "diatribe" and why is diatribe so likely in situations like this?

The Anatomy of Coordination

Coordination is more easily shown than described. The best way to understand it is, armed with some appropriate concepts, to watch persons interact in some normal surrounding. The key phrase is "armed with some appropriate concepts." These concepts might be best presented in three layers, starting with the analysis of very simple dialogue and ending with a metaphor. Here is an example of a well-coordinated conversation:

(1) "Did you hear what happened downtown today?
"No, what happened?"
"Well! Let me tell you! The bank was robbed, and . . . "

Not all conversations go so smoothly, of course. It might have gone like one of these:

(2) "Did you hear what happened downtown today?"
"No, what happened?"
"No, I'm asking you."
(3) "Did you hear what happened downtown today?"
"Yes. The bank was robbed."
". . . Oh. Yeah."
(4) "Did I ever tell you about my motorcycle trip through the Rockies?"
"Yes! Many times!"
". . . Oh."

In the well-coordinated conversation (1), the utterances of both persons mesh in such a way as to bring about a social event that both interpret as a completed pattern. The initial interrogative is heard as a request for a speaking turn. (It *might* have been heard as an accusation that the other is poorly informed, as a request for information, etc.) The second interrogative is heard as a turn-yielding signal, in which the speaker gives the other permission to launch into a long story. In the third line, the original speaker (with a satisfied grin?) takes the role of newscaster and starts what promises to be a lengthy story. Such an extended speaking turn would have been inappropriate unless some such conversational "work" had been done.

The difference between this and the three poorly coordinated conversations is a sense of having collaborated in producing a completed pattern. In example (2), the "did you hear . . . ?" was heard as a request for a speaking turn (just as in the well-coordinated example) but was intended as a request for information. The "no, what happened" response does not fit this pattern, and the final utterance, "No, I'm asking you" is an

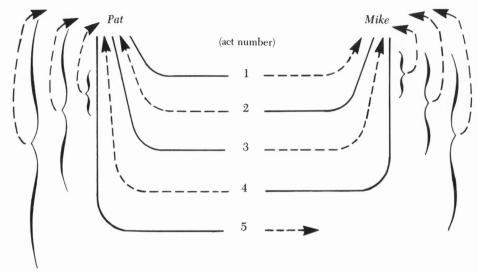

Figure 2–2. The process of coordination in communication.

awkward explanation/confession that the speaker cannot complete the pattern started by the combination of the first two utterances.

In example (3), "did you hear. . .?" was intended to be a request for a speaking turn. However, this role was preempted by "yes. The bank was robbed." The third utterance awkwardly closes down the conversation, leaving the pattern obviously disjointed.

The final example (4) shows a deliberate derailing of the emerging pattern. Again, the first utterance, "Did I ever tell you . . . ?" functions as a request for an extended speaking turn. It was both intended and heard that way. However, the second speaker did not want to grant permission for a telling of that story, and so responded as if it were a request for information. By answering "Yes, many times!," the emerging pattern in which all others must listen to the story of a motorcycle trip through the Rockies was successfully thwarted. In the final utterance, the speaker acknowledges not only defeat but recognizes that she or he has been either teased or insulted for retelling this story so many times.

These conversational excerpts are not unusual, but I wrote them as if the participants were not particularly gifted conversationalists. More competent conversationalists can detect the shape of the emerging pattern quickly and adapt their responses to fit it or modify it. A little of this skill is demonstrated in the "motorcycle trip" conversation, but there are many ways for both persons to negotiate a "better" pattern. In this way, conversation is an art form, and well-formed patterns of communication are the product of *poesis*, a collaborative artistic accomplishment.

Figure 2–2 describes the process of coordination. Persons A and B take turns exchanging and interpreting messages. As used here, "message" is a deliberately ambiguous term. It includes things people say, things they do, things they do *not* do when they are expected to, subtle inflections of voice or facial expressions, and the like.

The total sequence of messages comprises a *practice*, as discussed in chapter 1. Like "message," the term "practice" is deliberately ambiguous, referring to any situated, collaborative accomplishment of a social event/object. Practices may include conversations, conducting a class, a family dinner, a birthday party, a national election, a military invasion, and so on.

Practices Express Resources

Like other terms, "resources" is deliberately ambiguous. It includes all those stories, concepts, perceptions, memories, and so forth, by which persons make their world coherent. Today's conversation is guided by resources, and the memory of that conversation becomes part of the resources that guide our conversations tonight.

Resources are expressed in practices, because resources comprise a "logic" of meaning and action that defines what is obligatory, legitimate, dubious, or prohibited. This logic exerts a "force" that impells persons to interpret events in one way rather than another, to notice certain things about their environment rather than others, and to respond to social event/objects in one way rather than another.

"Logical force" is more like the force of an argument rather than a physical law; more like the "necessity" of drawing a conclusion or seeing the point of a joke than the "necessity" of a rock falling to earth. However, from *within* the logic, it can seem inexorable. As noted in chapter 1, persons find themselves in URPs ("undesirable, repetitive patterns") in which they report, with all sincerity, that "I had no choice; I had to act this way."

The strength of logical force became apparent in a study of domestic violence. A man had a long history of beating his wife. One of my colleagues was interviewing him and finally became exasperated with him. Asked why he hit his wife, he repeatedly answered: "It's not my fault. I can't control myself. Something just comes over me and I hit her." Because this seemed a too convenient way to dismiss his responsibility, she deviated from the planned interview protocal and demanded, "Well, why didn't you just kill her then!" His reply surprised them both: "I'd never do that!"

Both the "subject" in the study and the research team made a discovery. The resources that guided his actions and interpretations defined a situation in which he literally could think of nothing else to do but hit his wife. To make that coherent, these stories also included an explanation of wife-abuse as being out of his control. When he said "I can't control myself," he was sincerely telling the truth *as he knew it*. However, he was "in control"; he monitored the extent of his violence and made sure that he did not use lethal force. His logic of meaning and action prohibited him from doing anything other than hitting his wife; provided him with a rationale that absolved him from responsibility; left him in sufficient control to make sure that he did not do something contrary to his own values; and denied him awareness of being in control. (Sounds like the state of hypnosis, no?)

In the analysis of domestic violence, the research team came up with a startling discovery. Violent acts usually occurred when the logic of meaning and action simultaneously *demanded* that the person do something (that is, simply walking away or dismissing the situation with a smile or a hug was unthinkable) and *prohibited* every thinkable act. Violence becomes a communicative act, that which one does when nothing else will do (Harris et al., 1984).

There are many logics of meaning and action, and they differ from each other. "Cultures," "groups," "publics" are defined because their logics of meaning and action are simi-

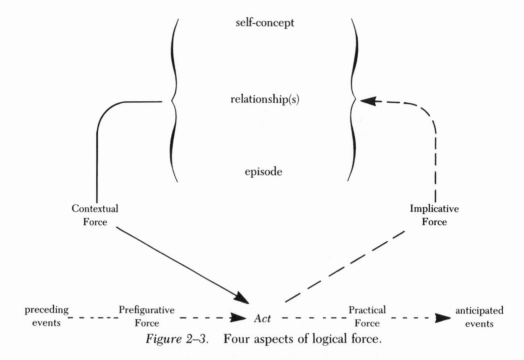

Figure 2–3. Four aspects of logical force.

lar—at least as compared with some alien standard. Yet even within these categories, individual members have quite different logics; and even within individuals, there may be very different logics for dealing with specific other persons or situations. A person may be sophisticated in dealing with religion and naïve about science, or vice versa.

Logics of meaning and action may be described in terms of four concepts. *Prefigurative force* is the sense of obligation that derives from things that occur before one acts. This is the "because" motive. "Why did you do that?" one might be asked, and respond "because he told me to." *Practical force* is the sense of obligation that derives from things that occur after one acts. This is the "in order to" motive. "Why did you do that?" one might be asked, and respond, "in order to get him to do what I want." *Contextual force* is the sense of obligation that derives from the definitions of self, other, relationship, situation, and so one, that one brings into the situation. "Why did you do that?" one might be asked, and respond, "because a person like me in a situation like this must do that." *Implicative force* is the sense of obligation that derives from the perceived/ anticipated effects that one's actions will have on the definitions of self, other, relationship, situation, and the like. "Why did you do that?" one might be asked, and reply, "because I wanted to redefine my relationship with him."

These four aspects of logical force are depicted in Figure 2–3. Taking a particular "message" as the focal point, contextual force comes from "above," prefigurative force comes from "before," practical force goes to "after," and implicative force goes to "above." The configurations of these logical forces are very important in differentiating forms of communication in later chapters of this book.

Practices express resources, but not all at once. The event/objects of social reality are not performed as a single act; they are the product of an unfolding sequence of messages performed serially (and sometimes simultaneously) by multiple persons, who

1. All conversations must begin with "◯";
2. Each speaker must respond to the other;
3. Everything not explicitly permitted is forbidden;
4. For *Pat*:

if the other says:	*then Pat must say:*
◯	☐ or ★ or △
★	◯ or △ or ★
△	◯ or ☐ or ★ or △
☐	◯

5. For *Mike:*

if the other says:	*then Mike must say:*
◯	☐
☐	★ or ☐ or △
★	◯ or △ or ☐
△	◯ or ☐ or ★ or △

6. For *Ellswood:*

if the other says:	*then Ellswood must say:*
◯	◯
☐	◯
★	△
△	☐

Figure 2–4. Rules for the game "Coordination."

may well be trying to express *different* resources. The message made by each participant at any given time becomes the "next" in an emerging pattern, and may extend that pattern, redirect it, block it, or simply confuse it. Well-shaped practices require the coordinated sequencing of messages by more than one person.

Practices express resources, but not necessarily accurately. The process of coordination often develops a logic of its own, which shapes a patterned practice that may not resemble the resources of any of the participants. This "logic of interaction" may be demonstrated by a simulated conversation using the artificial language shown in Figure 2–4. The entire vocabulary consists of the four geometric shapes (circles, squares, triangles, and stars) connected by various sets of rules stating that if the preceding message takes a particular shape, then the next "speaker" must respond in one of a limited and specified number of ways.

For the demonstration of the logic of interaction to work, three additional assumptions must be made. First, all speakers are rule-governed: they cannot do anything except what is expressly allowed in the grammar and vocabulary of this language. Secondly, "good" conversations in this language require that all four shapes be used. A conversation that uses all four (in any sequence, and not necessarily without repetition) is considered eloquent; one that systematically excludes one or more of the shapes is considered awkward and the speakers moronic. Finally, all conversations start with "circle" as the first shape.

Figure 2–4 shows that both Pat and Mike have a complex set of rules. Each can use the language with a great deal of flexibility; no matter what the other says, they should be able to respond in ways that ensure that they are able to produce an eloquent conversation (that is, to use all four symbols in a relatively small set of turns). This conversation might well occur.

Mike:　○
Pat:　　□
Mike:　★
Pat:　　△

Pat and Mike end the conversation feeling good about each other, congratulating themselves on being so clever and communicating so eloquently. However, they meet again the next day, and this conversation occurs:

Pat:　　○
Mike:　□
Pat:　　○
Mike:　□
Pat:　　○
Mike:　□

When they end the conversation, both feel frustrated and accuse the other of being a stubborn, uncooperative fool. What happened, they might ask, to change the other so much in so short a time!

From our vantage, we can answer that question: nothing happened to change them. Each person's resources—their rules for using the language—can mesh in any of several different patterns. On one day, they meshed in a way that produced the desired result; on another, they meshed in a way that did not. The explanation of the pattern of the practice cannot be found by looking at the rules of either participant alone; the fit—the interpersonal logic of the unfolding sequence of conjoint actions—must be examined.

Assume that Pat and Mike are sufficiently irritated with each other that they avoid speaking for several days. In the interval, each meets and talks with Ellswood, whose rules for using the language are also in Figure 2–4. The conversation between Pat and Ellswood is smooth, elegant, satisfying.

Pat:　　　○
Ellswood:　○
Pat:　　　★
Ellswood:　△
Pat:　　　□

However, Mike and Ellswood do not fare so well.

Mike:　　　○
Ellswood:　○
Mike:　　　□
Ellswood:　○
Mike:　　　□
Ellswood:　○

(To make this demonstration "work," find a friend and simulate these conversations— you will experience Mike's frustration.) When Pat and Mike meet again, they speak of their new acquaintance, Ellswood. "What a guy!" says Pat. "He and I can really carry on a good conversation!" ("Better than you and I can," she thinks.) "He's a dope!" replies

Mike. "I haven't been so bored talking to anybody in years!" ("Except when you and I last talked," he mutters.)

This demonstration permits three characteristics of coordination to be illuminated: that it is conjoint, nonsummative, and asymmetrical. The pattern of the "practice" in the conversations among Pat, Mike, and Ellswood is never simply the expression of any one of their resources. Practices are always produced by the *conjoint* expression of resources, in which the specific manner in which they intermesh may differ from instance to instance for no good reason except that one person chooses to say one legitimate thing today and another tomorrow, not necessarily knowing that one of those things sets off a logic of interaction very different from the other.

Practices are nonsummative expressions of resources. When we attribute praise or blame for someone's participation in the event/objects of social reality, we usually assume some form of connection between what happened and what that person intended to happen. There is a very unflattering pattern to these attributions: if good things result from what *we* do, we tend to cite ourselves as the cause; if from what *other persons* do, we tend to cite circumstances beyond their control. On the other hand, if bad things result from what *we* do, we tend to cite uncontrollable circumstances; if from what *other persons* do, we cite their incompetence or poor character. Not only is this pattern of attributions ungenerous, it exaggerates the extent to which practices resemble any individual's resources.

Is Ellswood brilliant because he can converse eloquently with Pat? Did Pat deliberately sabotage her second conversation with Mike? An alternative way of thinking, one guided by the communication perspective, is to consider all practices the nonsummative expressions of resources. It is possible—but hardly likely—that a particular practice perfectly and completely expresses one of the participants' resources. It is much more reasonable to start with the assumption that every practice is a (to some extent) surprising combination of two or more sets of practices, whose pattern is determined not only by those resources but by the emergent logic of interaction in the actual situated accomplishment of the practice.

The quality of life, it is fair to say, depends on the richness of the array of social event/objects in which one participates. These event/objects vary, of course, in the degree to which they are nonsummative. Rituals are perhaps the least nonsummative, in that they are reenactments of patterns assumed to be well known and rehearsed by the participants. "Enigmatic episodes" are at the other end of this continuum, in that none of the participants can make a realistic guess about what is going to happen. My hunch is that most of life lies somewhere between these two extremes, probably closer to the "ritualistic" end.

Finally, practices are asymmetrical. The research conducted by the various persons associated with the "coordinated management of meaning" project produced an interesting finding. Discourse *within* various groups in society is usually richer than that *between* groups. In speaking to those whose logics of meaning and action are similar to their own, persons use a sophisticated vocabulary, acknowledge the dignity and honor of those who disagree with them, and usually are able to put together well-coordinated episodes. However, when speaking to someone from another group, the form of discourse attenuates quickly. A simplified vocabulary is used; the personalities and motives of the other are posed in a desiccated vocabulary of human purposes; taunts and condemnations replace argument and evidence; and one's own reasoning and life experiences are protected from exposure and anticipated criticism. Discourse within one's group assumes rationality and good motives; that between groups often questions the potential of rationality—or at least of reasoning with "them." Instead, some nondiscursive means of coercion or compulsion is, regrettably, necessary, and thus enters "disinformation," censorship, firing squads, and other forms of domination.

The conversation among the two ministers and the rabbi is a case in point. The excerpt I quoted fails to carry with it the impact of the videotape. Missing are the red faces, heated voices, pointing fingers, contemptuous and outraged tones of voice that carried as much of the information as the verbal text; but you can imagine what it looked and sounded like. The point I want to make here is that these are not rowdy, inarticulate men given to verbal banter and caustic exchanges. Each is capable of discussing even this controversial topic sensitively and rationally—unless they are set off by the "logic of interaction" to oppose each other.

Scant moments before the rousing fight occurred, each of the men was asked to briefly state his own position. These statements were delivered in calm voices, with every sign of deep sincerity, and expressed positions whose "logic" could be "unpacked" into a comprehensive and, *within the frame set by its own assumptions*, valid picture of social reality. This is what they said:

Finnegan: "Let's begin this morning, if we can, with you, Rev. Wheatley, since you are the director of the Office of the Gay and Lesbian Concerns for the Unitarian Universalist Association. How is it that your church seems to have very little difficulty approving or at least lending some approval to the homosexual life-style?"

Wheatley: "Well, central to our theology and to our beliefs as individuals and as a group is the supreme worth of all beings, every person, and that means taking them in their entire personhood, their sexual orientation included."

Finnegan: "And therefore there is no discrimination in terms of the theological ground as to how I happen to practice my sexual . . .

[Wheatley: "That's right. . .yeah"]
preference."

Wheatley: "Yeah, that's right."

Finnegan: "Correct? Rabbi Waldorf, what do you say from the aspect of Judaism; is there some fundamental percept of Judaism which would make *verboten* the kind of activities that the Reverend just referred to?"

Waldorf: "In the traditional literature beginning with the Torah, there is prohibition against homosexuality, but as one talks to people in the Jewish community, it's quite clear that there's a great deal of ambivalence. The whole concern about how individuals feel about themselves and the desire to include each human being, and then there's a whole segment of the Jewish community very much into the civil rights movement and the desire to see there be openness and tolerance in American society. One of the historic facts is that in societies where homosexuals have been persecuted, Jews have also been persecuted. So there's a kind of a sense of desire to avoid all kinds of intolerance in American society."

Finnegan: "Pastor, what about you? You are opposed, I know, to some of the things that have just been announced. Tell us why from a . . .

[Crowell: "Yeah"]
theological standpoint, briefly if you would."

Crowell: "O.K., David. Those of us who are theologically conservative, whether they be conservative Catholics, Protestants, or the theologically conservative Jew, order their life after the Scriptures and believe that the Scripture is the standard rule for all matters of faith and practice. And in both the Old Testament and New Testament, the Scriptures state unequivocally that God has made a prohibition against homosexual practice and even says there is a death penalty for practicing such a sexual perversion."

Finnegan: "All right, well, three diverse views there. One obviously supportive, the other we ought to be tolerant, and the third saying nothing doing, it may even be punishable by capital punishment if we take the Scriptures literally at least. That's the kind of discussion we are going to get into this morning."

For Rev. Wheatley, the religious response to homosexuals is to support them, for the church should support everyone. He envisions an episode that starts with someone's self-ascription of homosexuality as a state of being. If someone says, "I am a homosexual," no further explanation or justification is necessary. This is one of the ways God creates persons. There is a well-worked-out process by which persons "discover" that this is part of their being and any challenges to this self-ascription are illegitimate. The church, he argues, is compelled (by contextual force: "this is the way that persons like us should act") to support homosexuals and (by prefigurative force: "if someone says that, then we have no choice except to respond in this way") to oppose those who do not support them.

For Rabbi Waldorf, the religious response is to tolerate homosexuals and seek tolerance within the community for all groups of persons. He envisions an episode that originates with expressions of intolerance and leads to a religious intervention in order to prevent undesirable repression of homosexuals or anyone else. The religious community is compelled by its own needs for a tolerant society to oppose any form of intolerance. It does so by inviting the community to engage in an agonizing deliberation of moral choices. Reflexive force predominates in this logic: intolerance is actively opposed in order to create a more desirable, better structured community.

For Rev. Crowell, the appropriate religious response is to articulate clearly the Biblical teaching, perhaps citing current statistics as proof, and call sinners to repentance. He envisions an episode that begins with a clarification of doctrine, and proceeds to a forceful application of that doctrine to all areas of life. The episode continues into the afterlife, and culminates in divine judgment, which supercedes all merely human rationalizations or practices. Contextual force predominates in this logic.

Each of these logics is consistent *within its own assumptions,* and each envisions a well-coordinated episode *if only the others would collaborate appropriately.* However, as their proponents interact with each other, they find each other's social realities opaque. Each denies fundamental assumptions on which the others rest, and each feels threatened by the others. As a result, the discussion soon turned into a pattern in which each attacked the others and defended himself rather than a collaborative effort to understand or resolve the issues. This case is very specific, but I think it exemplifies many situations in which the logic of interaction is more restricted and thus asymmetrical with the logics of participants.

Practices "(Re)construct" Resources

The model of the communication perspective depicted in Figure 1–1 shows a circular relationship between practices and resources. In any given practice, resources are drawn upon as a guide for interpretation and action. However, the outer brackets

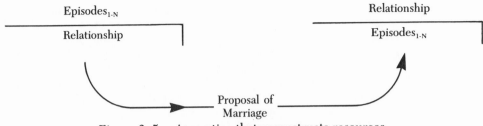

Figure 2–5. A practice that reconstructs resources.

in Figure 2–2 show a process by which communicators monitor the unfolding pattern of action in which they participate, and make judgments about what is happening. These perceptions of today's practices become part of tomorrow's resources.

Usually, the practices in which we participate reproduce the resources that guided them in much the same fashion that they existed before. When this happens, we think of the personalities or institutions involved as robust and permanent; we refer to them as being "real" even though they are the product of continuing "work." However, more often than we are aware, the practices in which we participate "construct" a set of resources that differ in significant ways from that which existed before. We call this "learning," "trauma," "growth," or "catastrophe," depending on the details.

Consider the perennial story of "boy meets girl." At some point in their relationship, what they are doing together (the "episode" they are enacting) is the context for their relationship. Perhaps they met at the beach, in class, or at work: these situations provide the "frame" for what kind of relationship they have. At some later time, they are husband and wife. Now their relationship is the context for the episodes they enact: it provides the "frame" for their trips to the beach and their work. How did this change come about?

At some point in their history, they engaged in some practice in which the reflexive force exceeded the contextual force in strength and differed from it in content. As a result, the practice changed the nature of their relationship and made it more important than the series of episodes they performed together. Perhaps this was a formal proposal of marriage, or perhaps over a period of time it happened behind their backs and they suddenly realized that their relationship went beyond their coordinated activities (Lannamann, 1980). This change is diagramed in Figure 2–5.

Resources are seldom, if ever, fully consistent. They are constructed from the flux of social experience, and thus include inconsistent reactions to particular events, internalizations of multiple influences, and so forth. Further, they are subject to continuous revision. They are changed on the basis of new experiences, contemplation of their own nature, and persuasion by others. As a result, they often include a variety of complex patterns, many of which directly determine in what way and to what extent resources are (re)constructed by practices.

One common structure of resources is a stable hierarchy. In this pattern (shown in Figure 2–6), the contextual force exceeds any and all other forces in the logic of meaning and action.

Persons "layer" their perceptions of themselves, their relationships, and the episodes in which they participate in such a way that their reasons for acting are always determined by perceptions that they brought with them into the situation. For example, if a particular "rugged individualist" made self-concept the most potent perception of

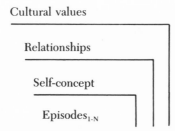

Figure 2–6. A stable hierarchy.

himself, with relationship and episode in a stable hierarchy under it, then he should be expected to act in a manner consistent with his self-concept regardless of what it means for his relationships with others or his success in bringing about the episodes in which he engages. Further, no matter what practice occurs, he is unlikely to change his perception of his self, his relationships, and the episodes in which he engages. At worst, this is the kind of person who persists in thinking of himself as wonderful even though all the episodes in which he participates should cause him to revise his opinion.

Permanence is the most striking feature of the resources (re)constructed in a stable hierarchy. Whatever changes might occur in practices, they are recognized by those involved as the "same." An aging man peers into the mirror and recognizes the "same" person who, as a young boy, kicked cans on the way to school and daydreamed about doing some great thing in his life. The practices of Christianity in the twentieth century differ considerably from those of the first, yet intelligent, knowledgeable persons celebrate the continuity of the "same" faith.

A second common structure is a strange loop. As shown in Figure 2–7, a loop occurs when the contextual force is equal in strength to the reflexive force; the loop is "strange" when the reflexive force changes the content of the contexts that guided the action. Figure 2–8 shows how this might look for a person who might well be called a "problem drinker."

An oscillation between two "opposite" forms of behavior is the characteristic practice that reconstructs a strange loop. In the case of an alcoholic, this often takes the form of a period of absolute sobriety followed by a period of drinking to excess, and so on. How does this pattern of practices come about?

One explanation focuses on a strangely looped relationship between the person's perception of episodes and concept of self. This explanation follows the arrows in Figure 2–8.

1. At one time, the alcoholic perceives himself as having a problem ("I cannot

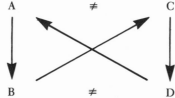

Figure 2–7. Abstract model of a strange loop.

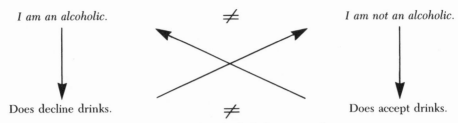

Figure 2–8. The alcoholic's strange loop.

control my drinking") and this concept of self becomes the context for his behavior in relevant situations: when offered drinks, he declines or takes a nonalcoholic alternative.

2. At some later date, however, he reflects on his recent behavior and notes that he has not taken a drink for what seems to him a long time. The episodes in which he has participated (as they have been incorporated into his resources) become the context for his concept of self, and persuade him that he can in fact control his drinking.

3. With this new concept of self ("I can control my drinking") as the context for subsequent actions, he begins to drink. Because he is an alcoholic, this leads to uncontrolled drinking and the familiar litany of problems deriving from it: perhaps he loses his job or offends his friends or family.

4. At some point, these episodes become part of his resources and, because this is a loop, become the context for his self concept. In this context, he thinks of himself as unable to control his drinking, and so it goes.

The Undirected Play: A Metaphor of Coordination

Imagine a very special kind of theater. There is no audience: everyone is "on stage" and is a participant. There are many props, but they are not neatly organized: in some portions of the stage are jumbles of costumes and furniture; in others, properties have been arranged as a set for a contemporary office; in yet another, they depict a medieval castle. There is no director—or, better said, there are many self-appointed directors each of whom bellows and swaggers in an attempt to impose order on the chaos. There is no script—or, better said, there are many scripts, each embraced with various levels of intensity by different groups. Actors move about the stage, encountering sets, would-be directors, and other actors who might provide the supporting cast for a production of some play. Imagine a wandering actor who encounters a particular group and, both to introduce herself and to suggest how they might coordinate, speaks a few lines as Ophelia. If the others respond with lines as Polonius and Hamlet, coordination has been achieved and they produce a pocket of order within the cacaphonous din. (We might call the group a "family" or a "culture.") But if Ophelia's lines are met with something written by Sophocles, Cervantes, or Simon, they may well have difficulty making the conjoint practice coherent.

The history of this theater shows that such babble produces confusion, frustration, and recriminations. If our actor feels that her Ophelia *ought to* fit into Don Quixote or Cyrano, then she may—literally—drive herself crazy trying to construct a story that makes the bizarre practices coherent. Perhaps she will drop the role of Ophelia and act like la Dulcinea del Toboso or Roxanne, in which case the practices have (re)constructed a *different* story, but a coherent one. Or she may cling to the role of Ophelia and wander on, hoping to find a group with which she can coordinate.

In your imagination, place yourself on a catwalk looking down on this theater. You see bedlam, with pockets of coherence and coordination. Some groups have oriented themselves around a prop—a church steeple, a boxing ring—which gives them a shared reference point and enables them to coordinate. Others have accidentally stumbled into a group prepared to enact the same script. Some move from group to group mouthing the only lines they know, cursing the others for their incompetence because they do not know their cues. Still others are locked into battles about what script they will enact: they seem unable to agree and unable to stop fighting about it. Some envision themselves as the "director" of the play and go about attempting to call everyone else to order. (Of course, the part of "director" is just another part, and adds to the confusion.)

Coordination and the Human Condition

Human beings are caught between two worlds. One is a world of stories in which cows can jump over the moon, heroes rise up to deliver their people from a fate worse than death, and—only sometimes, even in this world—stories have happy endings. Imagination fuels fantasy in this world; its logic allows us to start over from the beginning, entertain alternative endings, and so forth. The other world is one of interaction with our fellows, in which our capabilities to act are seriously limited by the rude characteristics of our nerves, muscles, and bones, and in which other persons often derail our intentions by stubbornly insisting on acting out their own stories. The human condition derives from being, simultaneously, hermeneutic ("interpretive"; an inveterate storyteller) and social, inextricably enmeshed in still unfolding patterns of collaborative action.

Because humans are social, coordination is a universal aspect of being human. However, not only humans coordinate. The characteristics of human coordination can be displayed by comparing it to the ways some nonhuman entities produce conjoint actions.

Machines

The relationships among machines may be thought of as communication, but what they do contrasts sharply with human communication. Coordination, coherence, and mystery are all jumbled together, for human beings; but for machines, communication is pure coordination.

In the second quarter of this century, mathematicians and engineers noted that systems function by the movement of *information* rather than that of energy or some commodity from one place to another. The organization of such systems consists in channels of communication.

This way of thinking resulted in cybernetics (the study of how systems can be regulated by devices that monitor and "steer" their function) and the development of sophisticated codes and channels for the transmission of information. For example, modems that enable computers to "talk" to each other over telephone wires, and data-based networks that permit users to manipulate a great deal of information, whether in numbers or alphabets.

This approach to communication has a particular notion of what communication is like, best expressed in the technical definition of "information." Information is a quantitative substance that "reduces uncertainty" in a system of symbols. For example, if one person chose a number between one and ten, and a second person wanted to know what that number was, there would be a certain, precisely measurable, amount of uncertainty. But if the second person cleverly noted that the first was using *both* hands to "remember" the number, he could assume that the number was between six and ten. The "message" of using two hands to represent the number reduced the uncertainty by half. In this view, "good" communication occurs when the message at the "destination" is identical with that at the "source." In fact, the existence of communication in a system can be inferred by comparing the information at various "places" in the system. A maxim used by engineers is that if the information is equivalent at two places, then there is a channel of communication between them whether it has been detected or not.

When two machines are "interfaced," messages can flow between them easily. A whole new jargon has developed to describe these communication practices. If one has a "smart" terminal, one can "download" a file from another computer—so long as the "software" is compatible and the baud rate of the modem is sufficiently fast—and have it printed as "hardcopy" and waiting when you get home.

Because communication among machines consists in pure coordination, the reduction of uncertainty, with nothing of coherence or mystery about it, it is good for some purposes but not for others. There is a cautionary tale about uncritical reliance on computers, summarized in the maxim "garbage in, garbage out," or GIGO for short. A computer will faithfully store, remember, even print "data files" that are meaningless as well as those that are profound. The lines you are now reading were written on a microcomputer, but that computer did not get self-conscious about what was said of it.

There is a lot of talk nowadays about "artificial intelligence," and some pretty impressive demonstrations suggest that sophisticated machines can engage in many practices previously thought unique to humans. The general structure of these demonstrations usually follows the so-called Turing Test: a machine is judged to be "intelligent" if a human observer cannot tell if the behaviors it emits are performed by a human or by a machine.

The Turing Test may say more about the quality of the intelligence of human beings—who seem capable of an incredibly broad range of behaviors, some of which seem machinelike—than about the "intelligence" of the machines to which they are compared. But for our purposes, the Turing Test is not the best point of comparison between machine and human communication.

Computers can certainly be programed to generate interpretations of *why* they are made to participate in the Turing Test. But they do not do so necessarily or spontaneously, and that is the point. Computers are very "content" to perform merely instrumental functions; unless instructed, they do not seem to have the human need to search for the significance of what is going on, or to be distressed if they do not know the purpose for which they were created or their immense powers employed.

Humans do, and thus they "clutter up" their communication with all sorts of things that get in the way of "high fidelity" transmission of "information" from one place to another. Humans persist in making meanings extraneous to the message, such as the relationship between the speaker and the listener, the cost of the other's clothing, what others will think if they see us talking together, and so on.

In Shannon and Weaver's mathematical model of communication (1949), these extraneous meanings comprise "noise sources" that interfere with the message. For human communication, they are the stuff of which coherence and mystery are made.

Honeybees

Human beings are variably enmeshed in multiple social systems simultaneously, each with its own logic of meaning and action. Honeybees are not. Demonstrating what truly sincere communication would be like, they are fully enmeshed in a single social system. They say only and all of what they mean—and a human being would die of boredom in this kind of communication system.

The communication patterns of insects and animals have provided a series of surprises. The first surprise was their complexity. Fish, snakes, toads, and crows, like humans, are confronted with certain "facts of life," and have sophisticated ways of coordinating their behaviors around them. These patterns are rich in the array of messages used, including ritualized movements (dances), facial and bodily displays (snarls, tail-movements), permanent or temporary coloration, the production of pheromones (scents), and rich patterns of vocalizations.

The second surprise was the nature of the differences between animal and human communication. Compared to human communication, animal communication is limited in terms of its content. Bertrand Russell wryly noted that "no matter how eloquently a dog may bark, he cannot tell you that his parents were poor but honest" (Farb, 1975, p. 259). Most humans are surrounded by others of their species, and do not have an opportunity to sense how barren the world is without other humans. Certainly the world is filled with a great variety of beautiful and complex entities other than humans, but the multileveled world of social reality depends upon human construction.

Your dog may be very accurate in detecting your mood and in begging for its dinner, but it cannot appreciate your puns or participate in a satisfactory discussion of the relative merits of the literary philosophies of Tolstoi and Conrad. A youthful Winston Churchill, campaigning for votes in a worker's section of Manchester, bemoaned the fate of the impoverished persons he met. "Fancy," he remarked to a similarly aristocratic companion, "living in one of those streets, never seeing anything beautiful, never eating anything savory—*never saying anything clever!*" (Tuchman, 1966, p. 431). In the most recent retelling of the "Tarzan" story, Greystoke pronounces himself half an English Lord and half wild, and returns to the jungle. The movie ends there on a melancholy note. It is clear that Greystoke is out of place in both worlds. His problems with human society are documented in the film; his troubles with the society of a band of chimpanzees *after* his exposure to human social reality are not. A sequel to the movie would certainly show him bored and frustrated with his companions, who—unlike the Manchester working class—really *cannot* say anything clever.

The dance of the honeybees provides the closest thing to an exception to this characteristic of nonhuman communication. Honeybees do "talk" of things removed in space and time. In fact, the distance and direction (and flying time to) a source of nectar is the subject of the "dance."

Honeybees are social by nature, and depend on a division of labor for survival. The queen must be fed by bees who do not reproduce but who must locate and bring to the hive sufficient food for the whole colony. These "facts of life" impose performance demands on the "worker bees" unlike those of most other animals. Unlike lions, for example, bees cannot consume their food where they find it, but must bring it back to a central place. Unlike birds, which can carry food in their talons, bees transport food in their stomach and it requires many of them to transport enough to feed the hive.

Bees have met this performance demand by a complicated communication system. A lone honeybee will arrive at the hive and engage in a dance, after which a large group of bees, not necessarily including the dancer, will depart and fly directly to a source of food. The dance conveys accurate information about the location, quantity, and quality of the food.

Information about the type of plant in which the nectar is to be found is conveyed by the odor of the flower that adheres to the dancer's body. Information about the quantity and quality of the food is conveyed by the liveliness and the duration of the dance movements, with sounds added if the food is unusually rich. The location of the food source is indicated by the rhythm of the dance and by the orientation of the axis of the tail with respect to gravity. If the food is very near, the dancer will turn round and round; if it is more than eighty meters away, the dancing bee makes a figure eight pattern, and shakes its tail when it is aligned in the proper orientation. The number of dance cycles is inversely related to the distance. If there are ten cycles in a fifteen-second period, the food is 100 meters away; if one cycle in a fifteen-second period, the food is 10,000 meters away. The angle to the verticle at which the bee shakes its tail is the same angle between the line of flight and the line to the sun. If the bee's tail is upward when it is wagged, then the food is to be found flying toward the sun; if downward, away from the sun (*Encyclopaedia Britannica*, 9:129).

The accuracy of this system of communication is vital to bees. Inasmuch as they have only their stomachs in which to carry food, they should arrive at a food source "empty." Before setting out on a flight, they eat just enough to give them the energy to fly there. Sometimes the signaling system goes wrong, and one may encounter bees crawling slowly on the ground far from their hive. They are out of "fuel" and unable to return to the hive, somehow having missed the promised food supply. They will soon die.

Bees seem to be born with a genetic "programing" to perform and interpret this message system. It is unique among animal communication patterns because it describes things that are far away, and does so with mathematical precision. Where, in the physiology of the bee, is the knowledge to measure angles and interpret numbers of cycles per second? It is amazing.

But note what bees *cannot* do and still achieve coordination around the "facts of life" in the hive.

A bee cannot dance for the sheer joy of dancing. If it did, the result would be dead bees. Observing the dance, a swarm of bees will set off in a precise direction and expect to find a food source. Eventually they will be on foot, unable to fly, far from the hive and with no food. How do you tell a bee that dancing can be for the sheer joy of living, not a task-oriented instrumental activity?

A dancing bee cannot improvise, throwing in a high kick here or a pirouette there simply for the artistic value. If it did, the result would be dead bees. How do you tell a bee that dancing can be for esthetic purposes or a way of "saying something clever"?

A dancing bee cannot change the subject. This communication system is remarkably efficient in saying, in effect, "nectar, at 120 meters, angle 30 degrees away from the sun.

Let's go!" A bee cannot say that the flowers are very pretty today, or that bees live not by nectar alone and that there must be more to life than this. Bees cannot say, "workers of the hive, unite! You have nothing to lose but your honey!" And if there were a genius bee who could say all of this by some sort of improvised dance, the result would be dead bees, not a revolution against the queen, a spiritual great awakening, or even a companionable flight to sniff rather than to rob the roses.

Wolves

Wolves have always been symbols of fear for humans. The vicious efficiency of the pack attack has inspired military leaders, and the unending war of farmers and shepherds against the resourceful predators has made wolves seem to be natural enemies of humans. Wolves are often thought of as the disembodied, frightening howl at night or the sudden flash of cruel teeth. A closer study of them, however, reveals that they are much more than just that.

Wolves are territorial. The dominant male and female in a pack establish a den in the center of a territory and mark the boundaries with urine or feces. Wolves have a remarkably keen sense of scent: they can detect one part of urine in one million parts of water. Hence they can recognize, even after extensive weathering, the territories they or other wolves have marked. Often they will urinate or defecate near the same spot, "accepting" the boundary between their territory and that of the adjacent wolf. Generally, if wolves are in their own territory, they act aggressively toward any intruder; if in another's territory, they will avoid confrontation.

Wolves spend much of their time in a pack. The members of the pack are organized in a strict hierarchy of dominance in which only the dominant male and female breed. This order is expressed in a variety of postural signals, and enables a high degree of coordination, particularly in hunting. Wolves use vocalizations to signal each other about the presence of prey, and a wide range of signals for expressing their "emotions" and "intentions." The position of the ears, the tail, the hair on the back of the neck, and the lips provide a rich communicative system.

Consider the "wolf's-eye view" of the world. It is primarily an olfactory world, with vision, touch, hearing, and taste used as supplements. If you and a wolf (or your family's pet dog) were to walk through the same path in the woods, you would sense a very different world. For you, the dominant sensations would probably be colors and shapes, and you would be aware only of things that were there at that moment. For the wolf, the dominant sensations would be smells, and they would tell the recent history of the trail. For you the walk might be a restful respite from the day's labors, a spiteful withdrawal from human company, a fearful ordeal, a spiritual quest, a shortcut to a destination; for the wolf, what? Surely not any of these. Whatever "coherence" the walk possesses, it would be in wolfish—not human—concepts.

What might a wolf think about the communication competence of a human being? If capable of such musings, a wolf would perceive humans as tragically crippled. Think of it: humans have no tail, and thus cannot signal their intent by wagging it, or holding it low and extended, or tucking it between their legs. Humans have almost immovable ears, and cannot lay them back, or cock them forward in a symboling system signaling emotions. Perhaps most tragically, humans have an atrophied, virtually useless olfactory sense. They cannot identify whose territory they are on by smelling the markings; they cannot differentiate between friend and foe by smelling them; they cannot follow the track of a rabbit by smell—pitiful!

The movie *Never Cry Wolf* portrays a naturalist studying wolves. He decided that the best way to proceed was to establish his own den and mark his own, comparatively tiny, territory by urinating around the periphery. His markings were "accepted" by the wolf in the adjacent territory: the wolf traced his steps and urinated alongside his markings. But, as the naturalist wryly reported, "what had taken me six hours and twenty-seven cups of tea, took him just a few minutes!"

Wolves have an effective communication system. Although limited in comparison to that of humans, it has some advantages in comparison to that of honeybees. A wolf cannot discuss philosophy or describe the curious practices of exotic peoples—but this "lack" is not particularly troubling, for it knows nothing of philosophy or exotic peoples. The wolf cannot describe direction and distance to a food source as effectively as a honeybee, but it can signal the hunt, or its desire to mate, or its challenge to any intruder on its territory. Wolves can "talk" about social status by signaling their place in the dominance hierarchy. Wolves can "talk" about food, enabling them to coordinate in pursuit of prey. Wolves can even "play." That capability deserves a bit more analysis.

Bateson (1972, p. 189) distinguished three types of messages: mood-signs, simulations of mood-signs, and messages about messages. He noted that the lower phyla in the animal kingdom emit mood-signs, to which others "automatically" respond. That is, a female ready for reproduction emits an odor that signals her "mood" (in this sense, physiological state). Males who perceive this odor respond automatically. Communication at the level of mood-signals is direct, immediate, and unsophisticated. It is analogous to two interfaced computers, the relationships among cells in an organism, or humans who display rather than report their emotions.

Communication among mammals, including wolves, is more sophisticated. It includes messages that simulate mood-signs. In adult humans, such simulations include commercially manufactured perfumes, deodorants, after-shave lotions, and the like, which are designed to be voluntary signals of what may or may not be the actual physiological state of the organism. Deodorants "protect" us from giving off mood-signals that would elicit an unwanted attentiveness by other persons. Perfumes simulate mood-signs that we might want to produce but may be unable to generate naturally.

Wolves do not use perfume—maybe. They do like to roll in the rotting carcass of a long dead animal. Does enveloping themselves with such a smell have some social meaning? Is it a way of (literally!) covering oneself with glory? A way of saying, in effect, "Lo! The mighty hunter comes!" Is it a dominance claim or sexual statement? Or does it have a meaning in a system of significance about which we humans know nothing?

Wolves do use simulated mood-signals in the form of "threats" and "play." They seldom fight among themselves, but more often engage in "displays" of threats that seem to answer the question of where each stands in the dominance hierarchy, or whether one wolf has come without permission into another's territory. They also engage in acts that look like fights, but are not fights: play. And this is a complicated message.

None of the animals described here can say "no" in any of its forms, such as "I will not hurt you." When your pet dog wants to play and says, in effect, "I will not bite you," the only way he can do that is to take your hand in his mouth and not bite. The potential for misunderstanding such a message while it is in the process of being delivered is quite high!

But wolves (and other mammals) manage to convey just such messages. Bateson described a trip he took to the Fleishhacker Zoo in San Francisco which, he said, caused him to revise his thinking about communication.

> What I encountered at the zoo was a phenomenon well known to everybody: I saw two young monkeys playing, i.e., engaged in an interactive sequence of which the unit actions or signals were similar to but not the same as those of combat. It was evident, even to the human observer, that the sequence as a whole was not combat, and evident to the human observer that to the participant monkeys this was "not combat.". . . The playful nip denoted the bite, but it does not denote what would be denoted by the bite [Bateson, 1972, pp. 179–80].

The message "this is play" is neither a mood-sign nor a simulated mood-sign; it is a statement about other messages. "Play" among higher mammals is a sophisticated form of coordination, but still less complex than that among humans.

Human Beings

Coordination is more difficult to achieve in human than in nonhuman communication. The difficulty arises from the greater capabilities, not the limitations, of human beings. There seems to be a general principle here. Increased complexity in the symbolic system(s) enables more sophisticated patterns of coordination, but at the price of greater difficulty in achieving these or any other patterns of coordination. Human communication contains in it the potential for patterns of coordination not paralleled in any nonhuman communication of which I am aware, but also displays a disconcerting tendency to produce unwanted patterns and unpatterned sequences of acts.

There are four ways in which the symbolic systems of human beings differ from those of nonhumans, and each makes coordination potentially more sophisticated and certainly more difficult: the ability to combine messages into an infinitely large signaling system; the ability to speak of and believe in counterfactual conditionals; the creation of moral orders; and the ability to be variably enmeshed in multiple systems simultaneously.

Combinations of Messages

Ever since Aristotle first speculated about human speech, it has been noted that humans share "the globe with a variety of animals that whistle, shriek, squeak, bleat, hoot, coo, call, and howl" (Farb, 1975, p. 255). Human speakers do much the same things. In fact, human speech does not differ very much from animal communication patterns in the number of vocalizations—phonemes—used in the signaling system. There are about forty-five different vocalizations in spoken English, twenty-seven in Italian, and thirteen in Hawaiian. Prairie dogs use ten, some monkeys twenty, chickens twenty-five, chimpanzees twenty-five, and foxes thirty-six. Given these observations, it is perhaps natural to assume that human communication "is only some superior kind of animal language" (Farb, 1975, pp. 255–57).

For example, Charles Darwin compared the facial expression of emotions in primates and in humans. Darwin argued that at least some human social behaviors could be explained by demonstrating their bestial origin. Following this lead, a number of twentieth-century social scientists have attempted to show that "human behavior was a thinly disguised version of the territorial and reproductive strife that was to be found in primate communities." Jonathan Miller (1983, p. 156) warned that "these misleading conclusions were widely publicized in a series of best-selling popularizations, and the reading public was given the false impression that biologists had identified in the human species an incorrigible tendency towards aggression and territorial ambition."

Although the array of signals available to a human speaker is not necessarily larger than that available to a chicken or a chimpanzee, humans get more "work" out of the system than do nonhumans. They do this by combining the message units into meaningful sequences—morphemes—and by combining patterns of morphemes into even larger meaningful sequences—sentences. The result is, quite literally, a signaling system capable of infinite expansion.

There is some evidence that the higher primates may be taught to use their signaling system in this linguistic manner, but they do not do so naturally. For example, chimpanzees employ one unit of sound in social play, another when a juvenile is lost, a third when attacked, and so on, but they do not combine two or more calls to generate a unique and more sophisticated message. In contrast, the thirteen morphemes in spoken Hawaiian can be combined in ways that produce 2,197 words with three morphemes in them, and nearly five million words with six morphemes in them. In English, the three sounds represented in writing by the letters *e*, *n*, and *d* can be combined in various sequences to make words such as end, den, and Ned:

> But the chimpanzee cannot combine the three units of sound that mean play, lost juvenile, and threat of attack to form some other message. Nor can the chimpanzee's call that means "here is food" ever be changed to talk about the delicacies it consumed yesterday or its expectations about finding certain fruits tomorrow. Generation after generation, as far into the future as the chimpanzee survives as a species, it will use that call solely to indicate the immediate presence of food.
>
> Even the most vocal animals are utterly monotonous in what they say in a given situation [Farb, 1975, pp. 257–58].

Counterfactual Conditionals

An apparently distinguishing characteristic of human communication is the ability to lie verbally. Many animals make mood-signs that deceive would-be prey or predators, but this is at the level of "false signals." The human ability to make messages about messages, coupled with the human ability to use the "negative," combines to enable humans to talk explicitly about things that do not exist.

In contemporary philosophy, such talk is referred to as "counterfactual conditionals," or statements of what might have happened if something else that did not occur had happened. For example, the statement "if it had rained today, I would not have gone to the park and would not have gotten into that trouble" is a counterfactual conditional. In fact, it did not rain, the speaker did go to the park, and the speaker did get into trouble.

Counterfactual conditionals resemble messages like "this is play," but go beyond them. In his analysis of play, Bateson noted that the playful nip denotes the bite, but does not denote that which would be denoted by the bite. But in human experience, what Bateson called "the opposite experience" sometimes occurs:

> A man experiences the full intensity of subjective terror when a spear is flung at him out of the 3D screen or when he falls headlong from some peak created in his own mind in the intensity of nightmare. At the moment of terror there was no questioning of "reality," but still there was no spear in the movie house and no cliff in the bedroom. The images did not

denote that which they seemed to denote, but these same images did really evoke that terror which would have been evoked by a real spear or a real precipice . . . . In the dim region where art, magic, and religion meet and overlap, human beings have evolved the "metaphor that is meant," the flag which men will die to save, and the sacrament that is felt to be more than "an outward and visible sign, given unto us." Here we can recognize an attempt to deny the difference between map and territory, and to get back to the absolute innocence of communication by means of pure mood-signs [Bateson, 1972, p. 183].

Of course, the attempt to get "back" to the innocence of pure mood-signs itself requires a sophisticated pattern of coordination. Failures to achieve these forms of coordination have resulted in some of the sorriest pages of human history: religious persecutions, nationalistic prejudice, deliberately inculcated closed-mindedness, and so forth.

Again, the general principle I cited above is evidenced. The ability to engage in sophisticated patterns of coordination precludes either ease or fidelity in the processes of human communication.

The Creation of Moral Orders

One part of the traditional understanding of the scientific method is the principle of parsimony. This principle requires theorists to accept the simplest possible explanation of any phenomenon. Given rival theories equally powerful in accounting for the phenomenon, the "residue" of the more complicated theory is described as "surplus meaning" and is to be contemptuously discarded as the results of "mere" imagination.

Following the principle of parsimony, some social scientists have tried to account for the wide range of practices in which humans engage by showing that they are really nothing but elaborate ways of coping with biologically based facts of life such as sex, hunger, social dominance, and the like. For example, Desmond Morris interprets "apologies" not as evidence of a distinctively human "moral order" but as a linguistic signal of appeasement, not really different from a wolf that will expose its neck to the stronger member of the pack, thus signaling that it has no intention to challenge the leader of the pack for dominance.

Other social theorists argue that such parsimony can be achieved only at the expense of fundamentally misunderstanding the nature of the human world. Language, they argue, "creates a domain which has no counterpart in the animal world—an elaborate system of rules and norms, rights and duties without which it is impossible to visualize, let alone describe the realities of human existence. It is only inside this framework that concepts such as shame, pride, honor, embarrassment, and humiliation have any meaning" (J. Miller, 1983, p. 156). In short, they argue that human beings create and then live within "moral orders."

"Morality" in this sense means being alive to issues of honor, dignity, and character. A "moral order" includes a set of practices and resources that promotes morality. In a moral order:

1. Rituals exist for the public markings of respect and contempt;
2. Actions are treated as displays of character, not just as instrumental ways of achieving purposes;
3. Moral commentaries are given that describe, prescribe, and evaluate conduct; and
4. There is an asymmetrical distribution of the rights to perform the practices listed above [Harré, 1984, p. 245].

Believe it or not, those of us who believe that *every* human society has a moral order, and that within the whole array of human societies there are *many, fundamentally different* moral orders, have had to defend our judgment from the attacks of those who want to "reduce" human existence to "smaller" units of analysis. Some of these reductionists argue that the whole concept of "moral order" is a "surplus meaning" generated by hyperactive imaginations or wishful thinking.

The ubiquity of concepts such as honor, dignity, and the like, is evidence that coordination among humans occurs within moral orders. If these are the result of hyperactive imaginations, then such imaginations have occurred in every culture and in every historical period of human existence.

Peter Farb identified the Great Basin Shoshone as the culture that was *least* likely to ensconce coordination within a moral order. The first Europeans who encountered them were uniformly appalled. In 1827 Jedediah Smith declared them "the most miserable objects in creation." Mark Twain, in 1861, described them as "the wretchedest type of mankind I have ever seen . . . (who) produce nothing at all, and have no villages, and no gatherings together into strictly defined tribal communities—a people whose only shelter is a rag cast on a bush to keep off a portion of the snow . . . [They] are manifestly descended from the self-same gorilla, or kangaroo, or Norway rat, whichever animal-Adam the Darwinians trace them to." In 1886 historian Hubert Howe Bancroft pronounced them directly kin to animals: "having no clothes, scarcely any cooked food, in many instances no weapons, with merely a few vague imaginings for religion, living in the utmost squalor and filth, putting no bridle on their passions, there is surely room for no missing link between them and the brutes" (Farb, 1978, pp. 18–20).

Having built the case "against" the Shoshone, Farb then countered it by noting that they are circumscribed by customs, rules of behavior, and rituals whose complexities rival those of the Kremlin or the Court of Versailles. At every moment of life the Shoshone must be careful to observe the complicated folkways of the group, to do reverence to superhuman powers, to remember the courtesies and obligations of kinship, and to avoid particular places. "Especially at those critical times of life known as the rites of passage—among them, birth, puberty, and death—an elaborate etiquette regulates their behavior . . . [They] can classify relatives, distinguishing the different kinds of cousins, and can set up rules about which relatives are appropriate marriage partners and which are not . . . [They] hold formalized rabbit hunts, share food during famines, and observe complicated rules of hospitality and exchange" (Farb, 1978, pp. 20–21).

Another way of defending the concept of "moral order" is to attack those who claim to be able to get along without it, such as Desmond Morris. Harré noted that Morris did his "man-watching" in "anonymous world(s) where nobody knows anybody else . . . [where] no autobiographies [are] at stake [and] where there is no institutional framework" such as London parks or the Naples promenade. In such situations, Harré claims,

All we have got to go on . . . is our biological inheritance . . . . Of course, very rarely do human beings live in those kinds of conditions. Mostly they know each other very well. Amongst other things they are constructing biographies and autobiographies of each other. They are living in very tight-knit communities. They have a delicately balanced system of performative utterances with which they construct the future and reconstruct the past. They do not live together by "happen" chance. People from infancy are already living in institutions, where there are roles to be fulfilled. Most importantly of all, there are rules by which high-grade social performances are specified. The rules are cultural artifacts, I believe, which act as the ultimate control of all sorts of institutional activities [in J. Miller, 1983, pp. 162–63].

One reason why theorists have resisted the idea of moral orders, I suspect, is that they too wish to return to the simplicity and innocence of communication by mood-signals. If the various practices of communication were nothing but elaborations of mood-signals, then a sufficiently powerful analysis could cut through the apparent complexity and enable us to coordinate with each other with the fidelity of honeybees. On the other hand, if one of the human characteristics is the creation and maintenance of moral orders, then there is no "anchor" for the various arrays of practices. Coordination is inherently difficult in human communication because the meaning of messages is determined by their enmeshment in various moral orders whose content cannot be assumed to be either constant or commensurate with each other.

Variably Enmeshed in Multiple Systems

Moral orders are socially created, expressed, and (re)constructed in the practices of various groups of persons. There are many such moral orders, and persons are enmeshed in many of them simultaneously. For example, some individuals are simultaneously fathers, sons, brothers, lovers, employees, friends, and citizens. Each of these roles denotes a whole system of rights, duties, and obligations. Further, these rights, duties, and obligations are not precisely identical.

In some cultures, the rights, duties, and obligations of these various roles are similar enough that persons do not find themselves often in moral dilemmas. When they do encounter inconsistent moral necessities, it is usually possible to solve the problem by being more deeply enmeshed in one morality than another. To protect his family, for example, a father might disregard his duties as an employee.

Problems occur in two types of situations. Within a single cultural system, a person may be equally enmeshed in two or more roles with conflicting moral obligations, or persons might find themselves enmeshed in two or more moral orders, such that it is difficult even to compare the incompatible moral obligations.

Difficulties in Coordination

At birth, human infants are far more helpless than those of most other mammals. A growing number of scholars believe that we are born "unfinished," expelled from the isolation of the womb to complete our gestation in webs of social relationships. When we are born, we have the physical capacity to be democrats or monarchists, and to speak Turkish or Japanese. When we begin to interact with others, certain of our abilities are extended through practice and by being embedded in the transpersonal logics of interaction. But every leaving is a returning; every learning a forgetting. As we continue to develop in some ways, we lose the ability to think/act/speak in others. This is most clearly the case with "accents." At birth, normal infants can utter all the sounds of all human languages. As they learn to speak the language of their parents and peers, they become very sophisticated in using the sounds of their own language at the same time that they are developing a trained incapacity to make, for examples, the clicks, *r*'s, and *l*'s of other languages. Much the same process, I believe, happens in the development of ways of thinking and forms of acting.

The point of all this is to subvert the illusion that coordination occurs easily. Just as speaking a grammatical sentence in your native language seems "thoughtless" or "natural" because it represents a lifetime of learning, so the ability to place an order in a restaurant, deliver a compliment without seeming ingratiating, or exchange greeting rituals with a stranger seems simple because it is the product of the mutual mastery of a collaborative art form.

Coordination is never simple; sometimes it is exceptionally difficult. In the following paragraphs, I cite three situations and one inherent feature that make coordination difficult.

Aggregates and Second-Order Cybernetic Systems

Coordination is inherently difficult because *practices* are aggregates, *human beings* are second-order cybernetic systems, and practices are essential to the process of being human. Human beings have "minds" that function as cybernetic monitors; practices do not. As a result, human beings frequently find themselves frustrated from trying to funnel into a less sophisticated structure their highest thoughts—as Campbell (1959, p. 3) said, to incarnate blazing, unearthly visions into earthly communities.

Let "aggregates" denote clusters of actions produced by persons who do not take each other into account. For example, if every person who walked through a garden picked just one rose as a memo, the garden would soon be bare; if every farmer shot every wolf he could find, the rabbit population would expand tremendously. Aggregate behaviors (of unrelated persons who do not observe each other's behaviors or monitor the consequences of their own actions) comprise practices that snarl traffic (when everyone takes the same shortcut), leave the front rows of auditoriums empty and the back rows full, crowd certain areas of national parks, and so on (Schelling, 1978).

Systems have a qualitatively different form of organization. In systems, the *occurrence* of particular acts depends on those that preceded and are anticipated as following them, and the *meaning* of acts derives from the pattern of the whole.

When systems reach a certain degree of complexity, they develop the capacity to monitor and direct themselves in accordance with their own purposes. Such systems are termed "cybernetic," based on the Greek word for the person who controlled the rudder and thus steered a ship. The simplest cybernetic systems are thermostats, which monitor the temperature and switch on heat or cooling devices in order to fulfill their "purpose" of maintaining a temperature within a predetermined range. In a standard configuration, thermometers are located throughout the building, a heating unit is in the basement and a cooling unit on the roof, and a computer is attached to a thermometer to turn on the heat when the building gets too cool and turn on the air conditioner when it gets too warm.

In a well-designed building, the thermostat keeps the temperature within a comfortable range. But consider what might happen if the designer was incompetent, lazy, malicious, or had a deep sense of irony. Imagine two adjacent buildings, each of which had a thermostat, but with a curious bit of cross-wiring. The thermometers in one building are connected to the heating and cooling units in the other, and vice versa. One day, building A gets too cool. This is detected by the thermometers and the computer turns on the heat in building B. Building B, of course, gets too hot, so the computer turns on the air conditioning in building A. But building A was already too cool, so the computer turns up the heat in building B, and so on. This is a pattern of symmetrical escalation familiar to therapists and communication researchers: persons feel compelled by the unfolding patterns of interaction to do what they had done before except in a more exaggerated manner. This pattern continues until something—a heating unit, a cooling unit, the face of one of the participants—gets broken.

No self-respecting architect would design such a system, and if such a system were designed, the architect would certainly be liable for lawsuits. But this is a structure that resembles Figure 2–2. Communication practices—the actual production of sequences of acts that, taken together, comprise the social world in which we live—have no cybernetic monitor. There are cybernetic monitors within the system—the minds of the persons involved—but there are too many of them for rational control and they are not able to monitor each other, only emerging practices.

When cybernetic systems reach a certain degree of complexity, they develop the capacity to monitor their own purposes as well as the way their behaviors serve those purposes. Second-order cybernetic systems can "choose" among other purposes; they can talk *about* as well as *within* moral orders; and they can move among various symbolic systems. The cross-wired thermostats described above might suffer mechanical malfunction in their benighted quest to maintain equilibrium in the temperature, but they will *not* reflect on the absurdity of it all, or become confused, or decide that one building is architecturally inferior and thus deserves to be very hot. Only second-order cybernetic systems act like this.

If coordinated practices were cybernetic—whether first- or second-order—they would have some systemwide monitoring unit that could *detect* patterns and *direct* the system in ways that would overcome them. However, there is no such systemwide monitor; instead there are multiple monitors—each of the persons involved in the process—none of which has access to the entire system. As a result, errors about *whether* the emerging pattern is coordinated occur along with potentially uncoordinated attempts to *repair* the pattern. Further, these second-order cybernetic monitors may make unpatterned changes in their purposes for the practices in which they are engaged, or bring confused, conflicting purposes to it.

The human condition, then, is that of being inextricably enmeshed in a process whose properties are significantly less complex than human capabilities. We cope with this condition in two ways: a search for surrogate systemwide cybernetic monitors, and the construction of coherent stories for whatever patterns are produced.

Persons often act *as if* there were a systemwide cybernetic monitor. These surrogates for the missing component of the communication process sometimes comprise the larger-than-life symbols by which human beings form the world into religions, philosophies, political systems, and the like. At other times, they comprise the more tangible "props" for the "undirected play," such as definitions of situations, roles, motives, or places. At still others, they may be any common referent presumed to be shared by all participants: the weather or the pulsating rhythms of the music at a dance.

Persons display considerable skill in constructing coherent stories for the patterns in which they participate. In fact, as second-order cybernetic systems that can invent and move among purposes, persons can "frame" any given practice in many ways. For example, three of the conversational excerpts with which we began this chapter ("Did you hear what happened . . .") were described as poorly coordinated. However, the skills of a great playwrite are not required to frame them in longer sequences in which they are clever, playful, mischievous—but well-coordinated—conversational games. (Simply reenacting the episode to demonstrate it to a friend or as a class example makes an initially uncoordinated episode coordinated.)

Incommensurate Resources

If communicators express different resources in the practices they collectively produce, they are likely to misunderstand and thwart each other's attempt to bring into being their vision of what is good and true. When a woman asks a man, "Do you want to go?" and he says "I don't care if I do," and means yes but she hears him as saying no, then she sadly goes alone, which makes him feel snubbed and left out.

Such misunderstandings are sometimes socially serious, but not theoretically interesting, for they yield rather easily to the ministrations of a good translator or therapist. However, certain types of differences in resources stubbornly resist the efforts of translators and are both socially important and theoretically interesting. Interpreters and researchers tell of concepts and phrases that simply cannot be moved from one language to another. Some social critics describe worldviews that are formally incommensurate, they cannot be "mapped" onto each other, because a faithful translation of the meaning produces a concept with radically different significance in the other worldview. In addition, incommensurate worldviews appeal to different principals or practices in adjudicating the conflict between rival interests or significations.

For example, the New Christian Right in the United States and those whom it calls "secular humanists" differ more radically than just taking opposing stands on issues. The moral orders from which their beliefs and practices derive significance differ so much that the arguments that seem best to one side are repugnant to the other. Some leaders of these groups have made heroic efforts to achieve coordination. Rev. Jerry Falwell, founder of the Moral Majority, and Sen. Edward Kennedy, whom the Moral Majority frequently identifies as the foremost example of a secular humanist, have entertained each other in their homes, appeared together in speaking engagements, and deliberately used a common vocabulary of "civility" (Branham and Pearce, 1987). But a closer reading of their public discourse shows that they draw from radically different resources. I think it likely that one or both of them will detect a failure to coordinate and accuse the other of some sort of betrayal (see Pearce, Littlejohn, and Alexander, in press).

Social interaction among groups with incommensurate resources is characterized by failed attempts at coordination. The participants—and most observers—usually explain the uncoordinated patterns—or the well-coordinated unwanted patterns—as the fault of one side or the other. However, it is more appropriate to say that the social realities of the various actors are mutually opaque.

Schoolrooms and football grounds in contemporary England have elicited concern because they are seen as "disordered." Newspaper accounts portray these settings as violent and unruly, and describe those who instigate unruly behavior as acting under the control of "primitive, almost animallike impulses and drives." The popular perception is that coordination in classrooms and at football matches is difficult because the "kids" have an irrational, inadequate social reality.

However, studies of the actual conversations between "troublemakers" and a research team forced a radical rethinking of the popular perception of the problem. The researchers found that "the 'kids' are knowledgeable about their situation and the meaning of their actions, and are capable of deploying a high standard of theorizing about their activities. . . .In short, they have an explanatory rhetoric at their command" (Marsh, Rosser, and Harré, 1978, p. 6).

If this is the case, why is it that the "kids" have so much difficulty coordinating with members of certain other groups? For example, why did a simple request by a homeowner that the "kids" move from in front of his house lead to an ugly incident? Perhaps because it is a confrontation of two plentiful but incommensurate sets of resources, the expression of each of which threatens and closes down the expression of the other.

In a newspaper retelling of the incident (*Oxford Times*, May 18, 1976), the kids were described as "shouting and screaming." This naming of their actions precludes further interpretation:

> While one may reasonably ask what someone shouted, it hardly makes sense to ask what it was they screamed. So the conjunction of these two words effectively prevents the raising of the question as to what it was that they were saying. Their vocalizations are consigned to the category of mere noise.
>
> Our interpretation of the predicament of the Joneses is simple. . . . Mr. Jones's reported "telling-them-to-go" belongs in a mode of speech instantly recognizable by the folk of the flock as part of the rhetoric of the very world they are closed to. No doubt there was speech addressed from them to him—speech he now glosses as "greeting with abuse and swearing." How could this situation fail to develop if he "failed to stop the nuisance" by appealing to the parents of the young people? It is just their dignity as selves that is at issue, and Mr. Jones has chosen the most powerful humiliation of all, that is treating them as within the social control of their parents.
>
> At this stage nothing remains but that each should present an opaque front to the other. Mr. Jones issues orders—the kids offer simplified abuse. Each has *achieved* opacity by progressive restriction of their modes of communication. The kids see Mr. Jones as incapable of anything but command, Mr. Jones sees the kids as incapable of anything but abuse. The newspaper reporter fails both sides to the dispute by adopting the rhetoric of only one of them, that of Mr. Jones. But then Mr. Jones has access to the reporter and to the apparatus of public statement in a way that the kids manifestly do not [Marsh, Rosser, and Harré, 1978, p. 7].

The "kids" and Mr. Jones comprise a prototype for many instances of failed coordination. I believe that the services of a good interpreter would illuminate a wide range of such situations, ranging from the street corner to the international conference table, as the confrontation of incommensurate social realities.

Mixed-Motive Encounters

The theory of games identifies three types of encounters: pure coordination, pure competition, and mixed-motive games. Pure competition encounters are "zero-sum" games: one participant can win only if another loses by an equivalent amount. Of such encounters are football schedules made: at the end of a season, whatever else happens, the number of wins and losses by teams in the league must be precisely the same.

It has often been noted that zero-sum games of pure competition in fact require a great deal of consensus and coordination. The participants must agree about what counts as winning and losing, and they must cooperate in order to mutually strive toward a goal

Person B
(choices)

	X	Y
1	+5;　+5 (A),　(B)	−10;　+10 (A)　(B)
2	+10;　−10 (A)　(B)	−5;　−5 (A)　(B)

Person
A　(choices)

Figure 2–9. The prisoner's dilemma.

that only one can win. A competitor hates a "good loser"; the thrill of victory is in some manner the inverse of the agony of defeat. In this sense, pure competition requires the greatest coordination.

Games of pure coordination and mixed-motives are "nonzero-sum." In games of pure coordination, both may win or both may lose. The clearest example of such a game involves coordination but not coherence: when on-coming cars meet, it does not matter if both keep to the left or to the right as long as both make the same decision. The deeper meanings of "keep to the right" may vary, but is of little importance. For one, it may be the reenactment of chivalric traditions; for the other, a mere social convention. Agreement, understanding, and being understood are superfluous: all "win" if everyone makes the same choice as everyone else and traffic accidents are avoided.

Mixed-motive games are more complex. The amount that can be won or lost, as well as winning rather than losing, depends on the combination of choices made by the players. The most common mixed-motive game is the so-called prisoner's dilemma (see Figure 2–9). The outcomes are the values in the boxes. "A" chooses either 1 or 2; "B" chooses X or Y. The combination of these choices selects one of the boxes, and "A" gets the first sum; "B" the second. The prisoner's dilemma game has a particular structure, such that each player has a "safe" and a "risky" choice. If "A" chooses "1," there is a risk of -10 and at best a gain of +5; if "A" chooses "2," there may be a gain of +10 and a risk of at most −5. However, if both chose "safe" (2,Y), both lose (-5, -5); if both chose "risky," both win a modest amount (+5, +5). Both have an incentive to trick the other; if one makes the risky choice, the other loses the maximum (-10) and the first wins the most (+10).

Perhaps the closest analogue to the prisoner's dilemma in human interaction involves the multiple meanings of messages. To be right in an argument about baseball may gain a sense of expertise but lose a friend. An old adage captures this insight: the boss isn't always right, but the boss is always the boss.

Unintended Consequences

Things seldom turn out as they were intended. There is a genre of stories—"thriller," or adventure stories—that depicts daring men and women laying out elaborate plans and executing them to perfection. Ken Follett is a leading storyteller in this genre, and in a pensive mood he wrote this introduction to a new printing of *The Modigliani Scandal* (1985, pp. 7–8):

> In a modern thriller the hero generally saves the world. Traditional adventure stories are more modest: The central character merely saves his own life, and perhaps the life of a faithful friend or a plucky girl. In less sensational novels—the middlebrow, well-told narratives that have been the staple diet of readers for more than a century—there is less at stake, but still a character's efforts, struggles, and choices determine his destiny in a dramatic fashion.
>
> I don't actually believe that life is like that. In reality, circumstances quite beyond our control usually determine whether we live or die, become happy or miserable, strike it rich or lose everything. For example: Most rich people inherit their money. Most well-fed people simply had the luck to be born in an affluent country. Most happy people were born into loving families, and most miserable people had crazy parents.
>
> I'm not a fatalist, nor do I believe that everything in life is blind chance. We do not control our lives the way a chess player controls his pieces, but life is not roulette either. As usual, the truth is complicated. Mechanisms beyond our control—and sometimes beyond our understanding—determine a person's fate, yet the choices he makes have consequences, if not the consequences he anticipated.
>
> In *The Modigliani Scandal* I tried to write a new kind of novel, one that would reflect the subtle subordination of individual choice.
>
> What I wrote, in the end, was a lighthearted crime story in which an assortment of people, mostly young, get up to a variety of capers, none of which turns out quite as expected. The critics praised it as sprightly, ebullient, light, bright, cheery, light (again), and fizzy. I was disappointed that they had not noted my serious intentions.
>
> Now I no longer look on the book as a failure. It is fizzy, and none the worse for that. The fact that it is so different from the book I intended to write should not have surprised me. After all, it rather proves my point.

As with this novel, so with life. The rules of meaning and action in many cultures produce outcomes quite different from those intended. For example, Lillian Rubin (1976) studied northeastern American blue-collar (lower income, manual labor) society. The moral order in this culture was one of responsibility, sexual purity, and frank acknowledgment of human nature. Any of these alone might be benign, but their combination provides an unintended "blueprint" for an undesired pattern of premarital pregnancy, early marriage with great economic difficulties, leading to marital problems and preventing upward economic mobility. Persons born into this culture are trained to lead lives of dignity, honor, and morality—that is, to be "good" men and women. But if the content of these rules were abstracted and posted on walls, it would look like this:

A Cultural Blueprint for Marital Discord and Economic Hardship

Some simple rules to internalize and follow

Premarital sex is immoral.

A "good girl" does not premeditate immoral behavior.

Buying pills or other birth control devices is a clear sign of premeditated immoral intent.

If a woman *knows* that she might get "carried away" on a date, she should avoid going so far that she puts herself in the position of losing control.

A person may be unable to resist the passion of the moment and have premarital sex. This is very human and forgivable if. . . .

When pregnancy results from premarital sex the man and woman must do the right thing— marry.

> If you didn't know that you might get carried away by the passion of the moment, then premarital sex is forgiven; but if you knew you might get carried away, then you should have avoided the situation.

The practices that result from these rules not only lead young persons to predictable problems, they re-create themselves generation after generation in ways that preclude economic prosperity, marital stability, and a fuller attainment of the ideals of the culture.

Some American families are known for being very much involved in politics, civic events, or charity. However, the level of involvement they sustain is very shallow. They are not particularly well informed; nor do they maintain their involvement in the face of opposition (Chaffee, 1978). These families do not, I suppose, set out to teach their children to be widely but shallowly involved in society, but if those rules were stated in a barren fashion—like the checkout time of a hotel or the rules for using a municipal swimming pool—they would provide a recipe for shallow involvement.

A Simple Recipe for Shallow Involvement

It is important to be involved in political and social action.
It is important to be informed.
You must be true to your conviction.
Disagreements count as threats to personal relationships.
It is insulting and presumptuous to disagree with persons of higher status.
It is dangerous and improper to insult persons of higher status.
It is most important that we do nothing that will threaten personal relationships.

Anthony Giddens (1979, p. 56) suggested that *all* practices proceed from unacknowledged constraints and lead to unintended consequences. I believe this is a very useful observation. There are contradictions in every set of resources, many of which are obvious only when expressed in practices, surprising most of those who produce them.

Summary

Coordination is a human universal. All human beings everywhere coordinate with their fellows. The question is not *whether* they will achieve coordination, but *how* and *in what form.*

A master mechanic is underemployed sweeping streets; a skilled surgeon underemployed driving a truck. In the same way, human beings are "underemployed" when they recurrently produce practices that are clumsy or simplistic. Coordination is so difficult, in part because humans are capable of great things; it is frustrating because we so often are able to produce only faint shadows of the blazing visions, to bring into being only flawed versions of our image of what is good, true, and beautiful. The structure of human communication makes coordination an inherently fallible means of expressing and (re)constructing resources.

3.
Coherence and Mystery

Like coordination, coherence is a human universal; something that human beings must do by virtue of their genetic composition as human beings. Coherence refers to all those processes by which persons invent, test, and tell themselves and others stories that make intelligible the world around them, tame the terrors of history, make familiar the unknowns that go "thump" in the night, and give acceptable accounts for their success and failures in coordinating with other persons.

That we tell such stories is no surprise. However, the "discovery" of communication brought with it the surprising realization of just how many stories can be fitted onto any given aspect of human experience, and a reassessment of the surprising importance of these stories. One such reassessment was offered by Wayne Booth (1974, p. xii), who described his *A Rhetoric of Irony* as "unabashedly in a tradition of evangelical attempts to save the world, or at least a piece of it, through critical attention to language."

To save the world? Through attention to language?

Citing I. A. Richards, Alfred Korzybski, Ludwig Wittgenstein, and the American New Critics as fellow travelers, Booth (ibid.) noted that "the list could be extended almost indefinitely. This has been a century of semantic and semiotic nostrums: the century of hermeneutical last-ditch stands. And here is another one, more modest than any I have named but still expressing the assumption that not just the practice of literary criticism but *life itself can and should be enhanced by looking to our language.*"

Without the "discovery" of communication, Booth's fascination with language would seem a poor choice as a means of saving the world. If one assumes the role of messiah, why focus on language rather than, for example, biology, physics, economics, or the exploration of outer space? And surely the practice of politics as it has developed in the twentieth century should claim our attention. However, standing on this side of the discovery of communication, Booth's claim seems less preposterous. Our sensibilities about language and about the human condition have been shaped sufficiently that we are prepared to grant Booth and his fellow travelers room to build their case.

The point is, of course, that biology, physics, economics, space travel, politics, and all the other vehicles for enhancing "life itself" are conducted *in* language. Like all arenas of human life, these are stories crafted to exacting criteria by skillful storytellers and told to sophisticated audiences.

"Life itself" is enhanced by looking to language because this shifts attention away from the *content* of various stories (e.g., that the state will wither away in the dictatorship of the proletariat) to the fact that they *are* stories and to the *form* in which they are told. This in turn illuminates human beings as storytellers, at once immersed in linguistic webs that they did not spin and busily weaving webs in which to immerse others.

Whether these "webs" are imprisoning snares or enabling scaffolds is, of course, a matter of opinion. The relationship between the storyteller and the story, perhaps, determines whether the world—or a piece of it—is to be "saved" (whatever that might mean) or simply reproduced:

> Unlike some of the earlier scourers of the language of the tribe, I cannot claim to have high general hopes. But then I do not, like some of them, think that if the *world* is not saved, all is lost. *For me, one good reading of one good passage is worth as much as anything there is, because the person achieving it is living life fully in that time.* The absurdity of this notion will be evident to everyone, but it seems only honest to get it out in the open from the beginning. Perhaps I should just add that I do not see how any such person can prove useless in the world [Booth, 1974, p. xii; italics added].

The delightfully enigmatic concept of a "good reading" points toward the relationship between stories and storytellers. Because human beings have the properties of second-order cybernetic systems, they must both live *within* stories and, at least at times, stand *outside* them as critics, judges, authors, or editors. We are not only characters in the stories we tell, we are authors; not only authors but anthologists (we call this "personality"); and not only anthologists but browsers in libraries filled with the stories told by others, deciding which to read and which to leave undisturbed on the shelf (we call this "living a life"). The skills demanded by each of these roles are not the same.

Stories: The Technology of Coherence

Human beings are confronted with certain "facts of life." We are born, we mature, and then we die. While alive, we eat, excrete, and interact with our fellows. And we invest all of these "facts" with meaning by placing them within stories. Making "meaning" is not an optional activity in which persons sometimes engage; it is part of what it means to be a human being.

Because they are ensconced in stories, births are political events as well as biological facts. They determine the succession of dynasties and provide the means by which mortal individuals attempt to achieve some manner of immortality. Bawling infants are central characters in stories they did not choose—stories that will shape their experience with the physical and social world. Deaths do not merely mark the termination of a particular life, but are invested with religious and legal significance. Sexuality has been endowed with so much significance that it complicates and enriches human life in everything from fashion to philosophy. The ingestion and elimination of food are surrounded by taboos and rules of etiquette in every culture, and those who do not follow these rules offend those who do. National or religious symbols become more precious than life itself, and our heroes would rather face death than dishonor. The quality of the stories we tell determines whether we confront the facts of life with equanimity, ecstasy, or dread. If we tell confused stories, we will be confused, and if we pursue confused stories too literally, they can drive us mad. If our stories are too far out of touch with the facts of life, we will experience recurrent problems; if our stories provide sufficient affordances, they facilitate coordination.

> The first sign that a baby is going to be a human being and not a noisy pet comes when he begins naming the world and demanding the stories that connect its parts. Once he knows the first of these he will instruct his teddy bear, enforce his worldview on victims in the sandlot, tell himself stories of what he is doing as he plays, and forecast stories of what he will do when he grows up. He will keep track of the actions of others and relate deviation to the person in charge. He will want a story at bed-time.
>
> Nothing passes but the mind grabs it and looks for a way to fit it into a story, or into a variety of possible scripts: he's late—maybe he was in an accident. Maybe he ran off to Tahiti with a blonde. Maybe he stopped on the way here to buy flowers. She will keep writing these "novels" until he shows up or till she finds one story in which all elements, emotional and circumstantial, blend. Then, whatever he says later, she will know what she "knows" [Morton, 1984, p. 2].

The Institutionalization of Coherence

None of us is ever thrown completely on our own resources to make the world coherent. Whatever language is spoken around us contains in it the plot lines of a thousand tales and semantic connections between some ideas and not others. Comparisons of the vocabularies and, especially, the grammars of languages show that there are several "families" of languages, each of which is oriented to tell particular kinds of stories. The Indo-European languages tell adventure stories best: "subjects" act on "objects" in a linear concept of time. On the other hand, some of the Amerindian languages and those of South Pacific islands are better at describing coevolutionary processes.

Families are a primary locus of institutionalized coherence. An adult's view of the world and the practices one is prepared to engage in are prefigured by one's parents' example. This is particularly true when the next generation comes along; new parents often surprise themselves by saying exactly what—and in the same manner—their parents said to them. Children are voracious interpreters, remembering with awesome detail the interaction patterns between their parents, their parents' commentaries about other drivers and their relatives, and modes of expressing love, anger, hate, and frustration. Even when children scandalize their parents, it is more because they exaggerate their parents' influence than because they were unaffected by it.

Friendship patterns institutionalize coherence. Persons of all ages form social patterns and invest their self-concept in them. At least one major function of such groups is to provide a cadre of storytellers who will assist in taming the terrors of history. Among the young, these groups seem very important in telling stories about self-identity and purpose in life. Such groups provide the operatives both for patriotic organizations and revolutionary cabals. The stories told by the Ku Klux Klan, the Young Republicans, the Weathermen, the Islamic Jihad, and the Americans for Democratic Action have different content, but they are all stories, and to a surprising extent, similar stories.

All cultures have enfranchised some of their stories in official organizations. In some cultures, almost every home has a shrine. One way of looking at these shrines focuses on the *object* of veneration: Shinto tradition, the Compassionate Buddha, the crucified Christ. From the communication perspective, however, each of these is seen as a *way* of institutionalizing a story that enables coherence.

Communication technologies add a new dimension to the institutionalization of coherence. They provide widespread access to particular characters or symbols; perhaps more importantly, they easily cross the various dividing lines that have traditionally compartmentalized stories. National boundaries, socio-economic levels, culture, religion, race: all of these are transparent to television broadcasts, videocassettes, radio signals, audiocassettes, and pamphlets.

Some nations have deliberately constructed stories intended to provide a basis for coherence and coordination. For example, the 1969 riots in Malaysia brought the racial and religious diversity of the nation to a new level of awareness. One of the responses by the government was to promulgate a 5-item "national ideology," which stressed commitments common to all Malaysians, regardless of race or religion. This national ideology was memorized by children in schools, recited in unison at sporting events and rallies, etc. The "Pledge of Allegiance to the Flag" serves much the same function in the United States, coupled with apocryphal stories of George Washington (telling the truth about chopping down the cherry tree; throwing a dollar across the Potomac River; sharing the hardship of the soldiers at Valley Forge) and Abraham Lincoln (freeing the slaves; besting Stephen Douglas in debate; born in a log cabin and working as a rail-splitter; meriting the nickname "Honest Abe"). From the communication perspective, stories like these function to enable groups of persons to achieve coherence.

Some stories are institutionalized in stone. From the Sphinx in Egypt to the statues in the National Park in Thailand; from the Arc de Triomphe in Paris to the church in West Berlin deliberately left unrepaired from World War II bombings; from Red Square in Moscow to Stonehenge on an English plain, humans have shaped the material of their world to fit their stories of meaning, honor, hope, and faith.

On Giving Stories a "Good Reading"

The existence of a story, of course, does not guarantee that it will make the facts of life coherent. Even a well-formed story can fail to satisfy if it is told badly, or if it does not sufficiently command the attention of a people. Creativity and enmeshment are two of the characteristics of a "good reading" of a story.

Creativity

The stories that sustain a people over long periods of time evolve, continually being reinvented and edited to fit the facts of life. These "natural" stories seem deeper, richer, and more symbolic than those written or told by any individual playwrite or novelist. In fact, the richest literature alludes to or retells stories that have emerged through a long process of cultural evolution.

When discussing coordination, I depicted human beings as second-order cybernetic entities who must live in practices whose *poesis* is structured in a way that would scandalize a design engineer. This is what folklorists call a "just so" tale; one that gives an explanation for, for example, the phases of the moon or the reason why hair turns gray. My intention was to give an explanation for the repetitiveness of communication practices (the same old patterns of greed, lust, and exploitation) and the fact that these practices tend to fall so far short of the visions that prompted them.

This observation about practices, of course, says as much about resources as about the patterns of interaction themselves. Unlike coordination, in which the successful achievement of a practice depends on the ability to perform particular acts in collaboration with others, coherence is limited only by the self-imposed boundaries of imagination. Stories are underdetermined by the "facts of life," and there is an inexhaustible array of stories that give a coherent account of the facts of life.

I believe that there are, literally, an infinite number of stories that fit any set of facts. Let "infinite" be defined operationally as a set to which it is always possible to add one more, no matter how large the set. That is, no matter how many stories you already have to explain why human beings are born and die, you can always come up with one more. Take the basic facts in any mystery story and set to work. With sufficient imagination, there is always another reading that can be given to those facts—a reading that shows that the culprit is really someone else. Anyway, comparative literature or mythology impresses me with the glittering variety and richness—not the parsimony—of storytellers:

> No human society has yet been found in which . . . mythological motifs have not been rehearsed in liturgies; interpreted by seers, poets, theologians, or philosophers; presented in art; magnified in song; and ecstatically experienced in life-empowering visions. . . . Man [*sic*] apparently, cannot maintain himself in the universe without belief in some arrangement of the general inheritance of myth. In fact, the fullness of his life would even seem to stand in a direct ratio to the depth and range not of his rational thought but of his local mythology [Campbell, 1959, pp. 3–4].

"Blazing visions" sustain the great civilizations of humankind as well as the little boy who has his own account for the whereabouts of his missing baseball and how the neighbor's window came to be broken.

Enmeshment: The Willing Suspension of Disbelief

As the young ballplayer's experience with the neighbor might show, not just any story will do. Some stories are easier to read than others, and some are more satisfying than others, but there are also differences in how stories are read. At one level, a good reading requires a deep enmeshment in the story, a "willing suspension of disbelief." To enjoy an action-packed adventure story, one has to somehow enter the world depicted in the novel or theater that is the carrier of that story; readers must in a sense forget that they are sitting in a theater and believe that they are tossed about on a sloop in a gale. The mechanics of storytelling must be transparent so that certain forms of credulity can be engaged. When the storyteller says "once upon a time . . . ," this is an invitation to enter a quality of experience, not a historical fact, a thesis for debate, or scientific test of a hypothesis.

The term "enmeshment" describes this quality of participation in a story. Those who are deeply enmeshed focus on the story rather than the mechanics of storytelling, and accept the limits and powers of the system as their own. Campbell (1959, p. 21) gives a powerful example of this way of "reading" a story in his discussion of the use of masks in primitive societies. At crucial points in rituals, members of the tribe don masks and enact the role of the gods. At one level, everyone involved "knows" that these are their neighbors wearing masks, but to read the story in such a way that it sustains their vision of themselves and of the universe, it is important that they *not* be mindful of this. They must see their masked neighbors *as* their gods.

Stories that cope with the facts of life must be "read" with deep enmeshment. The facts of life are tough: confronted with the inevitability of one's own death and that of everyone we love; with the concept of entropy, which indicates that chaos will inevitably prevail over those pockets of meaning and order that we are temporarily able to form; with the fact that the sun itself will someday cease sending its healing rays; and with the certainty that had we been born in another culture at another time, we would certainly be as firm believers in a different set of stories than those we currently use—confronted with all that, coherence, coordination, and mystery require reading stories with a willing suspension of disbelief.

Liberation from Mere Facticity

Stories in which we are deeply enmeshed create the world in which we live. In one sense, this emerses us in narratives; in another, it liberates us from mere facticity.

I do not know what life is like without language, and if I did, I could not express it. It is likely that such a life would be one of thoughtless immediate sensation. "The verbal process describes a 'reality' we can only approach through it—but approach without ever a hope of reaching the ultimate goal. . . . We are thus liberated by symbolic method from the emprisoning 'here and now' to which physiological process dooms all of our animal relatives" (Shands, 1971, p. 12).

A nonlinguistic existence may be described as "mere facticity," an existence—but not a "world"—of sensation without significance and the eternal present without past or future. Such an existence excludes the phenomena that comprise human existence: fashion, politics, arts, insults, compliments, victories, and so forth, which are linguistically created "artifacts."

To be sure, some scholars attempt to explain human life in strictly biological, economic, political, or behavioral terms. However, such explanations seem incapable of engaging what humans consider to be the most significant aspects of life. Clifford Geertz (1980, p. 3) contemptuously dismissed a book that attempted to explain "primary male-female differences among humans" in socio-biological terms. He did so simply by listing some of the things *not* discussed in *The Evolution of Human Sexuality*: guilt, wonder, loss, self-regard, metaphor, justice, purity, intentionality, cowardice, hope, judgment, ideology, humor, obligation, despair, trust, malice, ritual, madness, forgiveness, sublimation, pity, ecstasy, obsession, discourse, and sentimentality.

The liberation from mere facticity requires a willing suspension of disbelief. At least at some level, the symbolic world must be taken as real, tokens treated as that for which they stand, and conventions followed as if they were a part of the world.

Conventions, tokens, and stories *are* a part of the world. If humans and human activity are *in* the world rather than outside it, then the use of language to create events and objects is a natural process, as "real" as the life cycle of atoms or the rotation of the planets around the sun. Talking is not "just talk"; it is a creative process. It is not just a way of achieving our purposes within an objective, inhuman world; it is the means by which "we," our "purposes," and "the world" are created. "To create a sentence is to constitute reality; to put two sentences together is to create the world" (Peckham, 1962, p. 33).

The term "liberation from mere facticity" is deliberately provocative. I use it deliberately to name the emancipation that comes as an unintended consequent of naming the world around us and then ensconcing those names within the webs of grammar and the plot lines of stories. All at once we live in a world of our own creation—and whose nature we often forget, confusing the stories told with the process of storytelling.

I have tried to provoke this insight in the students I have encountered over a period of twenty years, and have been struck by the fact that all of them had to attain it for themselves. A line of argument that works wonderfully well for one person falls absolutely flat for another. With this in mind, I include in this section references to several lines of work, all of which make the same point, that coherence liberates us from a subhuman, merely factual way of life.

Kenneth Burke playfully scripted a conversation between "the Lord" and "Satan," which ostensibly occurred in heaven before creation, during which the Lord describes how purposes, economics, politics, philosophy, and religion all arise in language.

> Insofar as men "cannot live by bread alone," . . . they derive purposes from language, which tells them what they "ought" to want to do, tells them how to do it, and in the telling goads them with great threats and promises, even unto the gates of heaven and hell.
>
> With language, a whole new realm of purpose arises, endless in scope, as contrasted with the few rudimentary purposes we derive from our bodies, the needs of food, drink, shelter, and sex in their physical simplicity.
>
> Language can even build purpose out of the ability to comment on the nature of purpose. However, the purposes that arise through the tangles made possible by language are not merely the old bodily appetites in a new form. They are appetites differing not just in degree but in kind. . . . Simplest example: what hungry belly could be quieted by a poem in praise of food? Yet, as we have said, language will not let men be satisfied with sheer bodily purposes either, as other animals presumably are.
>
> In any case, obviously, the talking animals' way of life in a civilization *invents* purposes. Rationalized by money (which is a language, a kind of purpose-in-the-absolute, a universal wishing well), empires arise. Such networks of production and distribution, made *possible* by language, become *necessary*. So, they raise problems—and many purposes are but attempts to solve those problems, plus the vexing fact that each "solution" raises further problems. (Confidentially, that's "the dialectic.")
>
> But the very resources of language to which such quandaries owe their rise also goad men to further questioning. For language makes questioning easy. Given language, you can never be sure where quest ends and questions begin. Hence, the search for some Grand Over-All Purpose, as with philosophers, metaphysicians, theologians [Burke, 1970, pp. 274–75].

Language creates explanations as well as purposes. We never deal with facts-in-themselves, but always with patterns of facts that we perceive as interrelated into some mosaic that constitutes an interpretable world. For whatever reason, we name the events and objects in the world and describe them as related by "causes," "reasons," "karma," or "gravity."

The American psychologist/philosopher William James attempted to make us mindful of this organizing function of the mind. What is the "order" that relates events that happen at the same time?, he asked. "While I talk and the flies buzz, a sea gull catches a fish at the mouth of the Amazon, a tree falls in the Adirondack wilderness, a man sneezes in Germany, a horse dies in Tartary, and twins are born in France." The "real order of the world," James insists, is just this "collateral contemporaneity, and nothing else." However, it is an order that we attempt to escape. We break this array of facts into clusters—histories, arts, sciences—"and then we begin to feel at home: We make ten thousand serial orders of it, and to any one of these we react as though the others did not exist. We discover among its various parts relations that were never given to sense at all (mathematical relations, tangents, squares, and roots and logarithmic functions) and out of an infinite number of these we call certain ones essential and law giving, and ignore the rest" (James, 1881, pp. 7–9).

The liberation from mere facticity not only enables us to give multiple reading to the facts of life; it creates facts that otherwise do not exist. John Searle distinguished "brute facts" from "institutional facts." That which breaks our toe when we kick it is a brute fact; when we deal with it as a "brick" ("what is a brick doing in the road anyway?") or a toy ("who left this here?"), we locate them within particular social institutions that have in them human agency, moral responsibility, questions of purpose and competence, and so on. Bricks and toys, unlike the nameless things against which we break our toes, exist only because persons define them as existing and as having certain characteristics. Searle's own examples include baseball and money. "It is only given the institution of baseball that certain movements by certain men constitute the Dodgers' beating the Giants 3 to 2 in eleven innings. And, at an even simpler level, it is only given the institution of money that I now have a five dollar bill in my hand. Take away the institution and all I have is a piece of paper with various gray and green markings" (Searle, 1969, p. 53). Using this distinction, it is clear that humans very seldom deal with "brute facts"; following James's advice, we "get away from" the natural order as quickly as possible, taming and subordinating it to our own socially sanctioned forms of experience.

Ruth Benedict said that the facts of nature and of the biological nature of humankind function more as "hints" than as "causes" of cultural development. The overwhelming feature of humankind is its plasticity—in Benedict's terms, a "great arc" of potentials from which each culture takes selections and then elaborates into the institutions and facts of its own world. "Each from the point of view of another ignores fundamentals and exploits irrelevancies. One culture hardly recognized monetary values; another has made them fundamental in every field of behavior. In one society technology is unbelievably slighted even in those aspects of life which seem necessary to ensure survival; in another, equally simple, technological achievements are complex and fitted with admirable nicety to the situation. One builds an enormous cultural superstructure upon adolescence, one upon death, one upon afterlife" (Benedict, 1934, p. 24).

More recently, Clifford Geertz has claimed that not only culture but the persons who create it are constructed in social interaction: "Men [*sic*] . . . every last one of them, are cultural artifacts" (Geertz, 1973, p. 51). This startling conclusion was based on a concept of culture as a set of "control mechanisms" and of humans as genetically endowed not only with the capacity for but an absolute dependency on social learning.

Culture is best seen . . . as a set of control mechanisms—plans, recipes, rules, instructions (what computer engineers call "programs")—for the governing of behavior . . . [and] man is precisely the animal most desperately dependent upon such extragenetic, outside-the-skin control mechanisms, such cultural programs, for ordering his behavior.

Whatever else modern anthropology asserts—and it seems to have asserted almost everything at one time or another—it is firm in the conviction that men unmodified by the customs of particular places do not in fact exist, have never existed, and most important, could not in the very nature of the case exist [Geertz, 1973, pp. 44, 35].

Language liberates us from the mere facts of biological existence so that we can—and must—cope with sorrow, happiness, gloom, anticipation, and depression. Only in this "made up" world can we experience a joke, a clever remark, a sophisticated performance, a revealing comment, or an offensive remark. Daniel G. Hoffman's (1965) poem "In the Beginning" describes an excited little girl standing on a jetty jubilantly pointing out "boats!" in a harbor where her father can see none. "Kate's a joyous spendthrift of her language's resources," he explains as he tries to share her vision.

> That verbal imagination
> I've envied, and long wished for:
>
> the world without description
> is vast and wild as death;
>
> the word the tongue has spoken
> creates the world and truth.
>
> Child, magician, poet
> by incantation rule;
>
> their frenzy's spell unbroken
> defines the topgallant soul.

Not all transcendence of mere facticity involves the creation of sails on an empty bay; more commonly it occurs by the placement of the tangible within webs of significance. Consider the importance of art to Eskimos. The Arctic environment poses a uniquely stern test for survival for Eskimos. If art is merely a luxury, one would assume that the Eskimos would have little time for it. To the contrary, their lives are filled with esthetic values. Where life is reduced to the essentials, Peter Farb notes, one of these essentials is art. The presence and significance of art is shown by what is lost when a kayak is put in a glass case. "There are parts of a kayak that no one can ever transport to a museum. These parts, every bit as much belonging to it as to the wooden frames and skin cover, include who owns it, who is allowed to ride in it, taboos concerning it, rituals connected with its launching and its use, and so on. Only when these and many other things are known can anyone understand what the kayak truly means to an Eskimo. And the same principle applies to all other aspects of Eskimo material culture" (Farb, 1978, p. 60).

Just as a kayak is more to an Eskimo than merely a means of getting from one place to another, the stories of all cultures mean more than what they say. This applies even to our own culture, and even to those stories that purport to be about facts. Even those are vehicles for focusing belief, for creating community, or for galvanizing action. In the early days of World War II, a story was frequently told in Britain that it was normal for the British to lose the early battles of a war but then to win the war itself. The appeal of this story was obvious: the "Battle of Britain" was not going well, and this story permitted Britons to interpret their hardships within a story that promised a happy ending. The story became a self-fulfilling prophecy: believing that they would win because "schoolbook history" taught them this pattern, they continued to fight until the "Grand Alliance" won in 1945.

A purely rational calculation of Britain's chances was much more depressing, and that was why the story was so frequently told. "Action, irrational in the short run, proved rational in the longer run. Myth is what bridged the gap, remaking the reality of June 1940 into the reality of May 1945" (McNeill, 1982, pp. 12–13). This creative function of the story was missed completely by the scholar who reviewed military history since 1066 and loudly announced that this pattern occurred in only 37 percent of the wars in which Britain was involved. This scholar was not liberated from mere facticity by the same set of stories as those who deliberately led ("misled"?) the British people to persevere, no matter how dark the moment appeared.

Coherence and the Human Condition

Imagine a movie about unrequited love. In the audience is a Martian, a member of a sexless, genderless race of solitary individuals. How is the Martian to understand the story? Being human means participating in an array of stories dealing with love, honor, humor, dignity, frustration, pain, and joy. Martians may well have a different array of emotions, values, and purposes than do humans, such that the movie, poignant by human standards, would be literally incomprehensible to them. By the same token, the cherished and sustaining stories told by Martians may well be untranslatable into any human language.

Many problems in human existence stem from incomplete or unbalanced sets of stories. One way of understanding criminals, warriors, and mean-spirited persons focuses on their stories about generosity, empathy, and love. Perhaps they are incapable of giving a "good reading" to these stories. In the same manner, those with psychological problems are impaired somehow in their "reading" of their culture's stories about how to live a life.

The frontiers of human development may also be cast in terms of stories. Will social evolution produce new stories as well as variations on familiar themes? Will new vices and virtues be invented? Might our descendents eventually think of us as "deprived" because we cannot experience and have no name for ways of being human that they take for granted? Storytelling is a ubiquitous human process. We name the events and objects of our world in a hundred languages, and thereby seek to know and master them. We see connections among "collateral contemporaneity" and spin out stories of science, literature, music, history, and theology. We live in these stories and become them.

Inasmuch as stories are underdetermined by the ("brute") facts of life, there are many, equivalently plausible stories. The array of stories told through the ages and around the world comprises a glittering tapestry from which individuals can draw to make their interactions with others coherent. This is not always easy. To enable us to cope with the facts of life, we must read these stories with creativity and enmeshment. The result is a liberation from mere facticity. However, still more is involved in a good reading: mystery.

Mystery

With a single exception, all societies of which records remain have told themselves stories that included descriptions of the mysterious. The myths of primitive culture would merit an "X" rating if filmed in Hollywood. Their stories of explicit sex, cannibalism, and gruesome tortures would offend the self-appointed moral watchkeepers of the reading material in public school libraries. All traditional societies tell stories of gods, ghosts, and giants. Most name the mysterious (fate, God, karma, Valhalla, or paradise); others allude to that which lies unspeakably beyond human knowledge. Lao Tze wrote that "the *Tao* that can be spoken is not the true *Tao*," and warned that "he who knows, speaks not; he who speaks, knows not."

A good reading of these stories—that is, deep enmeshment in them—provides a sense of awe in the face of superhuman powers; a fear of the unknown (and unknowable) that satisfies curiosity by sealing stories from further inquiry; and an experience of worship derived from participating in the "deep matters" of the universe.

"Modern" society is the exception to this otherwise ubiquitous aspect of the human condition. The Renaissance initiated and the industrial revolution institutionalized a profound demythologizing impulse. The eighteenth and nineteenth centuries in Western culture witnessed a war between "science" and "religion," and between the comfortable mysteries of *Gemeinschaft* rural society and the stark liberties of *Gesellschaft* urban society. Alternately "hot" and "cold," this war recognized that the developing modernism was inimical to mystery as well as to coherence. As Karl Marx said, "All that is solid melts away; all that is holy is profaned." In modernist hands, the mysteries of the heavens are reduced to mathematical formulas; the glories of a sunset are described by physical laws about the refraction of light; the scourges of God upon the wicked are explained as the effects of poor sanitation to be remedied by public health programs rather than by prayer; personalities are interpreted as the results of early socialization experiences; and religion is treated as a quaint anachronism or as a set of theological propositions inappropriately inserted into political or scientific discourse.

Modernist attacks on particular incarnations of mystery may be seen in the early conflicts between science and the Church. The secular saints of science, Galileo and Kepler, both confronted a discrepancy between their observations of the physical universe and the sacred stories told by Church authorities. Both chose to believe their "data" rather than submit to religious orthodoxy (at least at first), and both ripped the veil of mystery just a bit.

Of course, it is possible to argue that neither damaged mystery *in principle*, only mystery as it was incarnated in the inadequate myths of medieval European science. However, in the twentieth century, there have been frontal assaults on the concept of mystery per se. One of the dominant schools of thought in the first half of the century was logical positivism, which eschewed anything that could not be tied to operational definitions. Such definitions determine the meaning of something by the "operations" an observer performs to observe it. Forget the significance of baking a cake for a friend, or the meaning of a cake presented on one's birthday; the operational definition of a cake is a recipe. (Take two eggs and two cups of flour, mix well . . . and when you take it out of the oven, what you have is a "cake.") All other meanings for cake are dismissed from proper discourse (by which they meant "scientific" discourse) as (shudder!) "surplus meaning."

The analysis of language by the "speech act" philosophers produced a thoroughgoing repudiation of mystery. John Searle (1969) proposed the "principle of effability," which stipulated that anything that can be thought can be said, and said clearly. Granting that some things are at any given time inexpressible in any given language, this is taken as a challenge to the ingenuity of the communicator rather than a commentary on the nature of things. In a spurt of linguistic Calvinism, Searle argued that, because the world is in principle effable, any inability to express oneself in language is evidence of personal inadequacy.

George Steiner bemoaned what he called the contemporary "retreat from the word." Western civilization, he maintained (1967, p. 12), has always tried "to order reality within the governance of language." The major documents of our culture "bear solemn witness to the belief that all truth and realness—with the exception of a small, queer margin at the very top—can be housed inside the walls of language."

The modernist attempt to expunge the mysterious is based on a moral commitment as well as faith in the powers of reason. Many contemporary thinkers attribute some of the horrors of recent history to fanatical devotion to irrational symbols or faith, and believe that increased rationality is required for the discovery of solutions to the difficult problems confronting society. The alternative to reason is chaos, nihilism, willful exploitation of the weak by the greedy, and political repression. They feel that rationality is vulnerable, besieged by forces that subvert hard-won gains and yet-to-be-won opportunities in everything from art to politics. "In our time, the language of politics has become infested with obscurity and madness. No lie is too gross for strenuous expression, no cruelty too abject to find apologia in the verbiage of historicism. Unless we can restore to the words in our newspapers, laws, and political acts some measure of clarity and stringency of meaning, our lives will draw yet nearer to chaos" (Steiner, 1967, pp. 34–35).

I believe that mystery is essential to the human condition, and that the attempt to expunge it cannot succeed. However, the fact that it is ultimately futile does not mean that the rationalizing, demythologizing effort has been unsuccessful. As is so often the case, it has succeeded brilliantly in achieving something it did not intend. Rather than *eliminating* mystery by spreading the clear light of reason, it has increased our sophistication about the mysterious and, I believe, set the stage for an enhanced appreciation of mystery by showing us a new dimension of what is meant by a "good reading" of the stories by which we achieve coherence.

The Familiar Snares of Language

Earlier in this chapter, the "liberation from mere facticity" was celebrated as that function of language and stories that makes the human world distinctive. Largely as a result of various efforts to eliminate mystery, we have become aware that what liberates us also constrains us. Liberation from "mere facticity" is bought at the price of enmeshment within the logics of particular stories. One aspect of a "good reading" of these stories is a sufficient enmeshment to make the stories "work" as interpretations of the facts of life; as sufficiently sustaining to provide meaning in a world that is disorderly and filled with unpleasant things that we cannot deny or avoid. We are to treat words as if they were things; to take seriously the symbols, status markers, fetishes, and taboos of the stories of the society in which we live. Its moral order is to be treated as if it were a brute fact of life.

Entranced by the liberating power of the stories in which we are enmeshed, we are often blinded to the alternative worlds created by the stories of our neighbors, our ancestors, and our descendents. We develop a trained incapacity to distinguish the "brute facts" of our physical world from the "institutional facts" of our society. We develop distinctive features of speech, dress, mannerism, hygiene, thought, and belief that incapacitate us for living a life in a culture other than our own.

The snares of language are not only exceedingly seductive, they are exceedingly subtle. They ensnare by capacitating; they limit by making things possible. Every symbolic system has an internal "logic" of meaning and action that facilitates some things and makes others difficult. There is always a close relationship between the characteristics of language and the ways of thinking of those who use it. Eskimos have many words for snow and characteristically make finer distinctions among types of snow than those who have only one word for it. The major languages in Europe have embedded in them a sense of time and agency—the relationship between "subject" and "object" of the verb—foreign to Trobriand islanders or to the Navaho of the southwest United States. Their ways of thought, relationship to "work," and forms of social life are correspondingly different.

This "linguistic relativity" is not inexorable. Rather, it is the result of convenience, habit, and the human predilection for learning. Particular symbolic systems encourage certain ways of thought and action, and *to the extent that those who use the language have suspended their disbelief in those stories*, they will think and act in those ways. For example, "health" is treated in American television commercials as a commodity that can be lost, regained, threatened, or preserved. Those *not* deeply enmeshed in this language game can think of health in a variety of other ways. Maybe health is an "organism" to be tended instead of a commodity to be obtained, or a "machine" to be oiled and repaired, or a "game" to be played.

However health is thought of, it initiates a logic of meaning and action in which "the rational thing to do" and the form of relevant institutions vary significantly. Given the "commodity" metaphor, the medical profession in the United States has developed enormous institutions and advanced technology for intervening after health has been lost. The People's Republic of China, on the other hand, emphasizes health issues more for those who are healthy than those who are not—what is sometimes called "preventive medicine."

Can the "health as commodity" orientation be pushed too far? How about prosecuting those who cough in others' faces, thus "robbing" them of health? If this seems too farfetched, it is because your willingness to suspend disbelief is slipping. How should we think of alcoholism or violent behavior? Is alcoholism a "disease" or a self-inflicted condition? Judgments made about responsibility and about "treatment" differ depending on what language game we use to think about it. Is violent behavior a "loss" of "mental health" or an appropriate response to irrational social settings?

Aware of the snares of language, at least three responses are possible. One is outrage; a petulant protest that language has not played with us "fairly." This response seems to characterize those who make a career of "exposing" the hidden snares of language; of "protesting" the oppression of various ideologies; and of "deconstructing" the sometimes hidden assumptions of various politicians and writers.

A second response is a celebration of the mystery of ineffability. Rather than try to "eff the ineffable," there are those who point to the ineffable as a constant reminder of the limits of the stories (and of the language in which we tell them) to guide coordination and achieve coherence.

A third response brings us full circle back to the beginning of this book: the "discovery" of communication as a formative process—expressing and (re)constructing resources in practices—rather than a supposedly neutral tool for describing the universe. This brings about a "second liberation," first from mere facticity and then from the snares of language.

Outraged Exposés of the Snares of Language

The "deconstruction" of various language games can be an important means of social criticism. Foucault's (1970) work, for example, is based on the assumption that no society allows anyone complete freedom of speech, and appropriates unevenly the right to speak about particular things and in particular ways. These restrictions and exclusions are in the service of power. His "archeological" work has shown how particular conceptualizations of madness and sexuality have had major formative influences on Western society.

Deconstruction is most commonly employed by literary critics. A poststructuralist school of criticism, it produces a seemingly endless array of "readings" of any given text, with special attention to the assumptions, metaphors, and linguistic practices of other authors (see Norris, 1982).

Although the purpose of these exposés of the snares of language is to free persons from them, for my purpose they serve best as demonstrations of the subtle snares themselves. I want to move quickly to other ways of responding to those snares.

Celebrations of Ineffability

One of the surprising developments in contemporary communication theory is a sudden sympathy for those mystics, visionaries, and poets who have claimed that their best insights were ineffable. This sympathy is sharply out of step with most persons in the Western tradition, who have little patience for claims that there are limits to what can be said. The very mention of ineffability seems to relegate someone to the academic trashheap.

Of course, ordinary discourse is filled with statements to the effect that "I just can't tell you how sorry I am." Over one-fifth of the sympathy cards received by two bereaved families contained some form of overt statement about "the inadequacy of language to communicate the true feelings of the sender or to aid the bereaved in coping with death" (Lippy, 1977, p. 16). However, such statements are commonly recognized as figures of speech, a perhaps too convenient way of signaling an emotional state, not a serious statement about the limits of language.

Searle's "principle of expressibility" captures a deep suspicion of those who know something they cannot tell. "Even in cases where it is in fact impossible to say exactly what I mean, it is in principle possible to come to be able to say exactly what I mean. I can in principle if not in fact increase my knowledge of the language, or more radically, if the existing language or existing languages are not adequate to the task, if they simply lack the resources for saying what I mean, I can in principle at least enrich the language by introducing new terms or other devices into it" (Searle, 1969, p. 19).

Searle's enormous confidence in the power of language to contain experience seems misplaced. The poor fit between language and the world can be seen in many places, including national parks. Many parks have a place where visitors can look at a distant range of mountains. A small map helps the visitor to identify each of the peaks, and *at this distance and level of imprecision* there is no difficulty in distinguishing one mountain from another. However, to those more intimately involved with the mountains, the task seems more difficult and the process of "naming" the mountains seems an inevitable distortion.

The problem is not the ambiguity of language but the converse: words are more specific and clearer than reality. They portray the mountains as if they were discrete, clearly differentiated from each other. But a climber sent into the mountains with the task of drawing a precise line showing where one mountain ends and another begins would find the task impossible. Whatever line he drew would be a distortion. Someone who took the task seriously and was sufficiently perceptive would return with some account of "ineffability."

As with mountains, so with persons, institutions, and emotions. To be a "native" of a culture is to use a particular linguistic "map" that names "Bill" and "Tom" and "Sally" as if they were discrete individuals; General Motors, General Electric, and General Aviation as if they were discrete institutions; and "love," "hate," and "respect" as if they were discrete emotions. Important decisions hinge on the ability to draw precise lines between "love" and "civility," between "work" and "play," and between "mine" and "ours" *as if* they were isolatable.

Of course, they are not. For *coordination,* it is only necessary that those who interact with each other draw the lines at the same place—this allows them to "dance" with each other. For *coherence,* it is only necessary that there be some lines drawn somewhere—this allows us to tame the terrors of history and impose meaning and order on the world. But *mystery* is the reminder that such lines are ultimately arbitrary distortions, no doubt necessary but not to be read with a complete suspension of disbelief. Without such reminders, hard-eyed men and women forget that, for example, "time" is the basis for coordination and coherence, not a map of "reality." The *New York Times* of May 11, 1985 (p. 8), announced that the last minute of the last hour of the last day in June was 61 seconds long. "The one-second lengthening of that minute," they explained, "is designed to match *perfectly kept human time* to the *imperfection of nature*" (italics added). The story continues to explain the difference between solar rotations (the basis of "natural" time) and "the average of many cesium-beam atomic clocks" (the basis of "human" time).

One of the most exciting and unsettling testimonies of ineffability comes from the most "exact" of sciences: physics. Tough-minded scientists are seriously, on the basis of their data, proposing the revolutionary hypothesis that the physical world has a structure incomprehensible to our minds. The problem is that we cannot (of course!) transcend our own human reference point, and our thought processes do not correspond to reality sufficiently to permit us to think about it. "We are now approaching a boundary beyond which we are forever stopped from pursuing our inquiries, not by the construction of the world, but by the construction of ourselves. The world fades out and eludes us because it becomes meaningless. We cannot even express this in the way we would like.

. . . It is literally true that the only way of reacting to this is to shut up. We are confronted with something truly ineffable" (Conant, 1962, pp. 21–22).

Scholars who have searched in other fields have arrived at similar conclusions. In the process of trying to relate and understand the stories with which human societies have clothed the gods, Joseph Campbell (1968, p. 84) made a curious statement. "The best things cannot be said; the second best are misunderstood. After that comes civilized conversation." It is not clear whether Campbell was referring to the myths of various peoples or to his own frustration in describing these myths to a contemporary audience, but his designation of "the best things" parallels Steiner's reference to that "small, queer margin at the top" of human experience.

Ludwig Wittgenstein's epochal analysis of language in the *Tractatus Logico-Philo-sophicus* stated that "everything that can be said can be said clearly" and developed a "propositional calculus" (in the form of "truth-tables") that set a standard for judging the "clarity" of a given discourse. This part of his work was, unfortunately (in my view), more celebrated than his insistent caution that "not everything can be said." He concluded that "whereof we cannot speak, thereof we should be silent," and later explained that it is the most important things in life—ethics, values, esthetics—that cannot be said clearly.

In his study of metaphorical uses of language, Philip Wheelwright stressed the fact that an inability to speak clearly does not necessarily imply a "defect" of some sort in language or in the speaker. It all depends on what one thinks is the nature of reality. If there is a "foundation"; if reality itself is composed of clear and distinct events and objects, then the language that most accurately describes reality is to be prized and will be distinguished by its clarity and distinctness. But "if reality is largely fluid and half paradoxical, then steel nets are not the best things with which to take samples of it" (Wheelwright, 1962, p. 128). Perhaps the most accurate language is one filled with stammers and protestations of ineffability.

The Second Liberation

In the process of liberating us from mere facticity, language ensnares us in the social world that it constructs. A good reading of the stories of the particular culture of which we are native requires us to be sufficiently enmeshed to coordinate with our fellows and to make the facts of life coherent. A particular kind of credulity, the "willing suspension of disbelief," deliberately overlooks the fabrication of the event/objects of the social world, and then forgets that it overlooked them. After all this, the socially constructed reality is read as "real."

But perhaps you noticed the tension between this and Booth's claim that "life itself" can be significantly enhanced by attention to language. To the extent that we *attend* to language, we undo the willing suspension of disbelief necessary for deep enmeshment; *discussions* of such things as the willing suspension of disbelief reinstates those critical faculties that were deliberately put out of mind by the collective amnesia that defines a culture.

This irony adds new teeth to the question with which we began this chapter. In what way does attention to language enhance "life itself"? Certainly not by making enmeshment in stories easier. In fact, it raises the spectre of alienation and relativism: the tendency to see all stories "from the outside," with the marks of human agency on them, and the conventions of storytelling all too opaquely obvious.

The issue is resolved by making a radical break from the traditional notion that language works by describing a nonlinguistic reality. Instead, language itself is a system within which persons live, and this system is far more complex than a wheelbarrow load of signifiers. This position militates against a "literal" understanding of language, whose virtues are clarity and precision, and which portrays itself as if there were no other way of making the facts of life coherent.

Muslims believe that Allah spoke the words written in the *Qur'an,* so many Muslims argue that any dispute about the faith must be done in Arabic. At the Council of Nicea, Christian leaders produced a set of words that, they insisted, expressed the true faith and condemned those who used any of a list of variations. However, each of the words in the Nicean Creed (and all of the other stories that have been treated as if they were clear and precise) are fundamentally metaphorical, used within socially imposed limits. A close attention to the "natural history" of languages subverts the possibility of clarity and precision. Words change and so do their meanings. Further, language is far richer than prosaic uses of it admit. Some who recite the Nicean Creed do so as a form of worship, others are repeating what is to them a meaningless ritual; still others mocking; and yet others making a point in some other argument.

Language is sufficiently complex that it permits stories that describe themselves as stories; it enables comparisons among stories; it is more naturally the stuff of metaphor, irony, and illusion than of prosaic description; and it provides a universe of discourse in which storytellers can complain about the limits of their ability to sustain sufficient enmeshment in stories. A famous Zen teaching says: "The finger points at the moon, but only a fool would confuse the finger for the moon." The aphorism chastises those who place too great an importance on language and rationality. But the lesson is *in* language! Is the saying itself more like a "finger" or like the "moon"? Either way, this new frame within which to think about the lesson demonstrates the capacity of language to describe itself, even to construct an image of itself that seriously exaggerates or underrepresents its own capacities.

The inevitability of mystery derives from an ironic relationship between deep enmeshment in particular stories and deep enmeshment in the capabilities of language itself. The kind of deep enmeshment in a particular set of stories that make the facts of life coherent is—often? usually?—achieved at the expense of an appreciation of the existence and beauty and viability of any number of other stories that serve much the same function. On the other hand, a deep enmeshment in the capacity of language itself to tell many stories, including stories about stories, is—often? usually?—accompanied by "the feeling—at least the feeling, no matter what one may think 'the fact' to be—of liberation into a new universe of experience" (Shands, 1971, p. 12). To achieve a sufficient enmeshment in the potential of language, one must see stories as arbitrary and local. They must be approached with a *willing suspension of belief*; a deliberate engrossment in the mechanics of storytelling and an openness to alternative stories. To give the kind of "good reading" that celebrates mystery, one must suspend *both* belief and disbelief in an affirmation of ironic tension. The stories are simultaneously "real" and "fictional"; deadly serious and playful.

Mystery is achieved in such "good readings" by a clear perception of the limits of the content of any story. However, the mysterious is not identified with some "thing" beyond the limits of what happens to be said, but with the inevitable, inherent existence of the limits to anything that could conceivably be said. The experience of mystery comes from contemplation of the fact that every story *must* leave something beyond itself rather than the specific *items* left beyond any given story. Even in a crime drama, the mystery derives less from the actual identity of the culprit than from the suspense of *knowing that you do not know* who it is. In communication, mystery is the explicit recognition that, as Campbell (1968, p. 84) said, "the best things cannot be said."

One aspect of the experience of mystery is an awareness of the open-endedness of the world. If communication is the process by which we create the world, then the world is still in the process of being created. There may be new things under the sun: new values, new roles of honor and dishonor, new patterns of interaction. A science fiction story told of an encounter between a twentieth-century man and a man from the far future who had been sent back in time (to the present) as punishment for his crime. Our contemporary was concerned; is this man one who should be shunned or helped; honored or condemned? Confused, he asked what the time traveler was guilty of doing. He replied, "you have neither the word nor the concept for it." Social creation is continuous.

A thousand years ago, the notion of who is the "author" of a book, and the rights and duties pertaining to that role, were very different from what they are now. The dastardly crime of plagiarism was not only unknown, but unthinkable. How would someone from that society evaluate one of our contemporaries who was fired from a professorship or flunked out of a class because of plagiarism?

In much the same way, the continuing process of communication creates the world in which we live. Usually, it (re)creates pretty much the same world with minor variations. We have a strong sense of continuity. We expect the bank, the church, and the school to be pretty much the same tomorrow as they are today. However, given the structural characteristics in the process of coordination, there is almost a certainty that something novel will be created.

Mystery also consists in the recognition that there is an open-endedness to the understanding of any given event. Events and objects do not come "prepackaged" with their own interpretation, and they are not incorporated into the human world until they are interpreted. Further, interpretation is an act by an interpreter, not an attribute of the event or object interpreted; as a result, there is no criterion by which one interpretation can be shown to be the "correct" one.

Consider a pattern well known to family therapists: the nag-withdraw syndrome. The "facts" of the matter are clear and undisputed: she nags and he withdraws from interaction with her. However, each "punctuates" the sequence differently. *She* says that she nags because he withdraws; *he* says that he withdraws because she nags. They agree about the facts, but disagree about which comes first and which comes second. So which one is "right"? He? She? Both? Neither?

Contemporary communication theorists refuse to answer the question about who is "right" in their punctuation of this—and similar—sequences. Because the stories that comprise the human world are "underdetermined" by the facts of life, many valid stories can be told about them. These facts may be put together in many ways, each of which is a legitimate *act* of interpretation.

Mystery comprises recognition of the limits of the stories in which we are enmeshed. These limits are not taken as confining boundaries, but the surest sign that there exists something beyond them. Mystery is a quality of experience of the human world, characterized by rapt attention, open-mindedness, a sense of wonder, perhaps even awe.

The second liberation is not a move into a nonlinguistic mode of knowledge or some transcendent form of existence. Rather, it is a way of treating words and language as "friends" instead of either "masters" or "slaves." It is an escape from "the kind of rationalism that maims and shackles the human spirit" (Janik and Toulmin, 1973, p. 200). It is a form of intellectual honesty that comes when one relaxes and ceases to force everything to fit "inside the walls of language" (Steiner, 1967, p. 14).

The second liberation permits attention to the potential discrepancies between one's own experience and the language one has learned. The creative function of language may be celebrated rather than treated as a source of error. This permits an appreciation of our position "inside" communication. "Words are the works of art that make possible science. Words are the abstractions that make possible poetry. Words signify man's refusal to accept the world as it is" (Kaufmann, 1961, p. 78).

The "second liberation" also permits us to disregard on occasion the language of the tribe and to explore alternative language games, to think in contradictions, paradoxes, and images as well as in syllogisms and grammatical sentences. The surprising discovery is that these nonstandard ways of thinking and talking make important contributions to the community. The "language of the tribe" customarily imposes a too simple, orderly pattern on the flux of experience.

> When a straightforward thinker sets out to free himself from symbolic and metaphorical thinking, what he actually means to do is to limit himself to those symbols and rigidified metaphors which have become habitual stereotypes in everyday life. The issue is not between symbolic and non-symbolic thinking, but between limiting one's thought and sensitivities to the plain meanings denoted by conventional symbols and learning to think with a more tensive alertness [Wheelwright, 1962, p. 128].

The second liberation allows persons to use words in full cognizance of their snares but without rancor. This emancipation is an antidote both to skepticism and to the outrage expressed by some when they discover that they have been ensnared by language.

Ursula Le Guin's description of how she works as an artist seems an excellent report of one who has achieved the "second liberation," able to use words as old friends, even when fully aware of the snares they set for thought, and their uneven usefulness for the twin goals of expression and communication:

> But it is words that make the trouble and confusion. We are asked now to consider words as useful in only one way: as signs. Our philosophers, some of them, would have us agree that a word (sentence, statement) has value only in so far as it has one single meaning, points to one fact which is comprehensible to the rational intellect, logically sound, and—ideally—quantifiable.
>
> Apollo, the god of light, of reason, of proportion, harmony, number—Apollo blinds those who press too close in worship. Don't look straight at the sun. Go into a dark bar for a bit and have a beer with Dionysos, every now and then.
>
> I talk about the gods, I am an atheist. But I am an artist too, and therefore a liar. Distrust everything I say. I am telling the truth.
>
> The only truth I can understand or express is, logically defined, a lie. Psychologically defined, a symbol. Aesthetically defined, a metaphor.
>
> The artist deals with what cannot be said in words.
>
> The artist whose medium is fiction does this *in words*. The novelist says in words what cannot be said in words.
>
> Words can be used thus paradoxically because they have, along with a semiotic usage, a

symbolic or metaphoric usage. (They also have a sound—a fact the linguistic positivists take no interest in. A sentence or paragraph is like a chord or harmonic sequence in music: its meaning may be more clearly understood by the attentive ear, even though it is read in silence, than by the attentive intellect.) All fiction is metaphor. Science fiction is metaphor. What sets it apart from older forms of fiction seems to be its use of new metaphors, drawn from certain great dominants of our contemporary life—science, all the sciences, and technology, and the relativistic and the historical outlook, among them. Space travel is one of these metaphors; so is an alternative society, an alternative biology; the future is another. The future, in fiction, is a metaphor.

A metaphor for what?

If I could have said it nonmetaphorically, I would not have written all these words, this novel; and Genly Ai would never have sat down at my desk and used up my ink and typewriter ribbon in informing me, and you, rather solemnly, that the truth is a matter of the imagination [Le Guin, 1979, pp. 157–59].

Mystery and the Human Condition

There have been many attempts to characterize the human condition. Most of them emphasize some attribute that supposedly distinguishes humans from other kinds of things. Humans have been thus identified as Homo sapiens (the thinking animal), Homo ludens (the animal that plays), Homo faber (the animal that makes things), and so on. The "communication perspective" shows that the human being is the animal that makes its own world and its own self—expressing and (re)constructing resources in practices—and that this is done in a process of which coordination, coherence, and mystery are the attributes.

From this perspective, the human condition is that of being *variably enmeshed in multiple symbolic systems, each with its own logic of meaning and action*. The "normal" human condition is to be largely unaware of those symbolic systems, living within them in a state of sufficiently deep enmeshment to achieve coordination with their fellows, to achieve coherence, and to experience mystery by participation in the stories and symbols of those systems. The stories of modern society, however, have made an "unusual" form of the human condition increasingly prevalent. This consists in recognizing the snares of each of these systems. This recognition makes coordination difficult (because one is aware that others use different logics, and that one can choose among logics); and it makes coherence difficult (because one must achieve it through the recognition of the limits of language rather than enmeshment in its content).

In contemporary society, it is not at all unusual to be, simultaneously, daughter, mother, and wife; owner, lender, and borrower; experienced and inexperienced. The rights and duties of these roles are seldom fully compatible and the conflicts among them are sometimes quite striking. We are not usually very much aware of the multiple language games we play. Our sentences may combine references to human rights, scientific method, divine revelation, freedom of choice, familial responsibilities, social duty, and the profit motive. Within a paragraph, we may have invoked not one world but many, incommensurate worlds.

If we lived in a single symbolic system not rigorous enough to expose its own limits or a set of systems compatible enough not to contradict from time to time, we would probably never detect the snares of language. But the characteristics of the contemporary world do not facilitate that. We are far too likely to come into contact with alien cultures, or to experience traumatic change in one's own culture, or to be exposed to a sufficiently powerful tool of inquiry to remain comfortably enmeshed in any given language game: "The problem is words. Only with words can man become conscious; only with words learned from another can man learn how to talk to himself. Only through getting the better of words does it become possible for some, a little of the time, to transcend the verbal context and to become, for brief instants, free" (Shands, 1971, pp. 19–20).

II.
Forms of Communication
and Ways of Being Human

4.
"Forms" and "Ways"

Part I described the discovery of communication in the twentieth century. The convergence of interest in communication quickly produced new concepts of how it works and what work it does. These new concepts suggest a more important function for communication than had previously been thought. Some (including myself) believe communication to be the primary social process. Rather than a tool used with varying degrees of skill for other purposes, it is the means by which humans construct the world in which they live, coordinate with their fellows, and experience mystery.

Part II deals with some implications of this new appreciation of communication. It makes three claims: that there are differentiable forms of communication; that there are differentiable ways of being human; and that these "forms" and "ways" have coevolved and are each the "cause" of the other. My concern goes beyond providing a description of these "forms" and "ways." I argue that the material and social conditions of the contemporary world are profoundly disordered. Not for the first time, there is a discontinuity between the contemporary form of society and the ways of communication it institutionalizes. A new round in the coevolution of society and communication processes is in progress.

Forms of Communication

Communication is not everywhere and at all times the same thing. It is not an either-or choice, which one does or does not perform; nor is it a continuum along which one may do more or less, or better or worse. Rather, communication is a ubiquitous aspect of human functioning, constitutive of being human. But it takes different forms.

To demonstrate that there are different forms of communication is quite easy; to specify just what differentiates them and to describe them is not. It requires no expert to see that three of the most successful men of the 1960s—John Kennedy, John Lennon, and Muhammad Ali—used different forms of communication. Successful participation in any society requires an ability to detect (and respond appropriately to) the differences between a lecture, a sales presentation, a sermon, and a helpful hint. Sometimes "the boss" is engaging in casual chat, sometimes making a suggestion, and sometimes giving an order—it helps to know the difference. Married couples will have recurrent troubles unless they can differentiate among sarcasm, humor, and serious talk. However, to go beyond noting the existence of different forms of communication requires a sophisticated vocabulary and theory. Among all the thousands of things that happen when humans communicate, only some are significant. How can these be illuminated?

There are any number of taxonomies of communication forms, each of which seems useful for particular purposes. Aristotle differentiated forensic, deliberative, and ceremonial discourse. Carol Gilligan (1982) described deep and pervasive differences between "feminine" and "masculine" ways of thinking and speaking. Basil Bernstein (1972) described "elaborated" and "restricted" codes of talk that keep the social classes in Britain separated. Ethnographers of communication such as Dell Hymes (1962), Gerry Philipsen (1975), and Donal Carbaugh (1988) have described distinctive patterns of speaking in various communities within the United States.

In the pages that follow, I propose yet another taxonomy. This one is based on the concept of communication as collective process by which resources are expressed and (re)constructed in practices. Forms of communication differ depending on how the communicators treat each other, and the nature of the "reading" they give to the stories that comprise their "resources." To get at these characteristics is to focus on the extent to which the participants treat each other "like a native" and whether they put their resources "at risk."

To treat someone like a native means to hold him or her accountable to your own evaluative and interpretive criteria; treating them not like a native involves discovering and using their own interpretive and evaluative criteria, even if these differ substantially from your own. Protecting your resources from risk refers to the suspension of disbelief that comes from deep enmeshment in your own stories. To put your resources at risk means reading your stories with a willing suspension of belief, comparing them with the emerging pattern of communication, intending to change them if it seems appropriate. The tensions among these ways of treating other persons and your own resources comprise the various aspects of giving stories "a good reading."

In the process of collaboratively bringing into being the events and objects of the social world, each person must engage in a process researchers call "conversational implicature." Persons seldom say all that they mean to be heard as having said, and often say something quite other than what they expect to be heard as having said. They joke; they allude; they use sometimes tortured figures of speech; and they depend on the willingness and ability of others to supply missing information, to invoke an appropriate context, and to interpret what they meant. The surprising thing about so ungainly a process is that it works so often. For the most part, we are able to perform "implicatures" sufficiently well to enable us to coordinate without too much difficulty.

For the most part, we do this by assuming that we know what resources the other person is expressing. This is a fiction, of course. There is no way in which we can get "inside the mind" of another person. We have no *direct* access to other persons' resources, only to their practices. When we infer what they *meant* by what they said, we engage in speculation for which there is no procedure for determining whether our descriptions match their avowals of what is meant.

Usually we assume that others are pretty much like us, and that we "know" their resources because they are the same ones that we have appropriated from our culture. As a result, we treat them "like a native" of our own culture, expecting them to interpret, evaluate, and respond to the events and objects of the world as we do because they tell the same story. Because they are different persons with their own personalities, we expect them to differ from us, but we expect even those differences to be interpretable by our standards.

What does it mean to wear green hair or white socks or earrings? When treating others like a native, we hold them accountable to our standards and assume that it means for *them* what it would for *us* if we were to do it. Whether we approve or disapprove, we think we know what it means. When we treat others "*not* like a native," we assume that their resources differ from ours. We may simply try to suspend judgment (I am not really sure what wearing punk clothes means to those green-haired youngsters, but I am quite sure that it means something to them other than what it means to me) or seek to find out what interpretive and evaluative criteria they bring to bear on their actions.

The imperfectness of coordination means that resources are always potentially at risk. The logic of interaction often leads to unintended consequences, and these can challenge the fundamental tenets of the resources of those who produced them. The greatest disillusionment possible is to discover that, unintentionally, our practices have made us into that which we abhor. (Samuel Donaldson's six-volume fantasy, *The Chronicles of Thomas Covenant the Unbeliever*, meditates at length on this theme.) However, persons are not uniformly sensitive to the potential "risks" to their resources of engaging in practices. In general, when contextual and prefigurative forces predominate, persons are not sensitive to the risks to their resources; when practical and implicative forces predominate, resources are very much at risk of change.

The combination of these criteria produces a taxonomy of four types of communication. In *monocultural* communication, others are treated like natives and resources are not at risk. The name denotes an attitude of acting as if there were only one culture (one's own, of course).

Ethnocentric communication occurs when resources are not at risk, but other persons are divided into two groups: natives and nonnatives. At least some persons are treated as if they do not share the resources of the others. This distinction often, but not necessarily or always, translates into patterns of treating others as if they were inferior.

When other persons are determinately treated as nonnatives, and resources are systematically placed at risk, *modernistic* communication occurs. The name derives from "modern society," a unique set of institutions, values, beliefs, and practices whose characteristics sustain this form of communication. This form of communication is inherently unstable and sharply at odds with the values upheld in other types of societies. As a result, it has spawned a variety of other forms of communication that, I believe, are best understood as alternatives to modernistic communication.

One of the virtues of *cosmopolitan* communication is that it strains the taxonomy set up by these two criteria. Cosmopolitan communication embraces the tension between the two aspects of a "good reading" of the stories by which coherence and mystery are achieved. Cosmopolitan communication requires a particular kind of resources, which simultaneously put themselves perpetually at risk and, because they do, exempt themselves from risk. These resources define others as "all alike" in that we have all been shaped by the particularities of our own culture and of our historical experience, and that this shaping has made us all, to some extent, a unique nexus of multiple social realities, and thus different from everyone else. By stressing coordination rather than coherence, and by developing a distinctive concept of ("social" rather than "rhetorical") eloquence, cosmopolitan communication derives from a commitment to find ways of coordination even among very dissimilar groups.

Each of these forms of communication is capable of achieving coordination, coherence, and mystery, but they do it in very different ways. These differences are not simply matters of taste, preference, or style. Because communication is the substance of social reality, these differences are crucial to ways of being human.

Ways of Being Human

Little sophistication is required to note that life is different in various cultures. Within complex societies, forms of life differ among those in various social and economic groups. These differences are not simply matters of style or appearance. A migrant agricultural worker lives in a different world of fact, value, relevancies, and affordances than an absentee, jet-set landowner who follows a different code of honor and dignity. An eighteenth-century Japanese samurai invading Korea had a different self and moral order than a twentieth-century American soldier serving in Korea as part of a United Nations "peace-keeping" force.

Further, there is a widespread recognition that something important has happened to us as a function of "modernity." Whatever might be meant by that ambiguous term, it has impacted in nontrivial ways on social institutions, practices, our concepts of self and the world around us.

The classic analysis of the effect of modernity was offered in 1887 by Ferdinand Tonnies. The industrial revolution, he argued, bifurcated society. *Gemeinschaft* society is rural and cohesive. Its members shun competition in order to practice mutual support and to preserve common beliefs. *Gesellschaft* society, on the other hand, is industrial and urban. Because it requires its members to compete, it breaks up social bonds, making its members feel like individuals rather than members of a cohesive group, and thus produces pervasive anxiety.

Gemeinschaft society is particularistic (local rather than universal standards prevail) and ascriptive (members are evaluated on the basis of who they are rather than what they can do). *Gesellschaft* is universalistic in that it holds the same standards for everyone and is achievement-oriented. Performance rather than parentage determines status (Johnston, 1972, p. 20).

I chose not to use this distinction for three reasons. First, it is too particular, addressing the characteristics of European societies as they were transformed by the industrial revolution. Second, these labels are intended to apply to the whole structure of society rather than to situated performances, in which I am interested. Third, I do not believe that these types of societies are discrete—at least not in "postmodern" society. For most of us, our experience is formed by an inchoate combination of a wide variety of social types. We are a bit of a lot of things, and this is our peculiar "way of being human."

The Coevolution of "Ways" and "Forms"

The question, "Which came first, the chicken or the egg?" poses a philosophical, but not a biological, problem. Chickens exist, and so do eggs, and it is impossible for there to be one without the other. The philosophical problem occurs only if the relationship between chickens and eggs is thought to be one-way or "linear," such that one must have preexisted and thus be the "cause" of the other.

A better way to think about the relationship is as a coevolutionary process, in which both chickens and eggs changed simultaneously in a patterned ("coordinated") way. So, "Which came first?" is a foolish question, from which we should escape rather than try to answer.

The relationship between forms of communication and ways of being human is similarly coevolutionary. This concept avoids a problem that has long bedeviled communication theorists: the relationships between ideology (resources) and material conditions (practices). Humanists stress the importance of religion, philosophy, and values of a people, arguing that its behavior is shaped by what it believes. Materialists argue that practices—particularly the means of production—are the true dynamic force in human history, and that ideology comprises an "illusion" used to legitimate the oppression of some persons by others. In this vocabulary, ideology is the "superstructure" and the material practices are the "infrastructure" of society, and the argument between humanists and materialists involves the question of which came first.

The model of the communication perspective in Figure 1–1 depicts it as a circular process in which coevolution rather than linear causality operates. As resources are reexpressed during a lifetime, they become institutionalized and taken as vital parts of a culture. For example, the collection of writings known as the Bible is so deeply imprinted in the consciousnesses of Westerners that it provides a constant subtext even for self-pronounced atheists. By the same token, as practices are reenacted, they too become institutionalized. But it is the circular process, whereby each of these re-creates the other, that is the causal mechanism.

We live at a time when many believe that new practices have outstripped resources. Pointing to nuclear weapons, an industrial society fully capable of polluting the oceans and the air, and a population threatening to expand faster than any reasonable forecast of the production of food to feed it, some have argued that the resources we inherited from less potent generations are inadequate as guides for the present. Because these developments have happened so fast, the reconstruction of an adequate set of resources has lagged behind.

This is a pluralistic, chaotic time in which a wide variety of very different forms of communication are practiced simultaneously. Of these, "cosmopolitan communication" seems to me the most appropriate response to the social and material conditions of contemporary society. Part II is an attempt to illuminate those conditions, depict the nature of cosmopolitan communication, and construct resources it will express and (re)construct. It is also a sustained plea for the dissemination and institutionalization of cosmopolitan communication.

5.
Monocultural Communication

Monocultural communication is the simplest, most natural, and—in the contemporary world—most fragile form of communication. At its best, it is a rich, satisfying, and effortless way of communicating; at its worst, it can be narrow-minded and coercive. Because it brings frequent news of different resources, practices, and cultures, contemporary society is not conducive to monocultural communication; the natives of postmodern civilization must work to achieve (or approximate) the graceful monoculturalism that those in primitive cultures find natural. For this reason, the practices of monocultural communication create the opportunity for contemporary persons to experience a way of being human far removed from the "normal" forms of everyday life.

Coherence is achieved in monocultural communication by treating others "like a native." Other persons are held to account according to one's own interpretive and evaluative criteria. Monocultural communicators assume (sometimes too readily) that other persons express and (re)construct the same resources as they do, and thus that "understanding" others is easy. "I listen to what they say and I know what they mean," a monocultural communicator might say, betraying the strategy of assuming that *they* mean the same thing that *I* mean by what they say.

Contextual and prefigurative forces are the most powerful aspects of the logic of meaning and action in monocultural communication. If pressed to explain why they acted as they did, monocultural communicators would likely cite the "contexts" in which they acted, such as their social role, the institutions of their society, or the need to respond as they did to the immediately preceding event.

However, conversations asking monocultural communicators to account for their actions are not likely to be very productive. Monocultural communication requires a kind of "mindlessness" about what one is doing and why. The *content* of their resources are stories that divert attention from explicit consideration of their reasons and do not contain an elaborated vocabulary of accounts.

Mindlessness is not a pejorative term, nor does it mean that the person's mind is empty. Rather, it means that the resources expressed and (re)constructed contain one kind of content rather than another. No less a thinker than Alfred North Whitehead

(1978, p. 40) extolled the virtues of mindlessness: "Civilization advances by extending the number of operations which can be performed without thinking about them. Operations of thought are like cavalry charges in battle—they are strictly limited in number, they require fresh horses, and must only be made at decisive moments."

Coordination is achieved through coherence. Monocultural communicators produce coordinated practices because they are expressing and (re)constructing the same resources—or at least they assume that they are. They tend to exaggerate the extent to which they share resources; they have little affinity for unintended consequences, paradox, existential angst, or nihilism. As a result, resources are not normally placed at risk. When practices are sufficiently disparate from resources, the whole set of resources—not just a particular story—is perturbed in a spasm of unexpected and unaccountable mindfulness.

The resources and practices of monocultural communication include mystery *within* the realm of knowledge and experience. There is no differentiation between the natural and the supernatural; the real and the imagined; the logical and the intuitive; and so on. The *content* of the stories of the mysterious is less important than the fact that they are integrated with other stories. Whether mystery takes the form of (what a contemporary would call) animism, the Tao, or simply the pleasures of the moment, monocultural communication involves an unthinking wholeness of experience that differentiates it from other ways of being human.

Three Contemporary Examples of Monocultural Communication

Many of the characteristics of contemporary society are inimical to monocultural communication, yet it persists and is even common. However, it does not call attention to itself and often requires some form of deliberate "work" to produce.

"Phatic Communion" and "Rhapsodic Communication"

Bronslaw Malinowski (1923) coined the term "phatic communion" to describe patterns of communication in which *what* is said is much less important than the fact that something is *said* at all. His observations of the Melanesians included quite a bit of what seemed purposeless, idle chatter, but which obviously served some more important social function. He concluded that in some situations talk itself, more than what was said, reinforced a sense of community. Those who participated identified with and reinforced the group; silence was taken as a signal of separateness.

It is tempting to identify greeting rituals as the contemporary, *Gesellschaft* analogue to phatic communion. These "hi, how are you?" routines seem like idle chatter but serve as an important social lubricant, allowing acquaintances to slide past each other without irritation. Like phatic communion, the content of what is said is of little importance; only a world-class boor would take "how are you?" as a request for a medical history. Like phatic communion, greeting rituals treat others like natives and do not place resources at risk.

And yet I am dissatisfied with the alleged equivalence between phatic communion among the Melanesians and greeting rituals among Americans. I have never met a Melanesian and I am sure their culture has changed significantly since Malinowski sojourned there, but I get the impression that phatic communion was more important for them than greeting rituals are for us. Without "proof" that this is so, I feel like I did when I heard eggs Benedict at Brennan's (in New Orleans) described as "sorta' like an Egg McMuffin without the top piece of bread." The fact that there is a certain similarity should not distract us from important qualitative differences. My hunch is that the closer analogue to phatic communion is a kind of talk that Abraham Maslow called "rhapsodic communication."

Maslow (1964, p. 84) defined rhapsodic communication as "a kind of emotional contagion in isomorphic parallel." More useful is his description of how he stumbled upon it. He was doing a series of interviews about "peak experiences," and found that "verbal description . . . in a sober, cool, analytic, 'scientific' way" was a poor method of telling his subjects what he wanted them to talk about. Without realizing it at first, he began to use more poetic speech, including figures of speech, tones of voice, and facial expressions in talking with subjects. This procedure sometimes produces "a kind of continuing rhapsodic, emotional, eager throwing out of one example after another of peaks, described or rather reported, expressed, shared, 'celebrated,' sung vividly with participation and with obvious approval and even joy" (ibid., p. 85).

Rhapsodic communication cannot create peak experiences, but it can facilitate participants' sensitivity to them and ability to express them. It depends upon common resources. Maslow (ibid., p. 89) claims that it is impossible to communicate about the feel and nature of a peak experience to a "nonpeaker." But if the "nonpeaker" becomes "more aware of what is going on inside himself, then he becomes a different kind of communicatee. It is now possible to communicate with him."

As Maslow described it, rhapsodic communication occurs anytime two persons compare moments of exhilaration. Talk at moments like this is liable to be a grammarian's nightmare, filled with evocative phrases, nonverbal utterances, and punctuated by disclaimers of effability ("I just can't tell you . . . !" "I know what you mean!"). Their coordination is an explicit affirmation of understanding what cannot and need not be expressed, which itself is part of the shared mystery.

Maslow concluded his description of rhapsodic communication with a powerful testimony to necessity of mindlessness when communicating monoculturally. He realized what he was doing, he reported, only when he was talking about it. Since being struck by the insight, however, "I have not been able to communicate in the same way" (ibid., p. 90).

Baby Talk

A coldly rational analysis of the content of the communication patterns between parents and children reveals nonsensical talk, poor grammar, untenable assumptions, and a curious one-sidedness. Some "progressive" counselors have gone so far as to advise parents not to engage in baby talk. Talking to babies like a baby, they say, teaches babies to talk like babies when they need to learn as quickly and efficiently as possible to talk like adults.

A coldly rational analysis of baby talk also misses the point. It is possible to speak more sensibly of the "functions" and "purposes" of baby talk. Researchers on parent-child interactions, for example, have noted that parents treat their children "like a native" in baby talk; that is, they treat the child *as if* it possessed the full range of adult emotions and intentions:

The baby is treated as if it had a full complement of moral and intellectual qualities. "Diddums want his bottle?" "Isn't she happy." "He's Mummy's naughty little boy." These are the sorts of things that are said. . . . Mothers have theories about how human beings should be and what they are trying to do is to fulfill the theory in the person of their infant. The way to do this is to anticipate the full panoply of social and psychological competence. It really is a vastly complex psychology and moral sensibility that they are ascribing to their infants. They do not talk *about* their infants' intuitions; they provide them with them, and then they react to the infant as if it had them [Harré, in J. Miller, 1983, pp. 168–69].

Children, so this reading of baby talk continues, abstract from that conversational matrix ways of talking that suit their own purposes, ultimately ascribing to themselves intentions and motives in stories experienced as "self" and "personality."

The monocultural nature of baby talk is illuminated by comparing it with Harré's *description* of it, which is not in monocultural communication (Plate 5–1). Most parents do not say "He's Mummy's naughty little boy" in a mindful, deliberate attempt to provide a vocabulary of motives from which the infant can abstract a self. I suspect that making parents mindful of the functions of baby talk shifts them from one form of communication to another.

Awe

Monocultural communication is perhaps most easily experienced by adults when they are mutually confronted by some awe-inspiring event or object. For example, one person is watching a spectacular sunset from the rail of a ship. A second person comes to the rail, watches quietly until the last rays fade into black, and then says, "God does good work when he sets his mind to it." The first replies, "Yeah!" They walk off in different directions.

An analysis of the text of this conversation might show it irreligious, uninformative, even rather simple. However, both may experience it as "good" communication, even an unusually successful attempt at communicating with another person.

Rudolph Otto (1923) analyzed the experience of awe resulting from confrontation with the "tremendous mystery." Regardless of the content of that mystery, whether the face of Yahweh, Allah, the Compassionate Buddha, the Star Maker, or nirvana, the experience is that of being overwhelmed by something much greater than oneself. The vocalizations by which we express such feelings are notoriously inelegant. Stapledon (1939, p. 418) said that he *should* "stammar" when trying to describe that which transcends his vocabulary, and Wittgenstein (1921) recommended silence as the responsible philosophic position regarding things that cannot be said. However lacking in elegance or syntax, such statements treat others like a native in that they assume that the other has shared an experience with the communicator. Resources cannot be put at risk when they define that experience in terms of its irrefutable, undeniable, inexpressible nature. Finally, the utterances we make when awestruck seem involuntary—a form of mindlessness.

The Practice of Monocultural Communication

The practices of monocultural communication coevolve with a particular way of being human characterized by deep enmeshment, a certain kind of mindlessness, and

Plate 5–1. Baby talk: A form of monocultural communication.
Photograph by Paul Franz.

a sense of social solidarity. Closer to *Gemeinschaft* than *Gesellschaft*, this is a distinctive way of life that, in contemporary society, seems to occur in sheltered pockets of preestablished social relationships.

Phatic communion expresses and (re)constructs an unchallenging friendship. Existential questions and policies of state are not at issue in phatic communion; it is itself its sole content. A "good reading" of phatic communion stresses deep enmeshment. One has missed the point, and is denied entrance to this way of being human, by answering its questions literally or by decrying its semantic emptiness.

Baby talk expresses and (re)constructs the most intimate human relationship. Whatever "functions" it might serve for later life are irrelevant to a deeply enmeshed participant. The content of baby talk is the shared enjoyment of mutual responsiveness. The often empty phrases are not intended to "convey" information or "refer" to events/objects beyond the couple; they are solely vehicles for the affirmation of connectedness. There is no thought of the difference between resources expressed by mother and baby; no mindfulness of the spectacle that adult partners make of themselves. Indeed, there must not be: when mindfulness of this nature intrudes, baby talk becomes artificial. To experience this way of being human, one must be mindlessly enmeshed, enraptured with the other.

The experience of awe is not common in contemporary society—or, better said perhaps, contemporary society contains relatively few situations and a relatively weak vocabulary for the expression of the experience of awe. Among these are the frontiers of scientific exploration where bathyscopes bring scientists face to face with strange life forms on the ocean floor, telescopes reveal fascinating astrophysical objects, spaceships set otherworldly horizons, and microscopes provide a unique perspective on what once seemed the ordinary world around us. Behind the avid research reports, the inhumanly scaled research apparatus, the pristine concern with methodological rigor, cleanliness, and order, lies some sort of driving motivation. Far more than is commonly realized, this motivation consists in an attempt to recapture the bliss of monocultural communication with God, although called nature, fate, chance, truth, statistical probability, or whatever. Memories of those times of mutual responsiveness (baby talk!) with the world around us—as it seems to unfold to us as we (finally!) learn to peek, probe, or inquire with the right tools—sustain scientists through many days of tedious observation and the disciplined development of methodology and instrumentation. A statistical analysis, like the quiet contemplation of a sunset or participation in a worship service in church, can be a form of praise. "The really good scientist," according to Abraham Maslow (1966, pp. 143–44), approaches his work "with love, devotion, and self-abnegation, as if he were entering the holy of holies. . . . His absolute morality of honesty and total truth can certainly be called a 'religious' attitude, and his occasional thrill or peak-experience, the occasional shudder of awe, of humility and smallness before the great mysteries he deals with—all these can be called sacred."

To the extent that contemporary persons are able to communicate monoculturally, they experience one of the possible ways of being human. There is considerable testimony that this is a particularly pleasurable way of being in the world. But the material conditions of *Gesellschaft* society militate against monocultural communication. We are now an educated society, and education erodes mindlessness. We are a well-traveled, mobile society, and this places resources at risk and makes coherence no guarantee of coordination: others express different resources and wind up doing the most surprising things. To engage in monocultural communication, one must be fortunate or seek it out.

Consider a fourth, contemporary example of monocultural communication: *aikido*. One of the newest and most sophisticated of the Japanese martial arts, *aikido* is distinctive in that it is noncompetitive and based on a metaphor of spherical motion within a boundless field of energy (*ki*). The name means the way (*do*) of harmonizing (*ai*) energy (*ki*), and the techniques stress blending the energy of the attacker and the attacked in such a way that the attack is neutralized. Training in *aikido* follows the traditional Japanese model: the *sensei* demonstrates basic forms and the students practice them repetitively. Virtually all practice involves sparring, in which all students alternate in the roles of *uke* (the attacker) and *nage* (the one who responds to the attack).

This practice *creates* a culture in which the participants can safely assume that they share the same resources. Coordination is achieved by a mutual subordination to rules of etiquette and the forms of the techniques. The necessary state of mindless, deep enmeshment is created by the physical demands of the activity: bodies fly, wooden swords are swung, and fists are thrown—one tends to pay attention to the moment. Mystery is achieved by a set of stories attesting to the oneness of the universe, providing a vast source of energy on which both *uke* and *nage* may draw. The "reality" of this energy is daily manifest in the power of *kokyu-ko* (a breathing exercise in which *uke* is thrown effortlessly) and the technique of the "unbendable arm," in which relaxed extension is far more powerful than focused effort. Finally, the practice of *aikido* is for the sake of practicing *aikido*: it is not the quickest way of learning how to win a barroom brawl; it does not lead to competition in tournaments with trophies and the thrill of victory; and the path to a black belt is longer than in other martial arts. Like baby talk and the expression of religious awe, one engages in *aikido* because it provides a way of being human that has its own virtues.

But *aikido* is done in a *dojo* (literally, "place" of the "way"), not on the street. One cannot practice *aikido* with an untrained *uke*: one falls down too soon, preventing *nage* from using the more elegant techniques; or the *uke* gets hurt, stopping practice before *nage* is ready. To experience this way of being human requires an isolation from the invidious outside world (particularly *Gesellschaft* society) and the company of others prepared to participate. Perhaps this is the case with other forms of monocultural communication as well.

In this discussion, I have been necessarily vague in describing the "way of being human" expressed and (re)constructed by monocultural communication. One reason for this is that monocultural communication does not contain powerful descriptions of itself—such mindfulness is inimical to the experience. Another reason is that monocultural communication in contemporary society occurs in "pockets," usually as a small portion of life. However, there is an example of what life would be like if monocultural communication were the norm rather than the exception: primitive society.

Primitive Society

When monocultural communication is institutionalized, (re)constructing itself through sequential iterations of the communication process, it creates a distinctive way of being human called "primitive society." "Primitive" does *not* mean simplistic or "backward"; rather, it denotes a complex but relatively uncomplicated way of achieving coordination, coherence, and mystery. It was the first form of human society. It has endured the longest, although it is now threatened. In the judgment of some, it is the best way of being human.

Primitive societies exist in the twentieth century, although they are quickly disappearing. They are known as prehistorical societies, not because they existed before historical records were kept but because they do not write histories. Illiteracy is not the problem; rather, such societies have a sense of time and of sacredness that precludes historical consciousness and differs markedly from modern and postmodern ways of being human. They live in an eternal "present" or in a time whose markers are mythic and ritualistic events, not the sequential passing of days or years.

Primitive society always occurs in small groups, usually between forty and eighty persons, and survives by gathering and hunting. It is, for the most part, a leisurely society. Even in relatively harsh climates, primitive peoples can meet the necessities of life by "working" only a few hours a day. They are unhurried, and not characterized by "instrumental" or "practical" reasoning. They place primary value on things because of their contact with the sacred, not because of their efficiency or their utility. Contextual and prefigurative forces far outweigh implicative and practical.

It is always a highly social life. "Mankind in its primary condition," wrote Robert Redfield (1953, p. 171) "lives in small and isolated communities . . . composed of one kind of people." In these intimate communities, "people come to have the same ways of doing things; they marry with and live almost entirely with others like them in that community" (ibid.). In these small communities, everyone knows, is known by, and probably is related to everyone else. Social relationships are determined by patterns of kinship and status within the group. (This type of society is about as far as one can get from the unstructured anonymity of a big city park, where persons are identified to each other solely in terms of their "displays" of insignia and mood-signs.)

Within the group, persons can safely act on the assumption that everyone shares the same resources. They have a strong sense of group solidarity based on common activities and a common array of stories. With the possible exception of the shaman, there were "no fulltime specialists . . . all men shared the same essential knowledge, practiced the same arts of life, had the same interests and similar experiences" (Redfield, 1953, p. 171). Further, "primitive and precivilized communities are held together essentially by common understandings as to the ultimate nature and purpose of life" (ibid., p. 174).

Redfield probably exaggerated the cognitive aspect of these resources: the intellectual heirs of the Greeks have trouble believing that not everyone shares their concern for articulating an analysis of the way the world works. The resources of primitive societies "for the most part had no creed; they consisted entirely of institutions and practices. No doubt men will not habitually follow certain practices without attaching a meaning to them; but as a rule we find that while the practice was rigorously fixed, the meaning attached to it was extremely vague, and the same rite was explained by different people in different ways, without any question of orthodoxy or heterodoxy arising in consequence" (William Robertson Smith, quoted by Ross, 1957, p. 17).

Figure 5–1. Relationships among the resources of primitive society.

The Moral Order

Primitive society is not well understood simply by observing it from the "outside," counting its members, and cataloguing the way in which it gathers food. Like all human societies, it has a rich and powerful moral order. In fact, primitive society has a stronger, more consensual, moral order than modern society. It is in modern society that institutions are created that deliberately strip away most of the distinctiveness of humanity, allowing participants to interact anonymously, with neither a past nor a future, on the basis of displays of mood-signs. At least, this is one plausible way to "read" the practices of singles' bars, escort services, and—at least one use of—public parks and public shopping areas. In primitive society, the moral order is "the essential order of society, the nexus which held people together. . .largely undeclared but continually realized ethical conceptions. . .predominate over the 'technical order'" (Redfield, 1964, pp. 174, 178).

In this and subsequent chapters, I want to compare the moral orders in several "ways of being human." Joseph Campbell argued that the myths of all cultures can be read as giving answers to four questions: (1) the "*psychological*" question, "Who am I?" (2) the *sociological* question, "Who are we?" (3) the *cosmological* question, "What is the nature of the universe in which we live?" and (4) the *epistemic* question, "What is the nature of our knowledge about the answers to all these questions?"

Figure 5–1 depicts the relationship among the answers to these questions that typify primitive society. One of the distinguishing characteristics is that the first three questions are not differentiated. The issue of individual identity is not separate from that of the group, and that of the group is not separate from that of the world in which the group lives. From the mind-set of a primitive society, the division of modern universities into separate departments—where faculty members of one department can neither read nor talk intelligently about the work done by those in the others—is foolish.

The second characteristic is that there is a division of function between those who deal with the epistemic question and those who do not. (In Figure 5–1, this is indicated by oblique slashes.) In primitive society, the shaman has undergone a unique set of experiences and has a special knowledge of the rituals of the tribe, and perhaps unusual personal power deriving from his or her familiarity with the spirits. Campbell (1959, pp. 252–53) described the "shamanistic crisis" as a traumatic experience that "ruptured" the connection between the shaman and the ordinary world, which satisfies the "tough-minded, honest hunters" of the tribe. This crisis is Janus-faced. On the one hand, the shaman discovers a sacred character in the external world; on the other, he or she realizes that this sacred character is deeply intermeshed with his or her own "internal" nature. The result is a depth of belief and function that sets the shaman apart from the tribe.

The third characteristic reduces the "distance" between the shaman and the other members of the tribe. It is the explicit assumption that whatever the shaman knows supports rather than contradicts those practices of the group that express the answers to the other three questions. The shaman, because of specialized knowledge, is trusted not to put his or her resources at risk.

The second and third characteristics, of course, pull in opposite directions. The shamanistic crisis separates shamans from the quotidian experience of the tribe, but it also co-opts the shaman as the primary defender and preserver of the group's resources. Campbell (1959, p. 462) described this as an antinomy in which myths and the practices of the shaman function both as "way" and "ethnic ideal." "As 'a way,' " he wrote, "mythology and ritual conduce to a transformation of the individual, disengaging him from his local, historical conditions and leading toward some kind of ineffable experience. Functioning as an 'ethnic ideal,' on the other hand, the image binds the individual to his family's system of historically conditioned sentiments, activities, and beliefs, as a functioning member of a sociological organism." The modern mind would pull these two functions apart, perhaps as "contradictions." However, focus on either alone constitutes a misunderstanding of the force of the mythological symbols and practices. Together, they "render an experience of the ineffable through the local and concrete, and thus, paradoxically, . . . amplify the force and appeal of the local forms even while carrying the mind beyond them" (Campbell, 1959, p. 462).

The fourth characteristic is that the myths of primitive society are "closed." They do not acknowledge the existence—far less the potential "correctness"—of alternative ways of life. The social situation is one in which members do not normally encounter anyone who does not share their own resources: "their interpretation of the world, while it has some internal complexities, is not tested in competition with other kinds of views. . . . It is not that it is irrational . . . [it] is that there is no other alternative available" (Geertz, 1983, p. 201).

Geertz is willing to explain the "closedness" of primitive resources in terms of their geographical and social conditions. To be sure, that makes their "closedness" possible. When those conditions change, primitive societies are shown to be very vulnerable: both their members and their culture almost always die when brought into contact with other peoples and other technologies. But even in a state of isolation, primitive society is characterized by practices that "defend" resources from being put "at risk."

Performance Demands: The Relationship of Resources and Practices

Persons in primitive society, like all humans, strive to achieve coordination, coherence and mystery about the facts of life. The distinctively "primitive" way of doing this is to achieve coherence by sacralizing everything important, and by treating the group as the whole of the world.

Sacralizing Everything Important

1. *Deep Enmeshment in Sacred Stories.* Those who are natives in a primitive society must be able to maintain deep enmeshment in its myths. Sacred stories and rituals in primitive societies are "participatory," not performances for the amusement or edification of spectators. An anthropologist may take pictures of the dance, may be able to recite the myths as well as any member of the tribe, and may even "act like a native" by joining in the rituals, but this is not equivalent to *being* a native. For that, one must

"believe" in and be a part of these myths and rituals without seeing them as "local" or "made up."

One of the earliest observations Europeans made about primitive society was the presence of "magic." For example, Bronislaw Malinowski (1923) observed that Melanesian fishermen would engage in ritualistic chants when they left their lagoon to fish in the more dangerous open sea. The first interpretation of this talk was that the Melanesians were doing "science"—but badly. Melanesians superstitiously believed, the Europeans assured themselves, that there was a causal connection between the ritual they performed and the consequence of good weather while they were out on the open sea.

For this interpretation of "science done badly" to be believed, it was necessary to think that the Melanesians were attempting to do the same thing that the scientists who were observing them would have done under the same circumstances. That is, the scientists thought of the Melanesians as thinking of the world as a complex machine whose structure is a pattern of "causes" and "effects," and in which human action has meaning to the extent that it affects and changes the social or physical environment. When stated this way, of course, the assumption seems far from plausible. The "scientific" worldview is a relatively recent achievement, limited to a rather small portion of some societies among the many on the face of the earth.

The alternative interpretation of magic-talk is that the practices of magic reinforce their enmeshment in a sacred world. The Azande have a rain-dance in which they throw water into the air:

> [They] are not trying to cause the rain in the sense that we would cause rain by seeding clouds or something; they are . . . trying to think about the way in which the various parts of the cosmos as they conceive it, explicitly or implicitly, connect up with one another. And the cosmos includes them, includes their dances, includes what they have to do in order to keep the cosmos whole, to give it that kind of order—sustain, if you will, its order. . . . When everything comes together, when you dance and you make all those long preparations that lead up to it, and then in the end it rains, what is reinforced is your conviction that you really understand what the cosmos is like and . . . your place and part in it.
>
> This is the point that I've been trying to get to; the ritual activity is not conceived as instrumental in the first place: It is considered as expressive or representational or some other term of that sort, none of them quite what one would want [Geertz, 1983, pp. 203–4].

There is a reason why so articulate a person as Clifford Geertz cannot find quite the right term for the place of ritual. In primitive society, deep enmeshment in the sacred is accomplished by *not* making a series of distinctions that Geertz has been trained to make since infancy. For natives of primitive society, Figure 5–1 is a distortion, because they simply do not see "self" and "group" and "cosmos" and "the gods" as separate entities, whose relationship is a matter of difference of opinion. Neither their actions nor their tools are differentiated from "nature" or "the gods." Every important thing they do is sacred.

The wholeness of primitive society makes it impossible for them to engage in deliberate "social engineering," or to think of themselves as "wearing a mask" by deliberate choice. In the *New York Times* of March 25, 1984 (section 1, p. 8), Sanjay Hazarika reported the efforts of the central government of India to revive the ethnic identity of the rural tribes in the troubled northeast. The Nagas and Mizos were converted to Christianity in the late nineteenth century, and under the influence of missionaries they abandoned their rituals and "their enjoyment of village feasts and merrymaking. The beating of drums, for instance, was banned as evil by early converts." The (secular) central government is encouraging the revival of "ancient dances, festivals, tribal law courts and ritual." However, other indigenous aspects of their society are not being supported: head-hunting, drunkenness, and sexual permissiveness. The Chief Minister of Mizoram, Thenphunga Sailo, explained, "We cannot keep alive all customs, but we can keep alive what is good."

Maybe.

But deep enmeshment in the sacred is already lost when one begins to pick and choose among the practices of one's society with the intention of deliberately reviving some and suppressing others. The preservation of ethnic identity may well serve laudable purposes in northeastern India and elsewhere, but the practices of social scientific research, ethical evaluation of traditional patterns of action, and political deliberation are inimical to deep enmeshment in the sacred.

Some think that primitive society is the best of the ways of being human. Much of the appeal derives from the fact that their life is filled with sacred significance. Eliade (1959, p. vii) said that "the man [*sic*] of archaic societies . . . feels himself indissolubly connected with the Cosmos and the cosmic rhythms." Campbell (1959, p. 470) judged that "primitive man [*sic*] could bring his mind to rest in the mystery of the universe and therewith attain to a knowledge that can be justly called wisdom."

I do not say of primitive societies that all their members achieve total enmeshment in the sacred all the time. Rather, I argue that primitive society is characterized by having "in place" a set of practices that facilitate deep enmeshment and make skepticism less likely. There are standardized ways of expressing deep enmeshment, and social supports for participation in those practices. There are even practices designed for those who see "beyond" the surface meaning of the myths: they become shamans and in that way are co-opted into the tribe.

Further, there is reason to think that these practices are potent. Any casual reader of ethnographic or mythological materials notes that much of the content would not be deemed suitable for American television and would be rated "X" at public theaters. Blood and sex are not only depicted, but are a part of many of the rituals. Why?

One answer is simply that primitive societies are not inhibited by Victorian prudishness; that their members are "earthy" persons, healthily in touch with basic life processes that modern society screens off behind butcher shops and delivery rooms and closed bedroom doors. Another interpretation is that blood and sex are—quite literally—matters of life and death, and whatever else they do, they command attention and enmeshment. The contemporary rituals of American football are certainly powerful. The stylized combat represents struggle and death; the dance steps of scantily clad cheerleaders suggest sexual activities. But these televised spectacles pale before participatory ritual cannibalism and sexual orgies. In comparison with primitive society, the practices of contemporary society are bloodless, lifeless, and often meaningless things. Most of us, I suspect, do not have the "stomach" for the kinds of practices normal for primitive society—but we can acknowledge that they are powerful means of maintaining deep enmeshment.

2. *A De-emphasis on Profane Talk.* For natives of primitive society, the "secular sphere" is not the "real world." Deeply enmeshed in their myths and rituals they see merely "secular" things as unusual or unimportant. "The archaic world knows nothing of 'profane' activities: every act which has a definite meaning . . . in some way participates

in the sacred. . . The only profane activities are those which have no mythical meaning, that is, which lack exemplary models" (Eliade, 1961, pp. 27–28).

The natives of primitive society are *not* ignorant or unskilled. To the surprise of the Europeans who mistook the absence of a high material culture for an inept manner of dealing with the physical environment, primitive societies are efficient and productive in procuring the necessities of life from their environment. Some of the modern "miracle" drugs are derived from herbs used by primitive shamans (e.g., curare). However, primitive societies require a kind of "double-think." Their members must be skilled, knowledgeable, and resourceful, but these skills, knowledge, and resourcefulness cannot be *seen by them* as important.

The nature of this "double-think," which also helps maintain deep enmeshment, is to sacralize virtually *all* the practices of ordinary life. Acts such as eating, hunting, gathering, love making, and tool building are never simply physiological or instrumental. They are, or can become, a sacrament (Eliade, 1961, pp. 4, 104–6).

There is a "technology" for sacralizing even ordinary events, and only those things that have been subjected to this process are "real." "Neither the objects of the external world nor human acts, properly speaking, have any autonomous intrinsic value. [They] acquire a value, and in so doing become real, because they participate. . .in a reality that transcends them . . . the object appears as the receptacle of an exterior force that differentiates it from its milieu and gives it meaning and value" (ibid., pp. 3–6).

Many of the ceremonial rituals are not so much a means of "controlling" nature in a "cause and effect" manner as they are a procedure for sacralizing profane events and objects, and thus making them real. This "technology" of sacralization is routinely applied to things that otherwise might threaten the meaning of life.

"History" itself, as an irreversible sequence of particular events, is a threat to the resources of primitive society. The routinized practices of contemporary journalists are perhaps the antithesis of those of primitive society. If a member of a primitive group performs heroic acts—for example, rescuing someone from drowning—the story as it is told does not supply details of the "actual" events, but describes the archetypal acts of the gods. The individual is not mentioned, but the god is.

Consider a well-trained journalist somehow transported to a primitive society. She volunteers to tell the story of a heroic rescue. If she follows the canons of good journalism, she will produce a story with a sensational "headline," a first paragraph (in an "inverted pyramid" structure) that summarizes the whole event, a series of graphs that give the factual sequence of events, complete with names and identifications, and then the reactions of bystanders.

It might go something like this: "Ug-Lak, 23, a member of the Tilsaday, today rescued his mother from a watery grave. The mishap occurred when Ur-Lag, 40, was gathering potatoes. The shaman, Ut-Yop, 51, said, "Never have I seen such a commendable demonstration of bravery and filial devotion! With no regard for his own safety, Ug-Lak dove into the swirling waters where three other persons have drowned during the last ten years, and rescued his mother. The tribe has debated putting guardrails around the waterfall to prevent future occurrences of this kind. We can only be glad that this reminder of the danger presented by this part of our territory was not at the cost of another life."

No. Not even "maybe"!

This kind of reportorial style is not likely to occur, but this is just the start of it. If it were to occur, the members of a primitive society would have great difficulty under-standing it. Drawing upon their resources, they would find the story to be told wrongly, if they recognized it as a story at all. And if, by some circumstance, they were to understand what was happening and its implications, they would certainly take some procedures to silence the journalist, for this kind of reporting makes "history" impor-tant—and that is a basic threat to their universe.

For members of primitive society, the function of myth and ritual "has always been, and surely must continue to be, to engage the individual, both emotionally and intellectually, in the local organization . . . through a solemn conjuring up of intensely shared experiences," which infuse even the ordinary events of life with meaning and significance (Campbell, 1959, p. 497).

The practices by which this enmeshment is accomplished are not limited to the formal enactment of rituals. They are a part of all of life. The Great Basin Shoshone, who have an extremely limited material culture, use sticks for digging, but even so simple a tool is invested with meaning. They do not use just any stick, but one intended for the special purpose of digging plant roots out of the earth. Any Shoshone can differentiate between digging sticks and sticks that are not used as tools. There are traditions and rituals associated with the preparation of a stick as a tool (Farb, 1978, p. 22). Communica-tion practices whose purpose is "merely" instrumental—whether a public deliberation on nuclear missiles, a journalistic report of how a hunt went, or a casual chat about the weather—are opaque in primitive culture. Whatever else they may be, for natives of primitive society, they cannot be perceived as important.

A "profane" or "secular" theory of human communication, such as reported in this book, would be a threat to a primitive society. If confronted with it, members would have to find a way to defend against it, perhaps by dismissing it as unimportant and communication processes as trivial.

Maintaining Boundaries *around* the Group but Not *within* It

Coherence in primitive society is achieved by sacralizing everything important. Coordination is achieved by maintaining an egalitarian society, which is perceived, quite literally, as the center of the world. Life in such a society imposes performance demands that are quite distinctive.

1. *No Concept of a "Self" as Separate from the Group.*   The modern concept of "self" as a unique, autonomous locus of meaning and value is a relatively recent "inven-tion," occurring first, according to one social historian, in Europe in 1750 (Lyons, 1978). The recency of this invention shows that various cultures have dealt quite differently with the concept of "self."

Every society "conspires" to reproduce itself in its children, and children are genetically programed to respond to those efforts (Calder, 1976). Language is a far from neutral "resource" provided to children; and parent-child interaction is a far from neutral "practice" in which children are co-opted.

There is a vast and important philosophy embedded in languages. When a child learns to talk, it is rewarded with approval and an increased ability to manipulate the world around it. In this sense, children quickly learn that the tongue is best understood as an organ for the manipulation of other persons' behavior. But the process of learning a language masks the process of learning to make a wide variety of discriminations and a system for relating some but not all the events and objects in the physical world. That the philosophy embedded in language affects the way we *perceive the world* is not news. But only recently the argument has been extended to cover the *we* who perceive the world. Our notion of "self" is constructed in coordinated social practices.

In primitive society, the moral order is based on a nondifferentiation between self, the group, and the cosmos. This is expressed in practices in which the particulars of history or individuality are not treated as important, as discussed above. It is also expressed in the absence of practices that call attention to individuals as separate and distinct. Birthdays are not observed, or if observed, then by "group" rather than by individuals. Some societies distinguish among persons on the basis of age, but all those individuals born within, say, a five-year period, are members of the same "set." "Once the set is closed you are no longer primarily an individual and you no longer go through life as such. From then on the set as a whole does whatever it has to do, and during the periodic rites of passage the set as a whole advances from one grade to the next" (Turnbull, 1976, p. 45). To a modern observer, there is a distressing lack of "individuality" among natives of primitive societies. One observer commented that the "Cooper Eskimo, as a rule, displays very little independence in either thought or action. . . . He follows the multitude, agrees to whatever is said, and reflects the emotions of those around him" (D. Jennes, quoted in Harré, 1984, p. 88).

2. *Maintaining Amicable Relationships within the Group.* The small, intimate communities of primitive society require the natives to take care of their interpersonal relationships. There are comparable situations in modern society. For example, the crew of a nuclear attack submarine engages in prolonged intimacy in highly cramped quarters for periods of six to nine months. For the submariners, this is an unusual situation sandwiched between times in which they have much greater privacy. For those in primitive society, this is the only life they know. Rather than demanding an extra amount of interpersonal care for a relatively brief period, their concern for amicable relationships is built right into the moral order. "To the Cooper Eskimo goodness means social goodness, that and no more. Whatever affects the welfare of the community as a whole is morally good or bad. . . . The foremost virtues therefore are peacefulness and good-nature, courage and energy, patience and endurance, honesty, hospitality, charity towards both the old and the young, loyal cooperation with one's kin and providence in all questions relating to the food supply" (D. Jennes, quoted in Harré, 1984, p. 89).

This moral order contrasts sharply with that of individualistic modern society, as Jean L. Briggs (1970) found when she was "adopted" by an Eskimo family while doing fieldwork with them. This experience juxtaposed "selves" constructed by very different ways of being human, and the predictable problems they had in coordination to illuminate the primitive Eskimo society. Briggs committed a serious offense: she was irritable and unhappy. Briggs describes three causes of conflict: (1) she was unable to perform skills required of a female member of the family (sewing, stretching skins, etc.); (2) she could not avoid being irritated when treated like a daughter in an Eskimo family addressed in the imperative tone and expected to show unquestioning obedience to parental authority; and (3) she found the roles of daughter and anthropologist incompatible. She often worked on her notes rather than helping with the family chores. Once she even questioned her "father's" judgment about leaving her tape recorder and field notes on a knoll, rather than carrying them with her during a flood. She writes:

> The Utkuhikhalingmiut are acutely sensitive to subtle indications of mood. They heard the

coldness in my voice when I said, "I don't understand," noted the length of a solitary walk I took across the tundra, or the fact that I went to bed early and read with my back turned to the others. Later, Inuttiaq might give me a lecture—phrased, as always, in the most general terms—about the fate of those who lose their tempers: Satan uses them for firewood. Or he might offer me an especially choice bit of fish—whether to shame me or to appease me I don't know. The contrast between my irritability and the surface equanimity of others gave me many uncomfortable moments, but I persuaded myself that the effects of my lapses were shortlived. When I laughed again and heard others laugh with me, or when they seemed to accept the generous gestures with which I tried to make amends, I was reassured that no damage had been done. I was wrong [Briggs, 1970, pp. 49–50].

There were three phases in the relationship between Briggs and her family: she was first treated as a stranger, then as a child, and finally as a simpleton. The first phase was characterized by ethnocentric communication, in which she was *not* treated like a native:

I was a stranger and a guest; and I was treated with . . . formal courtesy and deference. . . . Much of the time during this period the Eskimos must have been at a loss what to make of my behavior, and often when I did something that under other circumstances they might have defined as reprehensible—when I went to bed early, nursing a bad humor, or when I was silent in depression—they gave me the benefit of the doubt [ibid., p. 59].

The second phase was characterized by monocultural communication: Briggs's acts were interpreted according to Eskimo resources. She was expected to act like and be happy being treated like an Eskimo.

The third phase witnessed a cessation of any attempt to engage in sophisticated forms of coordination.

I was treated as an incorrigible offender . . . when it became apparent to the Utkuhikhaling-miut that I was uneducable. Inuttiaq no longer lectured me or used any other method to teach me. . . . Nothing at all was demanded of me. Though my physical needs for warmth, food, and protection from danger were still taken care of, socially I was simply "not there." There was one other person in the community who was similarly ostracized: a woman of about my age, who appeared to be of subnormal intelligence. Almost all of her personal qualities . . . were subject to comment behind her back, but hostility in her case, as in mine, centered on her volatility—the fact that she was easily upset and was unable to exercise proper restraint in the expression of feelings [ibid., p. 60].

The importance of amicable relationships does not imply that they are always achieved. Sometimes Eskimos have feuds that result in killings. But these are episodic, and then finished (at least for a while). Eskimos do not tend to be grouchy or argumentative.

3. *Egalitarian Relationships.* In primitive society, individuals are distinguished from one another by kinship relationships, and the like, but are not differentiated from the group in the modern sense. The *!kung* (Bushmen) who live in the Kalahari Desert in southern Africa employ a set of practices that keep successful hunters from becoming arrogant. Richard Lee (1984) learned about the practice by painful accident.

Lee lived among the *!kung* for a year, observing the way they gathered food. Part of his purpose for being there prevented him from sharing his own supplies of food, although by *!kung* standards he was rich. And not sharing food violated a cultural norm. He was sensitive to the fact that by *!kung* criteria, he was a miser. Near the end of his visit, he determined to provide the *!kung* a feast, and purchased the biggest ox he could find. He then immediately received a series of delegations of *!kung* complaining about his choice.

An old woman called the ox a "bag of bones."

"Bag of bones"! Its the biggest ox at /ai/ai," Lee responded.

"Big, yes, but old. And thin. Everybody knows there's no meat on that old ox. What did you expect us to eat off it, the horns?"

After everyone had feasted on his gift, Lee finally found an informant who explained that it is the normal practice to criticize anyone who makes a larger-than-usual contribution to the group, and to depreciate the value of the contribution. Such criticisms function to head off arrogance. "When a young man kills much meat," Lee was told pointedly, "he comes to think of himself as a chief or a big man, and he thinks of the rest of us as his servants or inferiors. We can't accept this. We refuse one who boasts, for someday his pride will make him kill somebody. So we always speak of his meat as worthless. This way we cool his heart and make him gentle."

Limitations of Monocultural Communication

Contemporary society's aversion to monocultural communication is not simply the unintended consequence of the material conditions of the age. Part of the difficulty is that monocultural communication is singularly inappropriate for many of the situations of contemporary society. It leads to practices that offend precepts of the moral order. In this section, I describe some of the negative aspects of monocultural communication.

Resources Not "At Risk"

The "resources" that human beings draw on to interpret the facts of life and to guide their actions are no small matter. They are the wall that seals us off from the chaos and terrors of an inhuman universe. The richness of our lives derives from the extent to which those resources can adequately "tame" the facts of life, and the fulness of life depends on their ability to tap and channel our own energy. The symbols in those resources "not only 'turn you on,' as they say today, but turn you on in a certain direction, making you function a certain way—which will be conducive to your participation in the life and purposes of the functioning social group" (Campbell, 1972, p. 89).

There are inherent tensions in the communication process that make these resources prone to disconfirmation or change. The flux of experience, with its disappointments and surprises, comprises a stern test for any set of stories. The wisdom of monocultural communication derives from the ways it "protects" an existing set of resources by "mindlessness." But this protection is not without its price.

Thinking may not always be the best policy, but neither is mindlessness. Mindlessness can lead to unfortunate (and, obviously, unforeseen) consequences. The history of military tactics provides a virtually inexhaustible source of examples of tragedies caused by too-successful "protection" of resources. In the fourteenth century, the English and French were often at war. Given the equipment and tactics in common use, war was a sporting event for the aristocracy but a matter of life and death for the peasantry.

Aristocrats went to war wearing metal suits and riding great, lumbering horses. Peasants went to war on foot, with little or no armor, and carrying rather light weapons. An exaggeration that nonetheless conveys the sense of the occasion has it that the aristocrats killed each other's peasants, occasionally taking each other prisoner and demanding (and getting) a ransom.

New technologies changed the nature of warfare. English peasants were armed with longbows, whose greater power enabled them for the first time to pose a real threat to an armored knight. At the battle of Crecy and subsequently, the English were victorious because their young men were able to kill the French knights. The French, on the other hand, were unwilling to adopt new strategies, because for them the tactics by which war was fought were closely linked to their myths about God, honor, and manliness. (The hilt and blade of a sword comprised a crucifix!) So they protected their resources—but not themselves—and honorably died in battle (Tuchman, 1978 and 1984).

The trial of Galileo, the arguments of Voltaire against the Catholic Church, the tribulations of *Don Quixote*, the efforts by the People's Republic of China to prevent "spiritual pollution" from the uncontrolled importation of Western culture—all these may be read as deliberations about the extent to which one should protect "old" resources of a culture or put them at risk because of new practices. But note: such deliberations cannot be conducted *in* monocultural communication, because they deliberately place resources "at risk." Monocultural communicators "do" rather than "ask," "are" rather than contemplate whether they should be this or that.

Treating Others "Like a Native"

In monocultural communication, coordination is expected to occur because all communicators are assumed to be "natives" of the same community. They treat each other "like a native" because they are mindful neither of their own interpretive and evaluative criteria nor of the (potential) differences between their own and others' rules for meaning and action.

To be mindful of the notion that persons are "natives" of different cultures precludes monocultural communication, but this vantage is necessary to understand what is involved in treating others like a native. By definition, natives of different cultures express and (re)construct different resources by engaging in practices that are overtly different or are subjected to different evaluative and interpretive criteria.

It is possible for a member of one culture to *act* like the members of another culture, but this does not make that person a *native* of the other culture. An Anglo-Saxon American who uses Korean greetings and honorifics perfectly is not treated by Koreans as a Korean; he or she is and will always remain an American who courteously, arrogantly, or pretentiously acts *like* a Korean. The only way to *be* a native of a culture is to be *treated* as a native by natives, and this is so when one's acts are subjected to the same evaluative and interpretive criteria as the acts of a native. The Anglo-Saxon American who speaks Korean may use the wrong honorific. If the Koreans to whom he is speaking treat it as an ignorant foreigner's "mistake," they are not treating him like a native; if they treat it as an intentional error (e.g., as a joke, an insult, a warning, etc.), then they are treating him like a native.

Treating others like a native gives monocultural communication the qualities of spontaneity and assurance that make it so appealing. Monocultural communication is the embodiment of the golden rule, which prescribes treating others as you would like to be treated yourself.

However, this aspect of monocultural communication seems naïve from the vantage of other, more cynical, ways of being human. For example, *if* persons are natives of different cultures, then a too literal (or mindless) application of the golden rule can be tyrannical—insisting that the natives of other cultures be evaluated and interpreted according to the criteria of one's own culture. A person communicating monoculturally would not be mindful of the differences in the meaning of time in various cultures. Prizing punctuality, he or she may treat the others' arrival thirty minutes late for dinner as an irreparable insult. Those who love to argue display the coercive aspect of treating others like a native if they insist on disputing every statement, even when communicating with those for whom consensus is important. These observations lead up to a moral argument that others should at least sometimes be treated as *not* natives; that they should be understood on the basis of their own evaluative and interpretive criteria.

This moral argument is buttressed by the observation that it is often difficult to achieve coordination if communicators persist in treating each other like natives. Clavell's (1975) novel *Shōgun* depicts the collision between two cultures, and some of the problems that occurred because—even though *aware* of the differences between cultures—they were unable to determine the rules for meaning and action of the other culture. The story describes the first Protestant European to reach Japan. When he arrived, he found Portuguese Jesuits already there, and deeply involved in the incessant civil wars among the Japanese. Blackthorne—called "Anjin" by the Japanese, who had difficulty pronouncing his name—was captured by one of the "lords" trying to become the next shōgun, and was seen as a potentially important pawn in this struggle. His captor, Toronaga, instructed that he should be guarded carefully but, for the moment at least, treated with courtesy. The only Japanese with whom Blackthorne could speak was Mariko, a woman who had been educated by the Jesuits.

But "courtesy," of course, is a cultural thing:

"In matters of the pillow, how would you compare your women with ours?"

"Sorry, I don't understand."

"Oh, please excuse me. The pillow—in intimate matters. Pillowing's our way of referring to the physical joining of man and woman. It's more polite than fornication, *neh?*"

Blackthorne squelched his embarrassment and said, "I've, er, I've only had one, er, pillow experience here—that was, er, in the village—and I don't remember it too clearly because I was so exhausted by our voyage that I was half dreaming and half awake. But it, er, seemed to me to be very satisfactory."

Mariko frowned. "You've pillowed only once since you arrived?"

"Yes."

"You must be feeling very constricted, *neh?* One of these ladies would be delighted to pillow with you, Anjin-san. Or all of them, if you wish."

"Eh?"

"Certainly. If you don't want one of them, there's no need to worry; they'd certainly not be offended. Just tell me the sort of lady you'd like and we'll make all the arrangements."

"Thank you," said Blackthorne, "but not now."

"Are you sure? Please excuse me, but Kiritsukusan has given specific instructions that your health is to be protected and improved. How can you be healthy without pillowing? It's very important for a man, *neh?* Oh, very yes."

"Thank you, but I'm—perhaps later."

"You'd have plenty of time . . . you don't have to leave until sunset."

"Thanks, but not now," Blackthorne said, flattened by the bluntness and lack of delicacy of the suggestion.

"They'd really like to accommodate you, Anjin-San. Oh! Perhaps—perhaps you would prefer a boy?"

"What?"

"A boy. It's just as simple if that's what you wish." Her smile was guileless, her voice matter-of-fact.

"Eh?"

"What's the matter?"

"Are you seriously offering me a boy?"

"Why, yes, Anjin-San. What's the matter? I only said we'd send a boy here if *you* wished it."

"I don't wish it!" Blackthorne felt the blood in his face. "Do I look like a godcursed sodomite?"

His words sloshed around the room. They all stared at him transfixed. Mariko bowed abjectly, kept her head to the floor. "Please forgive me. I've made a terrible error. Oh, I've offended where I was only trying to please. . . ."

The samurai leader, Kazu Oan, was watching angrily. He was charged with the barbarian's safety. . . . "What's the matter with him?"

Oan scratched his head in disbelief. "He's like a mad ox just because you offered him a boy?"

"Yes."

"So sorry, but were you polite? Did you use a wrong word, perhaps?" A sudden thought: "I wonder if it's because he's impotent. His story about pillowing in the village was vague enough, *neh*? Perhaps the poor fellow's enraged because he can't pillow at all and you brought the subject up. Ask him!"

Mariko immediately did as she was ordered, and Oan was horrified as the blood rushed into the barbarian's face again and a spate of foul-sounding barbarian filled the room.

"He—he said 'no.' " Mariko's voice was hardly a whisper.

"All that just meant 'no'?"

"They—they use many descriptive curse words when they get excited."

One of the older samurai said helpfully, "Oan-San, perhaps he's one of those that like dogs, *neh*? We heard some strange stories in Korea . . . they like dogs and. . .I remember now, yes, dogs and ducks. Maybe he wants a duck."

Oan said, "Mariko-San, ask him! No, perhaps you'd better not. . . ." [Clavell, 1975, pp. 329–31].

Mariko persistently assumed that Blackthorne shared her own cultural attitudes about sexual activities, and Blackthorne stubbornly interpreted her questions and offers as if they meant for her just what they meant for him. No matter how vigorously Blackthorne protested the proceedings, Mariko and Oan interpreted his anger in terms of the specific content of what he was offered, not the fact that such offers were made. Their sequential attempts to accommodate Blackthorne's apparently unusual tastes simply made the situation worse in a manner that they could not understand—as long as they continued to treat him "like a native."

Part of the charm of Clavell's depiction of Blackthorne's adventures in Japan is the clash of cultures and the painful, incomplete abandonment of monocultural communication. One example of cultural learning was Blackthorne's adoption of Japanese standards for cleanliness.

In the fifteenth century, when the story took place, European standards for personal cleanliness differed considerably from the modern sensibility. The Europeans thought bathing was bad for one's health, they were unconcerned about dirt or garbage in their living quarters, and they had only the most rudimentary processes for dealing with sewage. The Japanese, on the other hand, were fastidious. Early in his captivity, Blackthorne was forcibly bathed by the Japanese who were offended by his smell. He slowly became used to being clean and without knowing it, internalized the Japanese view of the Europeans as dirty. After being separated from the other survivors of his ship for some time, he was allowed to visit them—and saw them through "Japanese" eyes as loud, dirty, uncivilized barbarians. To the amusement and approval of his Japanese companions, when he left the house in which his crew was being kept, he took off and threw away his clothing as "soiled" and demanded a bath.

Another example of the problem that can result from being treated like a native is a story that deserves retelling, although I have no proof that it really happened.

The first European who came to Australia, according to this account, had a bad time of it. He was shipwrecked, washed up on the shore, and found by aborigines. His experience is known because he was tied near some rocks, and wrote on them in three European languages about his predicament.

The aborigines ate him.

Cannibalism!

Well . . . maybe not. Perhaps a victim of monocultural communication.

Think of the problem that his appearance posed for the aborigines. They lived in a society in which everyone was related to someone else, and in which each individual's identity was derived from a symbolic figure from their myths. To be human was to be a member of their family/tribe. When this creature suddenly showed up on the beach, they did not know what to do with him. He looked like a human being, but he did not have a name, could not identify his ancestry, and could not even speak (their) language. Whatever he was, he was not a human being.

The aborigines unquestioningly assumed that the strange creature on the beach was subject to their own criteria for differentiating between what is a human being and what is a fit entree for dinner. We assume that the shipwrecked sailor begged his captors for his life and liberty in at least three languages. He probably offered eloquent discussions of the morality of the situation; profound observations on the sanctity of sentient life; perhaps even inspiring homilies about the fatherhood of God and the brotherhood of man. Who knows what feats of rhetorical polish, philosophical rigor, or spiritual insight he performed while tied to a tree, watching the deliberations that led to his being defined as dinner! But because he could not speak the language of his captors, and because they believed that there was no language other than their own, his fervent appeals—despite their passion or enlightenment—*sounded* to them like the babel of an animal and were *treated* by them as the meaningless bleats of an admittedly unusual, but deserving candidate for the stewpot.

No one knows how the aborigines went about deciding what to do with their captive. But it is highly unlikely that some member of the group said something like the following. "Well, maybe this creature is a human, but not just like us. After all, the stories we tell to make coherent the facts of life are 'just made up,' the local expression of universal human themes. He probably has an array of stories of his own that he expresses and reconstructs in practices that seem as bizarre to us as ours probably do to him. Perhaps we should rethink our definition of what is 'human.' " Such statements involve a degree of mindfulness and a practice of treating the other as *not* a native that are incompatible with monocultural communication.

Summary

In contexts where it is appropriate, monocultural communication is the easiest, most satisfying, and most stable way of coping with the tensions within coherence, coordination, and mystery that humankind has yet devised. However, like all forms of communication, it can occur only when particular performance demands are met, and it is limited by its lack of fit with the material conditions of contemporary society and by the way its practices sometimes offend contemporary sensibilities.

The necessary mindlessness of monocultural communication means that we cannot talk *about* it *in* it. As soon as we begin to do communication theory, we have to use another form of communication. Mindlessness is the characteristic that makes monocultural communication particularly vulnerable in contemporary society. All factors that have led to the "discovery" of communication in this century impose a kind of mindfulness about communication processes—and an awareness that others are not necessarily natives of our cultures—inimical to monocultural communication. The remaining groups of primitive societies are quickly disappearing, and monocultural communication is institutionalized only in the most intimate of personal relationships (e.g., baby talk) or as a result of deliberate work (*aikido*). Other than that, our ability to experience this way of being human seems limited to contexts in which we stumble beyond normal resources and practices (e.g., awe).

6.
Ethnocentric Communication

In large, complex societies, ethnocentric is the most common form of communication. Also the most robust form of communication, its stories are structured in a distinctive manner, permitting them to be reconstructed virtually unchanged by a wide range of practices. Further, it co-opts mystery, using the energy of its most potent symbols to reinforce its most mundane stories and practices.

In ethnocentric communication, coordination is achieved by enacting patterns well known to all participants. The fact that these patterns are "known" has caused considerable difficulty for communication theorists, because participants in ethnocentric communication can often "recognize" a pattern and deviations from it, "perform" a pattern, but be unable to "describe" the pattern or the rules that govern it. I fail to see the problem, unless one privileges "verbal knowledge" to the exclusion of all other types and refuses to admit the rather obvious fact that persons know a lot of things that they cannot articulate verbally. It is far more useful to think of the patterns of ethnocentric communication as ranging from the explicit/formal to the implicit/informal.

Explicit/formal patterns are usually codified in books of laws, manuals of etiquette, or holy scripture. What one does, to whom, in what context, and what others do next is explicitly stated, and adherence to the requirements is compelled by official enforcement procedures. The sequence of actions that comprise the Catholic Mass permit easy coordination because there is no necessity for innovation; one follows throughout one's life the pattern learned as a child. Codes of military ethics and etiquette are good examples of coordination in ethnocentric communication: patterns of action are specifically described and deviation from them punished.

Implicit/informal patterns of ethnocentric communication are usually not written down and the participants are not capable of articulating the rules. Family communication patterns are a good example. In most families, members take the same seats at the dinner table at each meal. There is no formal discussion of this, and no explicit labeling of which chair "belongs" to whom, but coordination in dining is facilitated by the emergence of unstated rules for who sits where. In informal conversation patterns, unstated rules for what is permitted and what is prohibited enable strangers to coordinate. They know, without being able to articulate the rules and probably without ever thinking about it, that one does not return an insult for a compliment or ask intimately personal questions when being introduced. In formal organizations such as hospitals and businesses, an informal set of "standardized practices" is developed, which often differ substantially from the formal organizational chart, but which "natives" of the organization must know and follow.

The *content* of the examples given here derives from particular cultures, and is unimportant. The significance is that there are well-known patterns that provide the basis for coordination. There are several lines of research whose merit lies in articulating these patterns, known but not articulated by native practitioners of ethnocentric communication. In "artificial intelligence" research, Robert Shank (1975) writes the "scripts" that persons must follow to perform such apparently simple tasks as ordering and paying for a meal in a restaurant. By designing a computer to perform this social event "like a human," Shank is able to show just what humans have to know to function. Donald Cushman and Dudley Cahn (1985) studied the rules that persons follow in the process of "mate-selection" in several countries. Their description of that process, it is safe to say, does not resemble that of the participants', but seems to reveal patterns they follow without verbally knowing them.

An interesting category of patterns falls somewhere between these examples. This includes informal/implicit patterns that are made formal/explicit. Etiquette books and training manuals are the clearest examples. These are formulations of common practice (well, "common" among the "right persons") that shift from *descriptive* to *prescriptive* force. The use of a smaller fork in eating salad becomes not what *is* done but what *should be* done (by all cultivated persons, one assumes).

The process by which the resources in ethnocentric communication are created is revealed by this intermediate category. Somehow, through accident, historical necessity, or imitation of something else, an informal/implicit pattern of action was developed. At some point, perhaps to explain "us" to "them," or to perpetuate the achievements of this generation for posterity, these patterns were formalized, in the process being transmuted from "is" to "ought." At this point, contextual and prefigurative forces became much stronger than practical and implicative forces, and sequential repetitions of the pattern—often for hundreds of years—reinforced the "rightness" of doing it just this way. Deeply enmeshed in this kind of society, persons can find it literally "unthinkable" to act in any other way, and unable to treat like a native anyone who does not. The possibilities of coordination itself are seen as depending upon the maintenance of these patterns of interaction, and those who deviate from them are threatening, particularly if they are from one's own group.

As in any form of communication, coherence is achieved by the expression and (re)construction of resources in practices. The distinctive feature of ethnocentric communication is that these stories contain explicit distinctions between "us" with our stories and practices, and "them" with theirs. There is a mindfulness of the existence of others who differ from us, and some way of accounting for the fact that "our" resources and practices are "right."

Ethnocentric communication often contains patterns for interacting with those from outside the group. In some instances, this is an obligatory hospitality to stangers; in others, a studied disinterest. Tragically, in most it includes a variety of ways of exploiting or subjugating the other. European colonialism is perhaps the clearest example of

ethnocentric communication, in which ways of treating indigenous peoples were sometimes made explicit/formal in ways that now seem reprehensible. These patterns of
interaction were summarized by the sign over a bridge —*in China*—"no Chinese or
dogs allowed."

The term "ethnocentric" means viewing other cultures from the perspective of one's
own, and is popularly used to critique the accuracy of "travelers' tales" that emerged
from the first contact of explorers, missionaries, seamen, and "all the outer fringe of
travelers [from developed societies] who first made contact with primitive peoples"
(Severin, 1973, p. 348). These tales "are often superficial, nearly always ethnocentric
(that is, they look upon the 'natives' from the subjective viewpoint of another culture),
and they invariably offer an incomplete picture of native society, ignoring perhaps the
local religion, the art forms, or the social structure" (ibid.). However, I want to use the
term more generally to describe a form of communication that occurs within families
and neighborhoods as well as between cultures. In ethnocentric communication, whatever "we" are is defined in part by its contrast with "them," and "our" resources include
specific ways of dealing with "them" such that those resources are not put at risk. These
resources are robust because virtually anything "they" do merely confirms our perception
of "their" inferiority or maliciousness.

Ethnocentric communication is the norm in contemporary American society. It is,
of course, the stuff of racism, sexism, and the like. It also structures domestic political
discourse.

Robert Reich (1987) suggests that there are four "treasured myths" in contemporary
American life, each of which polarizes the individual against all others or one group
against other groups. These myths undercut the differences between liberals and conservatives. Conservatives see "them" as unruly and exploitive, requiring force and discipline; liberals see "them" as misguided and needy, requiring education and charity.

One myth is the "mob at the gates," portraying America as a triumphant beacon in
a sea of darkness, to be defended as the last, best hope of humankind. "They" are ruthless
enemies.

The "triumphant individual" portrays the opportunities of the little guy who works
hard, takes risks, and ultimately succeeds despite opposition. "They" are spoiled workers
whose wage demands could ruin the economy, or restrictive bureaucrats who would
shackle entrepreneurs.

The story of the "benevolent community" features the cooperation of neighbors and
friends who work together in pride and patriotism. "They" are dependent, selfish, and
irresponsible.

The "rot at the top" celebrates the essential goodness of the system, which is
threatened by "the malevolence of powerful elites, wealthy aristocrats, rapacious business leaders, or imperious government leaders" (Reich, 1987, pp. 12–13).

Mystery in ethnocentric communication is achieved by harnessing the most potent
symbols to the content of the stories by which coherence and coordination are achieved.
One of the most common moves is to link religion and the state, investing the ruler
with divine authority and the religion with state power. Within this arrangement, the
mysterious is expressed in the elaboration of stories and symbols. The facts of life—
birth, death, sexuality—are co-opted into the sacred story; in several traditions, the god
who is worshiped in culturally shaped temples is defined as the ineffable.

The genius of ethnocentric communication lies in elaboration. Mystery is taken as the inspiration for great art, impressive pageantry, erudite scholarship, mystic experience, and ethical rigor. Within the walls set by the content of its own resources, ethnocentric communication fashions a rich, often deeply satisfying way of being human in which specified categories of other humans are treated as nonnatives and resources are not put at risk.

Three Examples of Ethnocentric Communication

Misunderstandings: Your Fault

During the 1970s in the United States, there was a widespread sensibility that stressed the importance of personal integrity ("be true to yourself") and simultaneously noted the difficulty in being understood by others. This sensibility was expressed by placards bearing the statement: "I know that you think you understood what you thought I said, but I'm not sure that you realize that what you heard is not what I meant!" What led persons to purchase these placards and put them on display? I think it was the appeal of ethnocentric communication during a period in which many were criticizing it, a defiant statement of the purpose of returning from the babble of conflicting voices to a way of life in which resources were not put at risk by the responses of other persons.

A speaker's resources are clearly not going to be placed at risk. Assuming that there is a misunderstanding (such that "what you heard" does not equate with "what I meant"), there is no indication that the speaker will question whether "what I said" was an appropriate expression of resources ("what I meant") or whether those resources are good/valid/appropriate. There is a subtext of belligerence in the statement to the effect that "I" will remain deeply enmeshed in my resources no matter what bizarre interpretation you place on "what you thought I said."

The other person—the anonymous "you"—is treated as *not* a native. Again, a clear subtext alludes to the foreign interpretive and evaluative criteria employed by the other person, and declares them inferior to one's own.

Finally, coherence is celebrated despite the ability to coordinate. The fact of a misunderstanding is noted, but instead of seeking to identify or remedy the problem, the sentiment depicts the speaker as confidently reconstructing his or her own resources, which necessarily include a story about "you" that makes coherent the other's inability to understand "what I said."

Educating Kuwaiti Women

The *New York Times* (December 17, 1984, p. A12) reported a complex incident stemming from the Kuwaiti government's decision to allow female students to matriculate at Kuwait University. To understand the event, it is necessary to know that Kuwait has a (relatively) liberal social policy, including a commitment to raise the level of education for both men and women; that the Kuwaiti constitution specifies *Qur'anic* law as "the major source" of national law; that Kuwait is officially an Islamic country; and that Kuwait is sensitive to any other nation—including other Islamic countries—that might attempt to tell it what it should and should not do.

In October 1983, a leaflet was distributed outside the five hundred mosques in Kuwait. It was written by Abdul Aziz Bin Baz, a sheik from neighboring Saudi Arabia and known as a religious leader. He described himself as responding to a question asked by members of the Kuwait University's Islamic Students Society. The leaflet claimed that "coeducation is corrupting Kuwaiti women and is contrary to the teachings of Islam," and implied that coeducation turns women into prostitutes. It also "lashed out against those who taught or listened to music, against singing in public and against taking photographs of living things."

The effect of coeducational institutions on the women who attend them is being assessed in several countries. However, because they engage in qualitatively different forms of communication, it only *appears* that they are asking the same question. In the United States, the question was addressed by a study of women who attended coeducational and women's colleges. It compared levels of leadership positions held and academic performances achieved. The sheik, however, found his answer not in the *effects* of coeducational experiences but in the scriptures written centuries before there were coeducational colleges. For him, the issue involves prefigurative rather than practical force; it involves a process of finding a correspondence between present practices and the teachings of the sacred tradition. His conclusion: coeducation turns good Muslim women into prostitutes. I suspect that a survey of female graduates of Kuwait University would *not* show that a disproportionate number were prostitutes, but that is not the point for ethnocentric communication. Such a deliberate subjection of one's resources to "risk" is an inappropriate practice.

Like other Islamic nations, Kuwait is caught in an uncomfortable tension between its desire to achieve modernization and its adherence to its Islamic principles. At least a part of this tension is the discrepancy between two forms of communication: ethnocentric and modernistic. This tension explains the response by the government and the progressive elements in society. Rather than citing data from a survey of female graduates (as they might had they communicated modernistically), or challenging the sheik's interpretation of the *Qur'an* (as they might if they identified the sheik as one of "us"), they criticized the students for asking a foreigner for advice about a Kuwaiti practice. One professor explained, "We were angered . . . not only because a Saudi sheik had dared to tell Kuwait how to conduct its affairs, but also because Kuwaiti students had asked Saudis, rather than Kuwaiti religious authorities, to rule on an internal Kuwaiti matter." The editor of a daily newspaper, *Al Anbaa*, denounced in these intemperate words the students who involved Sheik Bin Baz: "The shoe of each Kuwaiti girl is cleaner than the teeth of the loudmouths who first raised these questions." Both professor and editor seemed more than willing to treat the Saudis as *not* natives.

Isms

Communication practices always stem from unacknowledged constraints and lead to unanticipated consequences. At least, I believe this is a useful perspective to talk about any form of communication. However, ethnocentric communication builds in a systematic insensitivity to the effects of one's actions on others. The preponderance of contextual and prefigurative forces over practical and implicative forces directs attention away from effects of actions toward reasons for them. Futher, the sanctity of one's own resources and the definition of others as "outside" the arena in which important things happen prevent ethnocentric communicators from empathizing with those they treat as nonnatives.

Ethnocentric forms of communication were the answer to Voget's (1975) interesting question of why anthropology was not developed in the same historical period as virtually all of the other humanities and sciences. The great accomplishments of Aristotle, Plato, Herodotus, and others were done in and shaped by ethnocentric communication. Despite their successes in other realms, they were not able to come to grips with other cultures. What descriptions we have of their contemporaries focus on what one would need to know to wage war or do commerce with them; it is all written from an unabashedly Greek or Roman point of view. The same insensitivity is manifest in Marie Antoinette's famous reply when told that the reason for the peasants' rebellion was that they had no bread. "Then let them eat cake," she replied in complete innocence of any understanding of the reality of peasant existence. In much the same way, an ethnocentric colonialist sincerely denied the accusation that his policies caused widespread suffering. "They don't suffer like we do," he said, "they don't even speak English." If you understand the reality in which these comments make sense, you comprehend the least savory aspect of ethnocentric communication.

The agricultural revolution enabled persons to live in groups too large for equitable distribution of status and materials, and started the evolution of social institutions such as church, state, banks, and police. It also required persons to interact with strangers, often daily. Some device had to be produced that would enable coordination without very much knowledge of the other person. The solution was a series of "scripts" or "patterns" to be enacted with certain "types" of persons. The latter is my focus in this section.

Stereotypes were developed based on race, gender, creed, social status, nationality, hair color, and so forth. At best, these stereotypes functioned as labels or cues, signaling which scripts should be followed by which persons. It is not always necessary or desirable to seek to know the persons with whom you coordinate, or to feel their pains and jobs as your own. At highway toll booths, supermarket checkout lines, crowded highway intersections, and the like, "mere coordination" is sufficient. However, the social technology that enables coordination without any specific knowledge of the other also permits callous disregard of the others. At their worst, stereotypes permit ethnocentric communicators to maintain distorted and dehumanizing perceptions of classes of other persons, and to "protect" those perceptions from disconfirming information or disquieting reflection about the others.

Public thresholds of shame and honor—that is, standards of civility—change. In the second half of the twentieth century, we have become sensitized to problems inherent in ethnocentric communication, and have constructed labels for those who coordinate with others on the basis of their membership in a group. We call them racists, sexists, and so on.

This evolution of civility has come at a great price. The waves of colonialism in recent centuries accidentally or purposefully destroyed many cultures; the Tasmanians and Caribs are gone. Many of the remaining primitive cultures "are dishearteningly vulnerable. Their loss will mean that we will have quenched the last vestiges of harmless cultures, whose manifold and variegated patterns will never be seen again" (Severin, 1973, p. 366). Racism has extracted a heavy toll from Jews, Armenians, American blacks, and others. Sexism has limited the aspirations of half the population of many nations. The bad name given to ". . . ists" is deserved because of some of the practices of ethnocentric communication.

Traditional Society

The contemporary social scene contains a sometimes confusing mixture of forms of communication, including ethnocentric communication. Successive iterations of the practices of ethnocentric communication create a very familiar way of being human, in which institutions like banks, hotel chains, and governments appear to be "real," and in which "scripts" exist for the coordination of practices. This way of being human is often called "traditional society."

Traditional society developed when primitive groups settled in one place and began to practice agriculture. This produced at least two "facts of life" for which primitive society had not prepared them. First, they had to coordinate with strangers, because the social group was larger. In primitive society, everyone knew everyone else; all were linked by multiple kinship ties. When towns and cities developed, natives simply could not know everyone with whom they had to deal. Further, because the world was becoming much more densely populated, they knew that there were other groups that lived a short distance away with whom they were probably not related. Second, they had to coordinate with others who lived in their group but who differed from them in expertise, knowledge, activity, social rank, and wealth. When agriculture and more sophisticated methods of tool making replaced gathering and hunting as the economy, a differentiation of activity occurred. "Crowding separated people as they had never been separated before. The hunter-gatherers' world had been a world of equals. . . . Now for the first time there were places for big men and elites, pomp and circumstance, arrogance and the accumulation and display of wealth" (Pfeiffer, 1977, p. 20).

It is hard to exaggerate the significance of the shift from a hunting/gathering society to one based on agriculture. Crowding, the accumulation of capital, and the specialization that came from division of roles set into motion a logic of interaction that, over the centuries, produced complex, often beautiful, and highly differentiated social and moral orders. Pfeiffer (ibid.) describes the sequence this way. With larger communities, persons worked to produce more than they needed for themselves alone. When the needs of communities were organized, new social event/objects were created: schedules, quotas, overseers, punishments for slacking off, money, taxes, and so on. To justify working beyond what was needed for survival, reasons were created to compel persons to work within the new social order. One of the most significant of these was religion. "People did not work primarily for their own ends. They obeyed the commands of gods as communicated by kings who, in due course, became gods themselves" (ibid., p. 21). Science and art were similarly co-opted into the expression and (re)creation of resources in practices. "Predicted eclipses, predicted sunrises at summer and winter solstices were taken as evidence that king and priest, the star performers in the pageants, were not only close to the gods but had a voice in the running of celestial affairs" (ibid.). All of this was wrapped up in mystery, expressed in sacred stories, impressive architecture, grand pageants, communal feasts and dances, and seductive music. "It was theater and more than theater, illusion and more than illusion, because nothing is as real as illusion believed collectively" (ibid.)

There have been countless traditional societies, and each has elaborated its own form of "theater" holding persons together. Seen from a sufficiently distant vantage,

Figure 6–1. Relationships among resources in traditional society.

however, there are some commonalities among all traditional societies. Regardless of their specific content, the resources of traditional societies can be depicted as in Figure 6–1.

Like primitive society, traditional society differentiates from the rest of society those who deal with epistemic questions. Indicated by oblique bars in the figure, this differentiation is usually accomplished by establishing a priesthood, marked by special vows, manner of clothing, a special language, and invested with a sense of power. These range from Buddhist monks begging to Roman pontiffs parading in medieval garb; from fiery evangelists to reclusive scholars; from gentle healers to leaders of armies; from kindly saints to the performers of bloody human sacrifice—depending on the particular content of the myths by which the society explains itself to itself. Also like primitive society, whatever answers are given to the epistemic question are explicitly assumed to support the ways of life governed by questions of "Who am I?," "Who are we?," and "What is the nature of the world in which we live?"

Unlike primitive society, there is a distinction between the sacred and the secular. In most—if not all—traditional societies, there is a sense that the sacred is long ago, high above, or far away from the present, although there are periodic manifestations of the sacred. Ordinary life is somehow an expression of or preparation for a life "beyond" the mundane—whether in mystic union with the "One," periodic rebirth, nirvana, or inclusion in the "Holy City" after the Judgment. This is the reason for the existence of a separate priestly caste: they are the intermediaries or contact points between the ordinary forms of life and those that make them significant.

Also unlike primitive society, the social order is filled with distinctions, groupings, and occasions, and these differentiations are thought of as expressing the "real" or divine order of things. The most obvious differentiation separated the rulers and the ruled. In Europe, social order was based on the alleged "divine right of kings." In Japan, the political structure was based on the direct lineal descent of the Japanese Emperor from the gods. But the practice of making such distinctions extends to virtually every part of life. In Europe:

> Medieval political speculation is imbued to the marrow with the idea of a structure of society based upon distinct orders. There are, first of all, the estates of the realm, but there are also the trades, the state of matrimony and that of virginity, the state of sin. At court there are the "four estates of body and mouths": bread-masters, cup-bearers, carvers, and cooks. In the Church there are sacerdotal orders and monastic orders. Finally, there are the different orders of chivalry. That which, in medieval thought, establishes unity in the very dissimilar meanings of the word, is the conviction that every one of these groupings represents a divine institution, an element of the organism of Creation emanating from the will of God, constituting an actual entity, and being, at bottom, as venerable as the angelic hierarchy.

The estates of society cannot but be venerable and lasting, because they all have been ordained by God [Huizinga, 1954, pp. 57–58].

In China, Confucius divided the social order into three virtues and five forms of relationship, with specific rights and duties in each. In India, the Buddha announced "Four Noble Truths," the last of which named the "Eightfold Path of Virtue."

The tendency of traditional society to divide itself into categories can perhaps best be experienced by wandering for a day through a walled city such as Dubrovnik, Yugoslavia. It is relatively small, with an enormous wall dividing "outside" from "inside." The wall is smooth, majestic, impenetrable. Inside the city, there is a complex, labyrinthian elaboration of narrow streets, sudden turnings, unexpected dead-ends, and open plazas.

A modern reader might see these categories and occasions as utilitarian; merely functional devices to facilitate coordination. In the modern view, such devices are useful if and only to the extent that they "work." If they ever should become obsolete or unnecessary, they would be discarded. But that is not the way they appear in traditional societies. Several times in the fourteenth century, the lower classes successfully revolted against particularly corrupt aristocrats. However, when they got the evil aristocrats in their power, they did not overthrow the feudal system. Usually, they simply required their prisoners to promise to be "good" kings or dukes or whatever, and let them go. Those promises did not usually result in profound social changes or redress of past wrongs (Tuchman, 1978); more profound reordering of social institutions was unthinkable within this form of communication.

Inasmuch as in traditional society the value of anything derives from its place in a fixed scheme of things, particular objects or persons are assigned to a category and expected to remain in it. The primary moral injunction is "know your place, and keep it." This means that a tool used for carrying rice will not also—normally—be used for carrying water, or that a warrior will not also be a farmer. In medieval Europe, every "function" was thought of as a "thing," and thus had to have its own special object. This led, of course, to a proliferation of artifacts and offices. For example, "the 'grand sergeanty' of the king of England comprised a dignitary whose office it was to hold the king's head when he crossed the Channel and was suffering with sea-sickness. A certain John Baker held this office in 1442, and after his death it passed to his two daughters" (Huizinga, 1954, p. 227).

Eliade (1959) characterized primitive society as meaningful only when it entails a repetition of the primal events performed by the gods. Traditional society is very similar. Every aspect of life is seen as "attached" to or emanating from the sacred, although only special events are sacred in themselves. Roles and situations are meaningful because they are seen as expressions of the sacred; each performance is meaningful because it repeats the "estate" or category of events of which the society is composed.

The morality tales of traditional society do not feature persons who do not know what to do; rather, they portray persons wrestling with the question of having sufficient "will" to do the right thing. Among traditional societies, Islam is distinctive for having an explicit theory of moral development, and even it is a morality that stresses the individual's power to act or refrain from acting, rather than the ability to make increasingly sophisticated judgments about what is right or wrong. "Hence all the will-strengthening techniques like the Ramadan fasts and the various other forms of self-denial. They are not to mortify the flesh, a kind of moral sadomasochism; they are to strengthen the will because that is the path of moral development. A Muslim knows what to do since it is prescribed in considerable detail in the *Qur'an*, but has he or she the strength of mind to do it?" (Harré, 1984, p. 244).

The moral order in medieval Europe also stressed "fitting" the demands of particular roles and situations. This was not expressed so much as a psychology of moral development as (in the church) the duty to avoid "sin" and (in the secular world) the desirability of "liberty." Sin was defined in just the manner I spoke about: categories and compartments within categories. There were two types of sin, mortal and venial, and a list of seven capital sins, and so forth. Morality consisted in avoiding those sins, and taking appropriate steps to be absolved of those that one did commit.

Liberty, for medieval Europeans, meant almost exactly the opposite of what it means for those in modern society. Interpreted from the resources of modernity, liberty means the *absence* of rules, regulations, and social constraints. In the medieval period, such a condition would have been called a "wilderness," where persons were "wild" and could do just what they willed, including imposing their will on others, unrestrained by law or convention.

> The higher one rose towards liberty, the more the area of action was covered by law, the less it was subject to will. The knight did not obey fewer laws than the ordinary freeman, but very many more; the freeman was not less restricted than the serf, but he was restricted in a different, more rational way. Law was not the enemy of freedom; on the contrary, the outline of liberty was traced by the bewildering variety of law which was slowly evolved during our period. The irksome rules and tedious gradations of society did not appear, as they did to a later age, as so many strangle-holds on liberty. High and low alike sought liberty by insisting on enlarging the number of rules under which they lived. The most highly privileged communities were those with most laws. At the bottom of society was the serf, who could least appeal to law against the arbitrariness of his superiors. At the top was the nobleman, governed by an immensely complicated system of rules in his public life, and taught in his private relationships to observe an equally complicated code or behavior [Southern, 1953, p. 108].

Figure 6–1 identifies some common elements in the structure of all traditional societies, but the content of the stories told by various traditional societies has varied tremendously. As a result, the specific acts that take place in ethnocentric communication differ in some striking ways.

The year 1500 A.D. is a convenient benchmark. Before that date, travel among the various land masses of the earth was relatively infrequent, usually hazardous, and always slow. After that date, the square-rigged sailing ships of the Europeans converted the oceans into trade routes with regular, frequent, and generally safe exchanges of persons, goods, and ideas among the major traditional societies. Before 1500, the peoples of the world had been separated by oceans, mountains, and ice. The stories told on either side of the Atlantic or the Himalayas were different. Campbell suggested that the means of coherence on the Eurasian land mass took four differentiable themes, each of which could be summarized by a symbol. The stories told in India and southeast Asia could be symbolized by the seated Buddha, who exemplified the desire to achieve a yogic arrest in the immanent great void. China, Korea, and Japan could be symbolized by the wandering sage, exemplifying spontaneous accord with the way of earth and heaven. Europe could be symbolized by Prometheus, exemplifying human reason and the responsible individual. The Levant, or as we now say, Middle East, could be symbolized by Muhammad, exemplifying supernatural revelation and the true community of humankind under one God (Campbell, 1962, p. 33).

The differences among these cultures are the product of many iterations of the process of ethnocentric communication. These practices were usually successful in expressing and reconstructing resources without placing them "at risk," and one crucial aspect of each culture was that of treating others as nonnatives. Europeans defined everyone else as "heathen" and "barbarians"; the Chinese confidently saw themselves as the center of the universe and the source of civilization, surrounded by "foreign devils."

The Practice of Ethnocentric Communication

Like all forms of communication, ethnocentric communication achieves coherence, coordination, and mystery. It does so in a unique manner, however, that makes it very robust but singularly insensitive to unintended consequences or to the hopes, desires, and fears of others.

URPs ("unwanted repetitive patterns"), discussed in chapter 2, comprise a fourth contemporary example of ethnocentric communication. In URPs, persons act *as if* their perceptions of self, other, situation, and the like, are "real" and compel them to act in particular ways regardless of the consequences (Cronen, Pearce, and Snavely, 1979). When two or more such persons, with different perceptions of self, other, situation, and so on, interact with each other, they can produce a tightly scripted, unwanted pattern that thwarts their attempts to realize their separate visions of the good, true, and beautiful.

When ethnocentric communication works well, however, it can lead to an unbelievable elaboration of a set of resources that deeply enmesh the participants. The brittle beauty of a sonnet or a Beethoven symphony, the intricacies of a Dostoevski novel or a Hegelian metaphysic, the sheer exuberance of the Sistine Chapel and the sharp edges of an academic debate—these art forms are instances of ethnocentric communication.

Resources Not "at Risk"

The stories ethnocentric communicators tell must have a certain form such that they are not threatened by the explicit recognition of other, dissimilar stories. At least two themes must be present: some account of the difference between one's own self or group and the others; and some explanation of how one's own stories are valid. Usually these themes take the form of stories of how one's own group is superior to the others, who are dismissed as subhumans, barbarians, less civilized, less educated, or less developed than the "chosen people."

More than the stories themselves, however, resources are protected by a quality of deep enmeshment that makes any questioning of the stories (beyond stipulated points, that is) a dishonorable heresy or foolishness. Laura Bohannan reports that the elders of the Tiv, a rural, tribal people in Africa, account for their customs in this way: "That is the way it is done, so that is how we do it." That pretty well stifles further debate. Their ability to maintain deep enmeshment even when brought into contact with an alien culture was evident when Bohannan attempted to explain "Hamlet" to them. A recurring pattern emerged in which she told them Shakespeare's story, and the Tiv elders, smugly confident in their own resources, patiently explained that she did not understand the story. They gently "corrected" her mistakes, attributing them to the fact that her elders had not yet told her the real truth of the story. When she finished, the chief elder invited her to "tell us some more stories of your country. We, who are elders, will instruct you in their true meaning, so that when you go back to your own land your elders will see that you have not been sitting in the bush, but among those who know things and who have taught you wisdom" (Bohannan, 1984, p. 15).

Unfortunately, history is replete with less gentle examples of practices designed to protect resources against the teachings/examples/influence of nonnatives. These practices include the Inquisition, book-burnings, censorship, deliberately inculcated stereotypes, xenophobia, crusades, zoned housing, and more.

A mural in a private house in Rome shows a Catholic cardinal quoting from a holy text to a penitent academician kneeling before him (Plate 6–1). One gets the impression of a scholar whose research led him a bit too far beyond the official doctrine, and who is being brought back into the fold by the priest. This impression is strengthened by the fact that the mural was painted just about the time the Inquisition under Pope Urban VIII declared Galileo's astronomical observations erroneous *because* they differed from the generally accepted interpretations of scripture. Under threat of torture, Galileo was forced to swear that he would act appropriately for ethnocentric practices. This is the text of the document he signed:

> I, Galileo Galilei, will for the future believe all that is held, preached, and taught by the Holy Catholic and Apostolic Roman Church. But whereas—after an injunction had been judicially intimated to me by this Holy Office, to the effect that I must altogether abandon the false opinion that the sun is the centre of the world and immovable, and that the earth is not the centre of the world, and moves, and that I must not hold, defend, or teach in any way whatsoever, verbally or in writing, the said doctrine, and after it had been notified to me that the said doctrine was contrary to Holy Scripture—I wrote and printed a book in which I discuss this doctrine already condemned, and adduce arguments of great cogency in its favour, without presenting any solution of these; and for this cause I have been pronounced by the Holy Office to be vehemently suspected of heresy, that is to say, of having held and believed that the sun is the centre and moves. . . . With sincere heart and unfeigned faith I abjure, curse, and detest the aforesaid errors and heresies, and generally every other error and sect whatsoever contrary to the said Holy Church; and I swear that in the future I will never again say or assert, verbally or in writing, anything that might furnish occasion for a similar suspicion regarding me; but that should I know any heretic, or person suspected of heresy, I will denounce him to this Holy Office, or to the inquisitor [quoted by Bronowski, 1973, p. 216].

Treating Some Others as Nonnatives

Coordination in monocultural communication is achieved through presumed agreement; communicators treat each other as if they drew upon the same resources. In ethnocentric communication, coordination is achieved by following a variety of scripts, some of which presume similar resources (for use when "we" communicate among ourselves) and some of them do not. The latter guide our behavior with those we treat as nonnatives, who are expected not to know or be able to apply our interpretive and

Plate 6–1. A Cardinal instructs a scholar: A form of ethnocentric communication.

evaluative standards. The scripts for dealing with nonnatives are very revealing, disclosing much about the resources of a culture.

Often these scripts comprise ways of exploiting other persons, and sometimes justifications for inhuman projects. Convinced that their own practices institutionalize the good, beautiful, or true in the guise of "civilization," "culture," "freedom," "God's will," and so forth, many groups have persuaded themselves that the "others" are "enemies" who must be destroyed at any price or whose practices must be subverted by any means. So it was that the members of the National Security Council in 1986 and 1987 deliberately lied to the U.S. Congress in order to sell arms to Iran and divert the funds to the Contras in Nicaragua. When ultimately called to account for their behavior, Lt. Col. Oliver North and Admiral John Poindexter justified themselves by explaining, without using the term, that they had to do what they did because it was an ethnocentric communication situation. Their own purpose was just and their motives noble, they explained, but Congress did not understand the issues and would not support their actions. Besides, members of Congress cannot keep a secret as "we" can, and this was a covert operation. As a result, they followed a script in which they reconstructed a false chronology of events, lied about specific actions they had taken, and shredded crucial documents to keep them out of the hands of the attorney general.

Scripts for dealing with nonnatives differ in ways that express the content of resources. In the period of European colonialism, roughly 1700–1950, several scripts for dealing with the inhabitants of colonized nations were followed. Resolutely perceiving their own resources/practices as superior to those of the cultures they dominated, the British allowed them to retain much of their own culture because there was no hope or interest in making them "natives" of British culture. This led to practices in which the British were awesomely confident of their social and moral rectitude and in which they created virtually impassible barriers between themselves and the subjugated cultures. On the other hand, resolutely perceiving their own religious resources/practices as both universally applicable and superior to any others, Portuguese and Spanish colonists made the process of converting the "heathen" their first task. The result was practices that linked colonists and colonizers far more than in the British empire. Brazil became Catholic; India remained Hindu. Brazilians are mixed ethnically with their former colonizers far more than are Indians.

Ethnocentric communication is not necessarily or even usually exploitive. Given the necessity of dealing daily with strangers in a complex, diverse society, there are ethnocentric scripts that permit groups to retain their own cultural heritage and to interact with those with other commitments. These may be labeled practices of "tolerant pluralism." For example, a family sojourning in an alien country may take care to preserve its religious and cultural resources/practices, clearly differentiating between themselves and those among whom they live. Governments may pass laws requiring toleration of different religious and ethnic groups, but these laws are useful in promoting pluralism only to the extent that these groups maintain their own traditions.

Competitive sporting events are ethnocentric practices. The fans of rival football teams derive great pleasure from perceiving themselves vastly different from those poor, benighted fools who unaccountably support other teams. "School spirit" is produced in high school "pep rallies" through practices that celebrate the communality of "our" resources compared with the detested "their's." The game itself is an arena in which honor and virtue are to be proven.

Ethnocentric communication emerged from particular patterns of lived experiences, and constitutes an important response to them. One aspect of these experiences is the fact that persons within our own communities often differ from us. To treat them "like a native," to impose our own evaluative and interpretive standards on them in monocultural practices, is coercive tyranny.

In the contemporary world, such tyranny sometimes seems preferable to the dangers of exploitation inherent in ethnocentrism, but Charles Krauthammer warned against it (1983). The doctrine of "plural solipsism," he suggests, emerges from a legitimate antipathy to the traditional distinctions between persons, racial groups, and political systems. It envisions a congenial world in which emancipating presidents, KGB chiefs, and Iranian ayatollahs are "folks just like us." There are two problems with the principled refusal to treat others as nonnatives in "plural solipsism." First, it ignores real differences between persons. In international conflict, it leads to the "broken-telephone" theory; a naïve concept that if the leaders would talk to each other, the causes of the conflict could be dismissed. This theory of conflict leads to practices in which "expert facilitators" or "mediators" are involved. Writing during the bloody and apparently interminable war between Iran and Iraq, Krauthammer (1983, p. 32) notes that "Iraq's Saddam Hussein and Iran's Ayatollah Khomeini . . . have perfectly adequate phone services. . . . Their problem is that they have very little to say to each other."

Plural solipsism's second problem is that it guarantees that certain forms of misunderstandings will occur. It is impossible for "us" to understand that the other actually wants something that is repugnant to us, or that they are motivated by desires—revenge, greed, conquest—that "we" have denied as legitimate. "When the U.S. embassy in Tehran is taken over, Americans are bewildered. What does the Ayatollah want? . . . It is impossible to believe that the Ayatollah wants exactly what he says he wants: the head of the Shah" (Krauthammer, 1983, p. 32). In the zeal to avoid xenophobia, various "isms," and exploitation, we forget that others may want or believe things that we cannot imagine. For example, Krauthammer notes, "The more virulent pronouncements of Third World countries are dismissed as mere rhetoric. The more alien the sentiment, the less seriously it is taken. Diplomatic fiascos follow."

Krauthammer's purpose is not to reinstate xenophobia, but to urge the readers of the *New York Times* Sunday "opinion/editorial" page to break through the comforts of their middle-class lives and to confront the realities of other ways of being human, including religious fanaticism, grinding poverty, and frustrating political impotence. His essay was sparked by a comment in the *New Yorker* magazine about President Lincoln, which claimed that the expression on his face clearly showed that he "would like to live out a long life surrounded by old friends and good food." Krauthammer confessed his inability "to recall the most melancholy and spiritual of Presidents" giving much thought to gourmet dinners. The author of that comment, Krauthammer might have said, was engaging in monocultural communication, interpreting Lincoln's expression according to his own, not Lincoln's, resources. In this case, ethnocentric communication is a liberation from narcissism:

> To accept the reality of otherness is not to be condemned to a war of all against all. We are not then compelled to see in others the focus of evil in the world. We are still enjoined to love our neighbor as ourselves; only it no longer becomes an exercise in narcissism.
>
> But empathy that is more than self-love does not come easily. Particularly not to a culture

as fixed on its own image that it can look at Lincoln, gaunt and grave, and see a man ready to queue at the pâté counter at Zabar's [Krauthammer, 1983, p. 32].

Summary

Ethnocentric communication developed in response to the "facts of life" in society after the agricultural revolution. It created a distinctive way of being human, historically known as traditional society and in the contemporary world institutionalized in the "cultures" that comprise organizations of various types.

Ethnocentric communication is robust, enabling particular patterns of resources and practices to perpetuate themselves in a complex, pluralistic social world. The way of being human that it creates may include many types of artifacts and belief, some of which have great beauty and some considerable ugliness.

7.
Modernity

Some of the astronauts and cosmonauts who have viewed the earth from space report an important change in perspective. From a few hundred miles above the atmosphere, the earth appears a single, fragile ball rather than an immense expanse divided into hundreds of artificial national compartments and thousands of natural geographic regions. This is a disturbing image to some persons, it is fundamentally incompatible with ethnocentric communication.

Imagine the world as if you were in orbit, but with an advantage over the astronauts and cosmonauts. You have a device that enables you to see and listen to individual conversations anywhere in the world. You hear monocultural communication in Central Park in New York City as a mother walks her baby, among isolated tribes in the headwaters of the Amazon, and in an *aikido dojo* in Tokyo. You hear ethnocentric communication in the U.S. Congress, in high school pep rallies, and in military training maneuvers. However, you also hear forms of communication that fit neither of these categories.

The primary characteristic of contemporary society is the *diversity* of forms of communication that one encounters, and thus the ways of being human that are available. Never having lived in primitive society, I have probably underestimated the diversity of its form of life, but my readings of those who have studied these societies indicate a fundamental difference in the range of lifestyles available in them and in contemporary society. I have lived in a segment of society that preserved at least some aspects of traditional society, and can testify that modern society is profoundly more open-ended in the ways of being human that it facilitates.

The diversity of communication forms in contemporary society is not accidental. The forms of communication that fit other societies did not disappear at the advent of the modern era. Monocultural and ethnocentric communication evolved in lived experience and comprise viable ways of being human. Just because some aspects of society have modernized to some extent, is no reason to suppose that contemporary persons are exempt from the circumstances in which these forms of communication developed. In addition, because we learn patterns of communication by imitation, it is likely that persons employ monocultural and ethnocentric communication even in situations where they do not fit, simply because they do not know what else to do. However, the major reason for the diversity of forms of communication is that the material circumstances of society have changed. There is a new lived experience, and a wide variety of new forms of communication have emerged from it.

The new situation is best characterized by the term "modernity." Like "primitive" and "traditional" societies, "modern" society refers to a distinctive set of values, practices, and institutions. It does not simply mean "recent." I use the term "contemporary" to designate the world in the present moment; "modern" denotes a particularly potent component of contemporary society.

Modernity originated in the West and spread unevenly first through Europe and then to every part of the world. One of the great unanswered questions of contemporary society is the extent to which "modernity" can be differentiated from "westernism." Many of the hundred or more "new nations" created after the breakup of European empires after World War II are faced with the practical question of how (and whether) they can maintain the distinctiveness of their own religions and cultural heritages while modernizing. At the time of this writing, this is very much an unanswered but often asked question, and the practices that stem from it have been extraordinarily violent. Modernity has been the most determinately evangelistic social movement in human history. From its European beginnings at the turn of the sixteenth century, it has now influenced every nation on earth. It is also the most unstable of all the ways of being human, devouring the cultural artifacts and ways of being human that it produces. This instability accounts for the fact that many forms of communication, not just one, have emerged as a response to modernity.

In this chapter, I tell the story of the development and of discontents of modernity. In chapter 8 I describe several forms of communication properly viewed as "modern." In chapter 9 I describe "cosmopolitan communication," which I believe to best fit the characteristics of the contemporary period. Taken together with the discussion of monocultural and ethnocentric communication, these chapters attempt to provide a "Peeping Tom's" (or a social scientist's) guide to the variety of communication forms in contemporary society.

The Development of Modernity

Everybody lives in "modern times," Crane Brinton (1963, p. 22) noted, "but they have not always been so much impressed with the fact. Our own time . . . is the first to coin so neat a term and apply it so consistently. . . . This awareness of a shared newness, of a way of life different from that of one's forebears—and by 1700 awareness of a way of life felt by many to be much *better* than that of their forebears—this is in itself one of the clearest marks of our modern culture."

Bold words have been used to characterize the effects of modernity, among them Renaissance, Enlightenment, Great Awakening, (cultural) maturity, and development. "Modern" has become a synonym for "better," reversing previous usage. To be called "old-fashioned" suddenly was an insult. By the time of the American (1776) and French (1780) revolutions, a sizeable and influential segment of the population shared "the feeling of living in a revolutionary age, an age that generates explosive upheavals in every dimension of personal, social, and political life" (Berman, 1982, p. 17).

Modernity developed in the West, and must be understood in that context. Even though modernity supplied revolutionary answers to many of the traditional Western questions, its concerns were shaped by the intellectual and cultural heritage of the West. This is well known in politics, where the institutions of democracy and capitalism clearly express resources grounded in the West, and it is readily apparent in the humanities. Northrop Frye (1982, p. xii) calls the Christian Bible a "great code," which underlies much of Western culture, so much so that "a student of English literature who does not know the Bible does not understand a good deal of what is going on in what he reads: the most conscientious student will be continually misconstruing the implications, even the meaning." Those who led the "Cultural Revolution" in the People's Republic of China recognized the link between modernity and Western influences. In an attempt to break that link, they banished even the playing of Western musical instruments and music. The Muslim leaders of Malaysia are aware that westernism penetrates the modern humanities. In an attempt to forestall Western influence, the students they sponsor in Western universities are restricted to majors in physical science or business administration rather than the humanities or social sciences. These precautions may all be for naught. We now know that science is more than technology; it is a cultural institution. We know that technology is not neutral; material artifacts such as refrigerators, airline services, and television sets carry with them far more cultural baggage than meets the eye.

Christianity (as a culture, including but not limited to theology) established the conditions in which modernity developed, and its concerns are the issues with which modernists (and postmodernists) continue to deal. Itself a mixture of Greek, Latin, Judaic, Arabic, and to a lesser extent, Norse elements, cultural Christianity included a set of resources that initiated an ironic development. As a result of the *extension* of practices fully consistent with those resources, discoveries were made and practices performed that forced a *reconstruction* of those resources with substantially different content. Specifically, its concepts of truth and of the relationship between humankind and nature produced the technological revolution, the result of which was to institutionalize modernity as a self-sustaining pattern of resources and practices that permeates all aspects of society (including those that would scarcely recognize the Christian concept of truth and the relationship between humankind and nature). Even devout know-nothings daily deal with the results of these practices and in so doing help (re)construct them.

The Relationship of Humankind to Nature

Like Judaism and Islam, Christianity told itself stories that portrayed nature as "dead." The Hebrew/Islamic understanding of creation separates nature from God and thus "disenchants" the world, leaving it to be perceived in a matter-of-fact manner, and exploited at the pleasure of humankind. The story of the Garden of Eden tells of Adam and Eve, even as they are being punished, being commanded to "subdue the earth, and have dominion over it." This perspective stands in stark contrast to, for example, animism, which sees nature as infused by the supernatural, or polytheism, which assumes that each of the many gods has a particular interest in some portion of the world. The Hebrew and Islamic traditions view the world as "entirely external to the creator God and therefore itself as profane, available for man's 'active disposing'" (Macquarrie, 1974, p. 30).

The writer of Genesis certainly never anticipated the many ways that humans would "subdue" and "dominate" the earth. Picture a chemistry laboratory where the elements of the earth are unceremoniously separated, labeled, roasted, mixed, pummeled, and bathed in acids. In physics laboratories, the most elemental particles of matter are hurled into each other at great speed and their tracks through a cloud chamber photographed. According to the Genesis account, the first humans were commanded to reproduce; in biology laboratories, scientists are experimenting with recombinant DNA, the basis of genetic reproduction. All of this expresses a particular way of thinking about the relationship between humankind and nature. "This disenchantment of the natural world," Harvey Cox (1965, p. 23) observed, "provides an absolute precondition for the development of natural science."

The same disenchantment permitted revolutions in agricultural methods, the effect of which was to confirm the idea that nature was a blank tablet on which humans could write their will. This all worked out unintentionally, of course. As civilization pushed north into Europe, farmers encountered a climate and soils that required a new kind of plow. Further south, it was sufficient simply to cut a furrow in the ground into which seeds might be dropped. The grasslands of the north made such plows useless. By 600 A.D., farmers had developed a plow that cut through and turned over the thick sod. However, this plow required a team of eight oxen, more than any one farmer usually owned. The farmers began pooling their oxen, apparently receiving an amount of plowed land proportional to their contribution. Lynn White, Jr. (1967, p. 23), noted the significance of what seemed a straightforward adaptation of agricultural technology: "Man's relation to the soil was profoundly changed." Ownership of land derived from technology and the social organization required to employ it, not on the needs of a family or the ability of an individual to till and reap. "Formerly man had been a part of nature; now he was the exploiter of nature." The new practices (re)constructed resources embodied, among other places, in illustrated calendars. Around 830 A.D., "the new Frankish calendars, which set the style for the Middle Ages . . . show men coercing the world around them—plowing, harvesting, chopping trees, butchering pigs. Man and nature are two things, and man is master" (White, 1967, p. 23).

This concept of the relationship between humankind and nature permitted the practices that produced modernity. Unlike other aspects of Western tradition, however, modernity never challenged this concept. To the contrary, it carried the program of exploiting nature to unbelievable extremes. So much was modernity comfortable with this concept that only recently have groups like Greenpeace and the Sierra Club been able to call it into question.

Truth

The Western tradition developed a unique concept of knowledge. Described as "foundationalism" in chapter 1, it assumes that truth exists independently of human agency, that it is rational and thus can be known by human beings, and that it can be expressed accurately in the careful use of language. Knowledge of the truth should be eternal, immutable, and out-of-history. This belief has had enormous influence in the shaping of Western culture. It is expressed in the articulation of "creeds," formal statements of what the church believed to which all persons had to assent on pain of death and excommunication; in the compulsion to offer logical explications of the scriptures, mathematics, philosophy, and even jurisprudence; and in the attempt to map the heavens, measure the earth, and deduce the gods.

This concept of truth provided a perfect rationale for the least savory forms of ethnocentric communication. As Crane Brinton (1963) noted, in the Middle Ages truth was thought to be "revealed" by God, and anyone who did not agree with the truth as known by the church was either ignorant or a heretic. "In the light of these medieval notions, the burning of heretics was understandable. They were rotten fruit and if left alone they might corrupt the sound fruit; moreover, they were damned, and to cut them off from actual living was doing them no real harm—they had done that to themselves already" (pp. 104–5).

Modernity significantly revised this concept of truth. First, it undercut the claim that revealed truth as enfranchised in the Catholic Church was perfect and complete. Although scientists made some contribution to this social movement, the early, decisive battles were fought by Protestants in the Reformation. Both the authority of the church as arbiter of truth and its particular doctrines were questioned, and "by 1700 there was a body of writings that defended the notion that religious differences *ought* to be tolerated, that Church and State are rightfully separable, that the individual should make up his own mind in matters of religious belief" (ibid., p. 104).

Western civilization never got away from the notion of a "foundation" for knowledge, but an important part of it—"modern" men and women—began to think about it differently. In modernity, the foundation lies in the present or future rather than the past; "revealed" truth is automatically suspect in light of tomorrow's research findings. The appropriate statement of truth by modernists is provisional rather than certain (although this rule is honored as much in the breach as in practice). With this goes an attitude of tolerance, based on the assumption that there is a new truth, deeper than that of traditional Christianity, which will eventually supplant or thoroughly modify whatever is known now, and that "truth is not revealed perfect and complete to men, but must be discovered progressively by trial and error, by investigation, by human effort" (Brinton, 1963, p. 105).

The Technological Revolution

The combination of the "old" relationship to nature and the "new" concept of truth was expressed in practices that produced the "technological revolution" about a century ago.

The West has had no monopoly on either science or technology. Many cultures have had active scientists, whose attempts to understand the nature of things are as sophisticated as those of the West, and all cultures have accumulated sophisticated technological skills. However, the Western mixture of resources and practices permitted a unique "marriage between science and technology, a union of the theoretical and the empirical approaches to our natural environment. The emergence in widespread practice of the Baconian creed that scientific knowledge means technological power over nature. . . . Its acceptance as a normal pattern of action may mark the greatest event in human history since the invention of agriculture, and perhaps in nonhuman terrestrial history as well" (White, 1967, p. 17). White's claim that the industrial revolution is "the greatest event in human history since the invention of agriculture" is not an attempt to praise it. His concern is with "ecology," and he feels that the technological revolution has enabled

Plate 7–1. The pursuit of knowledge: The practice of modernistic communication.
The Bettmann Archive.

humans to have a deleterious impact on the environment that endangers us all. But this
is a contemporary critique of modernity, not a part of the modernists' own awareness.

Broadly interpreted, "technology" means doing or making something. It has come
to be identified with machines, but need not be. Words may be used as a technology of
social relationships—this is Calder's notion (1976) when he defined the tongue as a
muscle used for controlling other persons' behavior. Rites and myths are the technology
of culture. In this sense, the "technological revolution" is the emergence of a distinctive
way of life, which includes but is not limited to the development of machines, factories,
and industries. Karl Marx, Thomas Jefferson, and Isaac Newton were contributors to
the technological revolution, thus understood, as well as was Thomas Edison, George
Washington Carver, and Eli Whitney.

A technological revolution in this broad sense seems the inevitable result of combining the new concept of truth with the old concept of nature. Persons came to believe
that there was a truth, larger and grander than had ever been known before, and that
if it were known, it would confer great power in achieving human purposes. That truth,
however elusive in practice, was not problematic in principle. It was to be sought
energetically and enthusiastically. The pursuit of knowledge was identified as the noblest
form of activity, producing the greatest possible boons to humankind. It was "a noble
intoxication!" (Plate 7–1; Durant and Durant, 1965, p. 607).

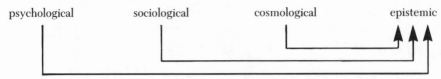

Figure 7–1. The apparent structure of modern society.

The Structure of Modernity

Modernity contains a set of stories expressed and reconstructed in practices, the process of which is the means of achieving coordination, coherence, and mystery. Like the stories of other societies, those of modernity address the questions of Who am I?, Who are we?, What is the nature of the world we live in?, and What is the nature of our knowledge about the answers to these questions? However, the content of these stories and the relationships among the answers comprise a distinctive form of life. This structure, shown in Figure 7–1, differs from those depicting primitive and traditional society in two ways. First, there is no demarcation between those persons who deal with the epistemic question and those who deal with the other questions. There is no separate caste of priests or shamans—or, better said, those who set themselves off as priests or shamans find their position encroached upon by persons who do not belong to the club.

This characteristic can be seen in the progressive diminution of the power-base of the clergy in Western society. In the medieval period, the clergy claimed title to not only sacred but secular mysteries. It lost some of this power when nonclerical professionals began studying the classical documents, writing secular philosophies, conducting research that contradicted the church, and so forth. It lost even more power when lay persons in the churches began reading the scriptures for themselves, rather than relying on the clergy for an uncontested interpretation. (The Catholic Church steadfastly opposed public education.) However, the truly revolutionary development was not the result of an unholy desire of secular scholars to talk about the nature of knowledge. Quite without meaning to, the results of research about the world, about society, and about individuals led to a concern with questions of epistemology and the nature of the stories that sustain any traditional or primitive society.

The second distinguishing characteristic of modernity is the direction of the relationship between the epistemic question and the others. In the other forms of society, the epistemic questions (what the priest or shaman knew) were foundational, and were presumed to support the content of whatever answers were given to psychological, sociological, and cosmological questions. In modern society, the direction of influence is precisely the opposite. The epistemic question follows (rather than leads) the methods and results of explorations of other areas of life. For example, contemporary philosophers of science view their role as explaining clearly what scientists do rather than prescribing for them the necessary conditions of valid knowledge or the methods they should employ in studying "cosmological" questions.

This pattern—from mundane to epistemic—can be seen in the activities of a number of the heroes of modernity. As a young man, Martin Luther wanted to be a good monk, not an enemy of the church. In fact, he was sometimes reproved for the detailed but boring list of transgressions he enumerated in his confessions. Whatever else the Reformation might have been, for Luther it was the application of a "psychological" technology for discovering for himself how *he* could become a good monk. This sharply contrasts with the (ethnocentric) technology of letting the church tell him what a *good monk* was. He was willing to study the scriptures *for himself* and come to conclusions *for himself* about the nature of the true faith, and was willing to debate his theses with all who disagreed with him. Apparently, asking questions about the "epistemic" areas of life, Luther's *technology* was that of individualism—most directly related to "psychological" questions.

Luther understood clearly the nature of the difference between his "modernist" communication practices and those of the "ethnocentric" society he abandoned. At a decisive moment, he declared, "Here I stand, God help me, I can do no other." The church also understood that a form of communication and way of life, not just the content of Luther's theology, was the issue, and refused to debate him. Instead, it insisted that he submit without question to the orthodox view—that is, that he return to the traditional way of life. Specifically, the church demanded that he renounce *all* his writings as a gesture of submission to clerical authority. He refused, citing the fact that his writings quoted scripture (which he could not renounce) and that much of his writing agreed with church dogma (which he should not renounce). This confrontation juxtaposed two forms of communication.

Other early modernists posed questions about the psychological question that led them to troubling encounters with epistemology. Their common characteristic, Brinton (1963, p. 26) claims, is that "they didn't like medieval art, letters, or philosophy." Dubbing them "humanists," he characterized them as tending to reject medieval habits of mind, medieval ideals, specially as embodied in Scholasticism, but not to accept Protestantism or the rationalist view of the universe as an efficiently functioning, regular arrangement (almost a machine). "The humanist is a great rebel against medieval cosmology, but he has no very clear cosmology of his own. The humanist is a great individualist—he wants to be himself. But he is not very clear about what to make of himself. He is much more in debt to the Middle Ages than he will admit, notably in what he most prides himself on, his learning" (ibid., p. 27). The restlessness of the humanists framed the question "Who am I?," which has bedeviled so many persons influenced by modernity. The pursuit of this question, armed with the technology of scholarship, soon turns into questions about the nature of our knowledge about questions such as these—that is, epistemic questions. In this way humanists, like scientists and theologians from other routes, eventually displace the traditional role of priest or shaman.

A particular form of social practice initiated a move from the sociological question "Who are we?" to the epistemic. In the late eighteenth and nineteenth centuries, many young persons were forming what historians politely call "intimate bonds," which violated traditional distinctions of family, class, religious and occupational boundaries. In fact, one characteristic of modernity seems to be an impatience with traditional social structures. In instances where couples stayed together, they often left the smaller towns for urban centers where they set the modern pattern for mobile, nuclear families. Either way, the new alliances—and their children who did not fit neatly into any existing social category—raised questions about the source, value, and function of social structures.

These questions soon became involved with epistemic concerns: What legitimate basis is there for inequitable concentrations of wealth?

The movement from cosmological to epistemological concerns is perhaps the most clear. Johannes Kepler, using the technology of modern research methods, attempted to prove the veracity of traditional stories about the solar system. Instead, he produced a scientific revolution. Believing that God created the planets and set them in their movements, and believing that the circle was the perfect geometric shape, Kepler agreed with medieval theologians who logically concluded that God had set the planets into circular orbits. However, when he combined the precise astronomical observations furnished by the newly invented telescope with the mathematics of geometry, he found an anomaly in the apparent motion of Mars. Confronted with a conflict between what he expected and what he observed, he changed his resources on the basis of his data. Reflexive force exceeded contextual force. His decision made a powerful statement not only about cosmology (planets move in elliptical orbits), but also about epistemology (when theory and data do not correspond, theory must be revised).

In summary, the technological revolution provided the natives of modern society an array of new ways of acting. These new technologies ranged from laboratory apparatus (telescopes; microscopes; accurate clocks) to forms of government (democracies; republics) and the daily rituals and commonplaces of life. These technologies appeared to be sufficiently powerful to expose and change the traditions of the past, and to offer the hope of a new, better "truth" that would improve humankind.

By 1750, the practices of modernity had constructed a widespread faith in "progress." It seemed clear that successive applications of these practices would improve both the quality of human life in the material world and lead to better, more capable human beings.

> There were better roads along which coaches travelled each year a bit faster; there were obvious, homely improvements such as water closets; there was even, at the end of the century, the beginning of the conquest of the air. . . .
>
> It was reason that would lead men to understand nature . . . and by understanding nature to mold his conduct in accordance with nature, and thus avoid the vain attempts he had made under the mistaken notions of traditional Christianity and its moral and political allies to go contrary to nature. . . . It was in the Church, and especially in the medieval Catholic Church and its successors, that the enlightened found the source of darkness, the unnatural suppression of nature—in short, the Satan every religion needs. . . . Reason had been suppressed, perhaps even atrophied, by the long rule of traditional Christianity. But now, in the eighteenth century, reason could once more resume its way, and do for all men what it had done for men like Newton and Locke. Reason could show men how to control their environment and themselves [Brinton, 1963, pp. 116–17].

Two Examples of Modernistic Communication

Ethnocentric communication is repugnant to those caught up in the practices of modernity. It seems superstitious, willfully ignorant, and laden with all the historical debris that they have tried to divest themselves of in their headlong pursuit of truth. Modernity requires the institutionalization of a new form of communication. Inherently unstable and deeply mystified about its own nature, "modernistic communication" has never become the dominant form of communication in any culture. However, its practices are widespread and have disproportionately large effects on the societies in which they occur.

Scientific Method

The idealized version of the scientific method, which is only sometimes realized in practice, exemplifies modernistic communication.

A scientist arrives somehow at a hypothesis, which is a story about the way the world works. This story is not acceptable until it can be stated in a manner that makes it potentially falsifiable. The scientist is then obligated to seek or create an opportunity to make observations that would show the hypothesis false if indeed it is false. If the data prove the hypothesis false, the scientist will revise it and advance another (better?) hypothesis.

The continuing practice of the scientific method is thought to produce a rational world freed from the limiting effects of antiquated tradition. As Karl Popper (1972) said, "our theories die in our stead," and differences of opinion, creed, or prejudice may be resolved by appeals to the data rather than by battle, pride, eloquence, or authority.

The scientific method requires an analytical, skeptical attitude to one's own stories. Scientists must engage in a willing suspension of belief, becoming at least an outsider (perhaps a permanent stranger) to that which they study. The sense of estrangement that this entails is tempered by the promise of mystery resulting from a penetration of the unknown and from the vital self-awareness characteristic of modernity. C. Wright Mills (1959, pp. 7–8) characterized the beatific vision that scientists pursue as feeling "as if suddenly awakened in a house with which they had only supposed themselves to be familiar." This feeling is accompanied by "a sense of power, progress, and wisdom. Correctly or incorrectly, they often come to feel that they can now provide themselves with adequate summations, cohesive assessments, comprehensive orientations. Older decisions that once appeared sound now seem to them products of a mind unaccountably dense. Their capacity for astonishment is made lively again. They acquire a new way of thinking, they experience a transvaluation of values" (ibid.). Recall the discussion of "paradigms" in chapter 1. After Kuhn's studies of the way scientists actually work, we know that the story they tell about "scientific method" is seriously distorted. Most of the time, scientists engage in "normal science," which is more like ethnocentric than modernistic communication. In "normal science" they take a "paradigm" as a set of resources with high contextual force, and they work out the "problems" set by that paradigm. If the results of a particular study contradict a popular theory, they suspect their methods, their materials, or the influence of some malevolent agent rather than announcing to the world that the theory is false. Their public statement is likely to be "more research needs to be done on this."

But paradigms do change. The fact that most scientists most of the time do research in a manner hardly distinguishable from ethnocentric communication should not obscure the fact that, unlike the situation in most traditional societies, the energies of scientists are oriented toward the weakest parts of the resources to which they are committed. They fully expect that the paradigm within which they work will change someday, perhaps as a result of their own work.

"Communication"

A distinctively modern form of communication has been institutionalized in contemporary American society. Katriel and Philipsen (1981) call it "communication." Contemporary Americans are required to know when and how to engage in "communication," and to distinguish it from "exchanges of information" or "mere talk." "Communication" is perceived as a form of "work"; a social technology intentionally engaged in for the purpose of (re)constructing one's self, relationships, and problems.

"Communication" requires three forms of performance. First, the participants must be "open," engaging in a great deal of self-disclosure. The talk involves the statement of information about the self that is normally judged "private" and that the other would not normally know unless the speaker revealed it. Secondly, participants must express willingness to accept and value others, regardless of what they say. Normal standards of evaluation of acts and of persons are suspended in favor of unconditional supportiveness. Thirdly, participants must express their support of the emerging, negotiated definition of self and of the relationship.

For example, if one person discloses that she has a socially stigmatic characteristic, such as homosexuality or alcoholism, this statement is accepted and the speaker is reassured of her value as a person. In the course of the subsequent talk, the person may "try on" one or more new identities, a process that the other person is expected to support.

The episode of "communication" is signaled by any of a number of acts, the most direct of which is a straightforward "I need to talk." Skillful communicators are able to request "communication" in more subtle ways, and to detect more subtle requests from others.

Great confidence is placed in the social efficacy of "communication." Refusing to participate in "communication" when there is a problem with self or with the relationship is considered reprehensible. If persons refuse to "communicate" about their relationship and a divorce occurs, they are held to be responsible. If persons refuse to "communicate" about their job, which is not going well, problems are seen as the result of their not using an available technology for change.

"Communication" requires placing one's resources at risk. There is no guarantee that one will exit from "communication" the same person as the one who entered. Indeed, that is explicitly the point: "communication" is seen as a powerful technology for changing self and social relationships, just as the scientific method is a powerful technology for changing one's knowledge of the world around us.

The Practice of Modernistic Communication

The practices of modernistic communication are inherently problematic. In primitive and traditional societies, persons could anticipate pretty well how others would interpret and respond to their own actions. The assumption was that the other's resources and practices were pretty well fixed and accurately identified by the external trappings of their role, the situation in which they found themselves, or even their manner of dress. Just these assumptions are put at risk in modernistic communication, where the only constant is the expectation of change.

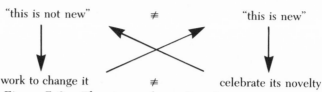

Figure 7–2. The strange loop of modernity.

Rather than the enactment of stable scripts (as in ethnocentric communication), coordination in modernistic communication depends on a reciprocated improvisation in which interactions are expected to be renegotiated even as they occur. To the extent that coordination is achieved, it is attributed to the skill of participants in extending "cues" to each other and being adroit enough to respond to the leads of others.

If this seems a risky business, it is. Modernistic communication institutionalizes a relatively cavalier attitude about coordination. Failures to coordinate are expected and taken as a symptom of "progress." When one's resources and practices change, as they do in "successful" modernistic communication, the communicator becomes a "native" of a culture unlike the one of which he or she had just been a member. The ability to coordinate with others in that group diminishes, and as the process continues, it is very hard to know on any given day what episodes are possible to enact with a person who recurrently engages in modernistic communication.

The development of slang is a useful example of the difficulties that institutionalized change poses for coordination. Virtually on a daily basis, the "in" word or phrase changes. Without close contact with the group, members' resources/practices cannot "keep up" and they will be exposed as "outsiders" by their inability to coordinate.

Another useful example of coordination problems is the pattern of communication between parents and teenaged children. Teenagers change so fast (not always in the same direction) that the parent's conversational partner may fluctuate within the course of a single discussion from a mature young adult to a rebellious youth and again to an immature child. No wonder such conversations often fatigue the older participant and frustrate the younger.

Coherence is stressed more than coordination. The primary moral injunction is to change resources and practices. As shown in Figure 7–2, this injunction is grounded in the notion of both truth and personal worth. The figure shows that the largest contextualization is foundationalism, here expressed as the belief that "truth is rational." Within this context, "change" counts as "progress" because it is assumed to make successive approximations of truth. Engaged in a collective quest for truth and control of the environment, individual worth is produced by being the agent of change. All of this frames a "strange loop" in which the individual is forever engaged in a process of creating "new" things.

Four characteristics distinguish modernistic from monocultural or ethnocentric communication. First, modernistic communication proceeds with a great degree of mindfulness. It requires communicators to be aware of their "old" or "current" resources/ practices, of another or "new" set of resources/practices, and of the difference between the two. When "new" resources/practices are evaluated as "better" than "old" ones, there is a powerful impetus to change, and thus change itself is celebrated in gleeful mindfulness.

Second, there is a sense that modernistic communication is somehow uniquely significant, or that those who engage in it are somehow uniquely alive. This is often a lonesome odyssey, because it happens within the patterns of resources and practices of individual communicators:

> A Napoleon without his army, an actor without his audience, is a nobody. The peculiarity of the poet, the man of creative imagination, is that he doesn't need other people to express his dominance. The great writer or thinker isn't writing primarily for other people; he is exploring the world of his own being. The huntsman needs a fox to give the chase excitement; the philosopher pursues an abstract fox across the landscape of his own mind.
>
> And yet he is not yet capable of remaining in that mental universe for more than an hour or so. After that, he becomes tired, bored, depressed; he has to get back to the physical world and his ordinary little concerns [Wilson, 1956, p. 298].

The sense of community among modernistic communicators, always fragile, is based on the recognition of others who have pursued their own abstract foxes across their own private landscape, not in the belief that they share the same resources. It is more like the sense of recognition among those who have experienced the shamanistic crisis, although they may describe it in myths other than the communalism of the "honest hunters."

Third, there is a sense of "time" as occurring in a mutable sequence. "Earlier" events are seen as "causing" later ones, and "new" event/objects are perceived as "better" than "older" ones.

Time is perceived as finite: a given day or moment will never recur, and all subsequent moments will be affected by what one does "now." This concept of time is far from that of monocultural or ethnocentric communication, in which the present moment is seen as an instance of the eternal rather than a thing in itself. The modernistic concept of time is best exemplified by the efficiency expert who teaches workers on an industrial production line how to eliminate unnecessary movements in their work; or by time-management consultants who offer advice about how to "save" time by organizing and planning one's activities. In sharp contrast, the monocultural and ethnocentric concepts of time are best exemplified by a religious activity such as the Catholic Mass, in which the point is that of re-creating something timeless. If something happens to make a particular Mass distinctive and different, its value as monocultural or ethnocentric communication is challenged.

Fourth, there is an explicit awareness of the process by which practices (re)construct resources. Practical and implicative forces exceed prefigurative and contextual. In traditional society, an elaborate array of supposedly immutable situations and roles provides the contexts for action, and the practices of ethnocentric communication are accounted for by showing that they "fit" those situations. In modernistic communication, on the other hand, the array of situations is made problematic. One can never know (but one always hopes) whether practices that express a set of resources will result in changing those resources.

Mystery is difficult in modernistic communication. The closest approximation to mystery is delight in change and unfeigned faith in "progress." Any other kind of mystery is an irresistible goad to the kind of investigation that will "explain" the mysterious by showing it to be an ordinary process.

Modernistic communication proceeds by placing resources at risk, and by treating others as nonnatives. The combination of these features achieves awareness of differences among sets of resources and a willingness to change one's own resources if it will achieve progress. Or at least this is how modernistic communication represents itself to those who find in it an antidote to the limitations of their tradition and the harbinger of a better way of life.

Disillusionments with Modernity

Modernity institutionalizes change; modernistic communication is the technology by which resources are expressed but then changed in the reconstruction. There is little disagreement about this characterization of modernity, but opinions differ substantially about how it should be evaluated.

The public myth of modernity is that it has no myth; that it is a technique of discovery of truth and of increasing human control over nature. I call those deeply enmeshed in this myth "happy modernists."

"Happy modernists" use modernistic communication as the technology of liberation—a heady and healthy escape from the dead hand of tradition and a license to explore new ways of life. For them, life consists of recurrent, coordinated patterns that start with the recognition that a particular way of thinking or acting is not new, followed by some form of work that changes it into something that is new, and end with a celebration of the new. Successive iterations of this pattern produce a lifestyle comprised of a series of celebrations, themselves the best evidence of the efficacy of this way of being human. Happy modernists continue to practice scientific method, "communication," and other forms of modernistic communication, secure in the belief that they are helping to change themselves and the world around them.

Sustained by an unquestioned belief in the rationality of truth, as shown in Figure 7–2, happy modernists are confident that whatever confusions, doubts, or frustrations we now experience will be eliminated by "more" practice of modernistic communication. Sustained by this faith, happy modernists have calmly discarded as "ignorant superstition" the wisdom accumulated through thousands of years of human life; they have contemptuously disregarded the practices and forms of life of all other cultures, sometimes charitably assuming that they are on the same evolutionary path but not so far along, needing "help" to get past the point where their evolution is "arrested." They have put their own social institutions to the torch or guillotine in the name of progress and they have deliberately disrupted other societies inculcating discontent with traditional beliefs and institutions in order to "modernize" them.

The equation of change with progress shown in Figure 7–2 is expressed in a variety of distinctive practices. It is the rationale for the Marxist call for a continuing revolution in which "self-criticism sessions" are an institutionalized practice. The same belief is expressed in the capitalist practice of planned obsolescence in which products are deliberately fabricated so that they will be superceded in a specified period of time.

The identification of self-worth with the capacity to be the agent of change is the impetus for the role of the "developer" or "entrepreneur." Natives of modern society are impelled to "make a difference" in the world, either altruistically leaving it a better place or selfishly achieving a position of respect and affluence in it. Modernists work harder and longer than natives of any other society because work fits into their moral order differently. In primitive society, resources facilitate seeing one's work as part of a union with all that is sacred. In traditional society, work is a way of finding one's place in a world linked through various means to that which is right and holy. In modern society, one's work is an effort to achieve "worth" in one's own eyes.

What a happy modernist cannot see, on pain of disillusionment, is that these beliefs contextualize a "strange loop." Recall the description of the happy modernist given above. Life is perceived as a continuing sequence of episodes, each of which changes some undesirable state and leads to celebration. This perception requires a particular "punctuation" of the sequence of events. So long as the happy modernist commands technologies of sufficient power to produce change, and can maintain this punctuation of the sequence of events, an exhilarating lifestyle comprised of a series of celebrations can be experienced.

For whatever reason, many modernists become disillusioned (Plate 7–2). Although they explain their disillusionment in their own vocabularies, many of them amount to a perception of the sequence of events in modernistic communication as a strange loop.

As Paul Watzlawick (1976) argues persuasively, there can be no "right" or "wrong" punctuation of a series of events. That being the case, there is no compelling reason to start the sequence depicted in Figure 7–2 with "this is not new." An alternative linear sequence could start with "work to change," leading to "this is new" and "celebration" but then to "this is not new." Successive iterations of this coordinated pattern—which simply punctuates differently the identical sequence of events—produce a life of repeated frustrations, beginning in work and ending with the ego-shattering realization that what one has achieved is not new, and hence worthless. I hear the whisper of "mid-life crisis" behind this punctuation, an ominous melody made relevant by the fact that there is no protection against the possibility of using this punctuation rather than the more desirable one of the happy modernist. Is the difference between joy and despair, between a happy and a disillusioned modernist, simply a matter of punctuation with no criterion for which is "right"?

But there is yet another level of disillusionment possible. Both examples of punctuation above presumed that the sequence of events, wherever it started and stopped, was linear, a four-step sequence that ended and then started over. But Figure 7–2 shows the pattern as a strange loop in which there is no starting or stopping, just a pattern that continues. The "strangeness" in the loop derives from the vagueness of the pronoun "this." Looked at as a whole, the loop portrays the "this" that is new and celebrated as the same "this" that is subsequently not new and the object of efforts to change it. It takes less than a certified ring-tailed genius to figure out that something is lost (or gained) in what is designated with the pronoun "this" as modernists move around the loop. How long can you celebrate something's newness before it becomes no longer new? What is the social alchemy by which things change from modern artifacts to historical relics, from the avant-garde to stifling tradition?

There are, perhaps, many forms of disillusionment with modernity. One form of disillusionment consists of punctuating the sequence of events in modernistic communi-

Plate 7–2. A disillusionment with modernistic communication.
Copyright 1988 M.C. Escher c/o Cordon Art, Baarn-Holland.

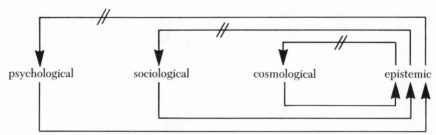

Figure 7–3. The actual structure of modernity.

cation in a way that does not end with a series of celebrations. For such persons modernity is seen as depressing rather than exhilarating; as a voracious set of practices that devours all that is good and beautiful. Marshall Berman (1982) found three metaphors in nine-teenth-century literature that captured just this fear of modernity: the vision of all that is solid melting away; the spectre of finding oneself naked and unprotected in public; and the vertigo of being a pedestrian in the middle of a busy street filled with large, noisy vehicles.

A second and more sophisticated form of disillusionment with modernity focuses on the deep mystification required of those who would achieve coordination, coherence, and mystery in modernistic communication. Happy modernists must be deeply enough enmeshed in the resources and practices of modernity that the terrors of history can be tamed, their lives made coherent, and their practices sufficiently well coordinated with other persons that they can act effectively in changing the world. However, those deeply enmeshed in modernity *cannot* understand it very well; this level of involvement requires several forms of "managed awareness" that limit their knowledge of constraints and consequences.

A fictional example of this managed awareness is perhaps more permissible than the analysis of a real person. Goethe portrayed Faust as a happy modernist, spurning tradition in a relentless quest for knowledge and daring all—including a pact with the devil—in order to harness sufficient technology to change the world. He also never seemed cognizant of the effect his practices had on other persons until it was too late. Early in his adventures, Faust fell in love with Gretchen, a traditional village girl who ultimately was executed for their extramarital affair. The night before the execution, Faust (whose affection for Gretchen had waned but who felt responsible for having debauched her) managed to break into her prison and offered her escape and a modern life in the city. To his consternation, she refused both. Later, Faust turned from personal to social adventures, concerning himself with public work. He decided to reclaim land from the sea by building dikes across what were family farms. His plans were thwarted by an elderly couple whose home was "in the way" and refused to sell. Enraged by their ability to block "progress," Faust had them killed.

Gretchen's conscience and the commitment of the old couple to their farm are antithetical to modernistic communication, but the three graves are not the stuff of which "celebrations" are made. To understand modernity, it is important not only to hear the testimony of happy modernists, but to observe the effects of modernistic communication and be advised by those who are "in the way," like Gretchen and the old couple.

Figure 7–3 provides a convenient way to organize some of the major criticisms of modernity. The concept that truth is rational has come under considerable challenge. Mathematics and natural science might be expected to provide the strongest bastions of support for foundationalism, but not so. Kuhn's (1970) analysis of "paradigms" shows that science is a social activity, and specifically raises the question of whether there can be any rational discussion between paradigms. At the time of this writing, this is a hotly debated point with no clear resolution (see R. Bernstein, 1983, for a lucid discussion of the issue). In mathematics, the twentieth century has been characterized by "the loss of certainty" (Kline, 1980). There are many mathematics equally rigorous and useful, whose principles contradict each other. A choice among them seems more a matter of faith or choice than grounded in "necessity."

The loss of confidence in the existence of any "foundation" suggests an alternative reading of the structure of modernity. The pattern depicted in Figure 7–1 portrays a triumphant progression of the results of the psychological, sociological, and cosmological questions toward a final revision of the epistemic question. Instead, we find a strange loop.

As shown in Figure 7–3, the revisions in the epistemic question are not final; on the contrary, they specifically undercut the notion of any "foundation" on which "final" knowledge can be achieved. Unexpectedly, the epistemic grounds on which the psychological, sociological, and cosmological inquiries were based have been undercut. The result has the same logical structure as the "liar's paradox," in which these two statements refer to each other: "I am a liar" and "I am telling the truth." If the speaker is truly affirming that he is a liar, then he is lying about telling the truth, which implies that he was not truly affirming that he was a liar, and so on.

As bizarre as it may seem, this complex, confusing pattern is the structure of knowledge in much of contemporary society, specifically those disciplines that have developed a critique of modernity. It is this vertiginous, paradoxical loss of certainty that has produced the series of "turns" (linguistic, structural, poststructural, rhetorical) that I described in the first chapter, and which provides the context for the emergence of the communication perspective.

The facile identification of change with progress cannot withstand the lesson of 1914–1917, the so-called Great War. At the close of the nineteenth century, there was a worldwide optimism that a new era of peace and prosperity was at hand, and that the technologies of modernism were to be thanked.

> Society now had running water and lighted streets, sanitation, preserved and refrigerated food, sewing machines, washing machines, typewriters, lawnmowers, the phonograph, telegraph and telephone, and lately, beginning in the nineties, the extraordinary gift of individual powered mobility in the horseless carriage. It seemed impossible that so much physical benefit should not have worked a spiritual change, that the new century should not begin a new era in human behavior; that man, in short, had not become too civilized for war [Tuchman, 1966, p. 272].

The war that ravaged in Europe from 1914 to 1917 was a bewildering surprise, and the savagery with which it was waged and the inability of civilized reason to gain either diplomatic or military success thoroughly crushed the high hopes for progress. The subsequent barbarisms of World War II seem in retrospect superfluous.

The same painful lesson has been learned in other contexts. The most rationally planned attempts to "develop" the nations of what has come to be called the Third World have resulted in an increase in their gross national products, but at the same time have given rise to an unwanted increase in the gap between the affluent and the poor, and an absolute reduction in the quality of life for most of the citizens of those countries. The first casualty of the development effort was the confidence of developers that the problems of development would yield to intentional, rational planning.

Finally, the belief that self-worth derives from being the agent of change could not withstand the demonstration that successive changes destroy value per se. Note that the only value identified in Figure 7–2 is "newness." There are no intrinsic values acknowledged in modernity, only the attribute of having only recently been created, and this attribute depreciates rapidly and irrevocably. In a deliberate pun, it is accurate to say that *nothing* (no thing) has value in modernity other than the extremely perishable quality of novelty.

Taken together, the resources of modernity establish evaluative criteria that desacralize events and objects. The intent is clear: "to rid the world of extra-mundane values. It is a systematic banalization of the world undertaken for the purpose of conquering and mastering it" (Eliade, 1961, pp. 156–57). In this spirit, Faust was enraged by ocean tides, whose vast energies are "wasted" because they do not serve humankind and thus "nothing is achieved":

> This drives me near to desperate distress!
> Such elemental power unharnessed, purposeless!
> There dare my spirit soar past all it knew!
> Here I would fight; this I would subdue!
> [Goethe, quoted in Berman, 1982, p. 62].

The attempt to make the world fully mundane can be seen as a necessary liberation that facilitates the improvement of the human condition. However, an unintended consequence is the loss of the belief in "truth" and "progress" that is necessary for deep enmeshment in modernity. Nisbet (1980) argues that the early modernists retained more of the medieval heritage than they knew. Specifically, they continued to treat knowledge as sacred even after they had formally repudiated the grounds for its link to the sacral. However, in the twentieth century, the scions of these crusaders have finally expunged the sense of sacredness from their treatment of knowledge, and with it has gone respect for and confidence in knowledge. "The present age of the revolt against reason, of crusading irrationalism, of the almost exponential development and diffusion of the occult, and the constant spread of narcissism and solipsism make evident enough how fallible were and are the secular foundations of modern thought. It is inconceivable that faith in either progress as a historical reality or in progress as a possibility can exist for long . . . amid such alien and hostile intellectual forces" (Nisbet, 1980, p. 355).

From a sufficiently great distance, the self-deceptions and unanticipated consequences of modernity might be amusing. But to those who must live in a society influenced by modernity, or—worse—to those "happy modernists" who will lose their innocence, the situation is far from funny. Like all other human beings, quondam happy modernists must confront the facts of life and achieve coordination, coherence, and mystery. Aware that their practices comprise a strange loop and that their resources cannot withstand precisely the type of scrutiny they bring to bear on other stories, how do they function?

Once the comfortable enmeshment in the levels of context shown in Figure 7–2 is gone, the remaining practices of modernity make it difficult for enmeshment in any set of stories to achieve coordination, coherence, and mystery. To fight a battle, filled with danger and disgust, in a "war to end all wars" or "for king and country" can be glorious; but to fight that same battle to protect the economic advantage of big business is foolish and profane. To labor far into the night as a form of love nourishes the soul; but to work the same hours just to pay the rent leaves the soul flat and dusty. If you watch the Olympic Games' opening ceremony—the parade of national teams—and are choked up about it so that your palms sweat and your heartbeat is fast and your attention is closely focused on what is happening, then the ceremony is working to evoke and channel your energy. But if you watch the same telecast and criticize the costumes worn by your own country's representatives, wonder how much all of this cost anyway, and how much longer it will last, then it is not functioning as an enmeshing story.

Lured by the glitter of modern entertainment and the convenience of home appliances, or entranced by the promise of knowledge or power, millions of persons have abandoned their traditions in favor of modernity. However, many of them have discovered that they paid more than they expected and bought something other than they knew. Now they are required to live in a world whose stories demand a specific kind of self-deception and destroy all that they value.

Practices that explain away and thus deprive stories of their power to enmesh threaten our ability to achieve coherence, coordination, and mystery. No one expressed this threat more powerfully than Karl Marx:

> In our days everything seems pregnant with its contrary. Machinery, gifted with the wonderful power of shortening and fructifying human labor, we behold starving and overworking it. The new-fangled sources of wealth, by some weird spell, are turned into sources of want. The victories of art seem bought by the loss of character. At the same pace that mankind masters nature, man seems to become enslaved to other men or to his own infamy. Even the pure light of science seems unable to shine but on the dark background of ignorance. All our invention and progress seem to result in endowing material forces with intellectual life, and stultifying human life into a material force. . . .
>
> All fixed, fast-frozen relations, with their train of ancient and venerable prejudices and opinions, are swept away, all new-formed ones become antiquated before they can ossify. All that is solid melts into air, all that is holy is profaned, and men at last are forced to face . . . the real conditions of their lives and their relations with other men [quoted by Berman, 1982, pp. 20, 21].

But how do we live with such self-consuming stories? How can we coordinate the energies of large populations without a shared enmeshment in some common stories? How can we make death and birth tolerable without mystery? With the communication revolution has come the realization that modernity imposes more difficult performance demands than any other way of being human.

Five proposals for coping with the disillusionments of modernity have been advanced.

1. Freud said that there is no solution to the "discontents of civilization" and acted as if the best way of coping was to be a useful, productive, and well-integrated member of society. His concept of the "mature" man (he had little to say about mature women) was a description of the civic virtues of his culture. Particularly after the First World War, Freud "saw the problem of human evolution as an essentially tragic one. Whatever man did, it ended in frustration; if he should return to become a primitive again, he

would have pleasure, but no wisdom; if he goes on as a builder of ever more complicated civilizations, he becomes wiser, but also unhappier and sicker" (Fromm, 1962, p. 37).

2. Others believe that the solution lies in reviving and restoring life to the "old" myths. For example, Bruno Bettelheim (1976) compared the current offerings of "children's literature" with traditional fairy-tales, and found the modern television versions pale and insipid, unable to provide the necessary symbolic enchantment. An educator and therapist, Bettelheim said that severely disturbed children have a problem finding meaning in their lives, of living "not just from moment to moment, but in true consciousness of [their] existence" (p. 3). Modern, demythologized literature written for children "fails to stimulate and nurture those resources [they need] most in order to cope with [their] difficult inner problems" (p. 4). Books designed to teach reading are devoid of meaning, and attempts to entertain or inform are "so shallow in substance that little of significance can be gained from them" (ibid.).

In the same vein, Le Guin stressed the importance of fantasy as a vital anecdote to the mechanization of life, which makes it vulnerable to exploitation by vulgar pragmatists. "Those who refuse to listen to dragons," she predicted, "are probably doomed to spend their lives acting out the nightmares of politicians. We like to think we live in daylight, but half the world is always dark, and fantasy, like poetry, speaks the language of the night" (Le Guin, 1979, p. 11).

3. Others shudder at the prospects of a reinstatement of the "old" myths. The contrast between the many successes of modern technology and the same old sorry story of politics and social relationships strikes many as bizarre. "Prometheus reaches out for the stars with an insane grin on his face and a totem-symbol in his hand" (Koestler, 1978, p. 3). The practices of modern society have changed, and our capacities to reach out to each other—in peace or in war—have been dramatically increased. Can the old myths be grafted onto new practices? "Surely it is folly to preach to children who will be riding rockets to the moon a morality and cosmology based on concepts of the Good Society and of man's place in nature that were coined before the harnessing of the horse," Joseph Campbell (1959, p. 12) exclaimed. "And the world is now far too small, and man's stake in sanity too great, for any more of those old games of Chosen Folk . . . by which tribesmen were sustained against their enemies in the days when the serpent still could talk."

4. Some say that new myths are what we need. If so, Joseph Campbell (1972, p. 275) skeptically observed, they will simply be the "old mythology . . . poetically renewed" to encompass modern conditions. Whatever else such a new mythology contains, it must envision "a new kind of man—a man who transcends the narrow limits of his nation and who experiences every human being as a neighbor, rather than as a barbarian; a man who feels at home in the world" (Fromm, 1962, p. 171). Bateson called this a "new epistemology" and got downright apocalyptic about it. "If you put God outside and set him vis-à-vis his creation and if you have the idea that you are created in his image, you will logically and naturally see yourself as outside and against the things around you. . . . The environment will seem to be yours to exploit," he warned, adding, "the whole of our thinking about what we are and what other people are has got to be restructured. This is not funny, and I do not know how long we have to do it in" (Bateson, 1972, p. 462). There is no shortage of self-nominated shamans who will convey the new mythologies. The Reverend Moon announced himself as the third advent of God who did not make the mistake that Jesus made, and invites adherents. The Reverend Jerry Falwell

is pleased to announce his availability as a guide to the application of Christian teachings to current affairs. The Ayatollah Khomeini is rather insistent on leading his nation to a reaffirmation of his understanding of Islamic traditions. Pope John Paul II has issued renewed claims that his office provides moral leadership for the world.

Not all would-be gurus present themselves in the guise of religion. Every social theorist is a myth-maker, offering a set of stories that can enable others to make sense of their experiences, and perhaps even guide their practices. Even more, the writers of popular self-help books claim that their brand of "transactional analysis," "transcendental meditation," "theory Z," jazzercise, or vitamins is the sure guide to—they do not call it this, of course—coherence, coordination, and mystery.

5. In sharp contrast, Berman argues that the cacophony of proposed "solutions" is misdirected; what is needed is not less modernistic communication but more. Granted that the new practices of modernity force a revision of old resources, and that revised resources in turn compel changes in new practices, and so on—the trick is simply to keep ahead of the changes. Problems occur only when changes outrun one's ability to adapt to them:

> To be modern . . . is to experience personal and social life as a maelstrom, to find one's world and oneself in perpetual disintegration and renewal, trouble and anguish, ambiguity and contradiction; to be part of a universe in which all that is solid melts into air. To be a modern*ist* is to make oneself somehow at home in the maelstrom; to make its rhythms one's own, to move within its currents in search of the forms of reality, of beauty, of freedom, of justice, that its fervid and perilous flow allows [Berman, 1982, pp. 345–46].

In the moral order of modernity, the worth of individuals derives from knowing the latest thing, wearing the newest fashion, being "into" the most recently developed patterns of actions. Berman applauds.

One thing is clear: we cannot follow *all* the advice of the various experts who would instruct us about coping with the disillusions of modernity. Further, I am deeply skeptical about whether the solution will be reached in an armchair, either mine or someone else's. The cacophony of communication forms in contemporary society contains a variety of responses to modernity. I suspect that a modus vivendi with modernity will be worked out in social practices, not in formal deliberations.

8.
Neotraditional Communication, Wails, and Relativism

Among the various forms of communication in contemporary society, the three named in the title of this chapter may be seen as "responses" to modernity. Disillusioned with modernity, various persons have been inventive, developing other practices and other stories. Neotraditionalism, as its name suggests, is an attempt to reverse or undo the effects of modernity; wails and relativism are attempts to achieve coordination, coherence, and mystery as best one can, given a full awareness of the "real" structure of modernity and the problems with its basic premises.

Neotraditionalists

Neotraditionalists have been influenced by modernity and are trying to regain some of the qualities of life they forfeited. Many were "happy modernists" for a while and, disillusioned, are trying to re-create the practices and resources of ethnocentric communication.

"Happy modernists," I argued, perceive the events depicted in Figure 7–2 as a joyous linear process, each iteration culminating in a celebration. The sequence *starts* with the perception that some situation is "not new," leads through a process of change to a perception that some new event or object has been constructed, which, of course, is a sufficient cause for celebration.

The disillusionment leading to neotraditionalism results from punctuating this same sequence as starting with celebration and ending with unwanted change. Consider the plight of a happy modernist who has worked for many years to bring about some important change—for example, tax reform, political revolution, an intellectual breakthrough, or a new genre of art. Before the celebration even gets properly under way, *other* happy modernists begin defining this hard-won accomplishment as the dead hand of tradition that stultifies the continuing pursuit of progress. They set themselves to the task of bringing about an additional change. If the original happy modernist is deeply enmeshed in the logic of modernity, he or she has no choice but that of agreeing to cut short the celebration and begin to undermine the results of previous work. However, not everyone is so deeply enmeshed in modernity. Some insist on celebrating the results of their own efforts; others are deeply enmeshed in particular stories they are unwilling to put "at risk". Both see modernistic communication as a threat to that which they value.

Religious Neotraditionalists

There is virtually unanimous agreement that modernity is "bad" for religion. The practices of modernity undercut the resources of traditional society, particularly claims for a sacred warrant for its institutions and practices. For example, it shows that kings rule by coercion and deceit rather than by divine right; that some nations are rich and others poor because of international trading practices rather than as the work of the divine hand of Providence that governs the affairs of nations; and that many of the institutions of society function to protect the privileges of the aristocracy or affluent classes rather than to express the rightful structure of the universe (M. Harris, 1979, p. 110).

This aspect of modernity is not accidental. The early modernists fully intended to achieve secularization, and through it a great boon to humankind (Berger, 1982). In the United States, secularist intellectuals fought against various forms of clerical control all through the nineteenth and twentieth centuries. When they won, they rewrote history. Before the middle of the twentieth century, "the Protestant roots of the nation had been uncritically lauded and sentimentalized; now they were presented as repressive or, more often, were simply ignored. Evangelical religion was regarded as though it had been peripheral and hence all the more dispensable to American culture" (Marsden, 1982, p. 150).

In some instances, desacralization is overt, mandated by the state. At the time of this writing, there is great controversy in Poland about the government's attempts to remove the crucifix from public classrooms. In the United States, the Supreme Court ruled in 1962 that an officially sponsored prayer in public schools violates the constitutional provisions of the separation of church and state. Subsequently, it ruled that the "Ten Commandments" cannot be displayed on school walls and public buildings cannot be used for religious club meetings.

There are less official, sometimes more subtle practices at desacralization. Religious topics are portrayed in the mass media in a way that subjects them to ridicule, and—in the name of pluralism and tolerance—powerful role models are portrayed as engaging in nontraditional, secular practices.

In the 1970s, many secular scholars believed that traditional religion had been destroyed by modern practices, and that such institutions that continue to exist do so because they appeal, as Isaac Asimov (1981, p. 6) said, only to "ignorant people, the most uneducated, the most unimaginative, the most unthinking among us, who would make of themselves the guides and leaders of us all, who would force their feeble and childish beliefs on us." This conclusion was based more on ideological preference than on good data; we now know that much of the academic dismissal of religion was wishful thinking (Hunter, 1981, p. 1). Scholars who predicted the end of religion were surprised by the turn of events and were forced to recant a lot of their embarrassingly well publicized words by a major resurgence of religious activity in recent years (e.g., Cox, 1965; 1984).

In Africa, the Middle East, and in much of southeast Asia, politically powerful movements urge Muslims to adopt a more purely Islamic way of life. In the Soviet Union, there seems to be a comparable movement among conservative factions of the Orthodox Church as well as among Protestants. In Latin America, "liberation theology" with its Christian base communities is a major political force opposing the alleged affinity between the affluent social classes, the secular state, and the mainstream Roman Catholic Church. In the United States, the New Christian Right has become an important force, obliging the nation to confront the issues on its agenda, including prayer in the schools, abortion, defense spending, school curricula, and pornography.

The Liberty Foundation (before 1986 known as the "Moral Majority") is one of the most prominent conservative Christian organizations in the United States. Its stated purpose is to "turn America around" by "returning" society to "moral sanity." This purpose derives from a particular reading of history and a very special way of thinking.

As they see it, the founding fathers planned the United States as a society based on biblical virtues. Because of its righteousness, God has blessed the nation with prosperity, and is using the United States as the basis for a program of worldwide evangelism so that souls may be saved before the "return" of Jesus, which is the end of history and initiates the "judgment." However, in recent years, "secular humanists" have gained control of the government and have enfranchised their philosophy into it. For example, they have legalized the "murder" of babies by abortionists; they have banned prayer and enforced the teaching of evolution in public schools; they have biased the news media against conservatives and toward secular humanists; and they have glamorized sinful lifestyles in the media.

This story provides conservative Christians a means for achieving coherence, coordination, and mystery in a society that has enfranchised "secular humanism." The rival story, they charge, has become so taken for granted that government officials and liberal opinion leaders no longer see it as partisan—that is, as one of a set of rival stories. According to religious advocates, the peculiar perspective of secular humanism appears as simply "right" to the secular humanists who dominate government, education, and the arts, and they are prepared to use any available political weapon to force it on those who might disagree. The institutionalization of secular humanism reached its climax in the 1960s when liberal churches became very active in politics, promoting such causes as civil rights and the antiwar movement, and when the government initiated an unprecedented wave of social legislation.

Because it teaches that all individuals have to generate their own ethic, leaders of the New Christian Right argue that secular humanism is inherently defective as a basis for achieving coherence, coordination, and mystery. "Moral sanity," on the other hand, requires communal ethical standards that are not placed "at risk" and suffice to produce clear ethical precepts. "We believe that it is impossible to maintain a morally sane society without some basic framework for moral decency, some standards that we live by," Tim LaHay (1981, p. 19) said. "I have noticed that humanists talk a lot about moral values, but haven't been able to define them. We Christians, however, have easily defined moral values."

In a book revealingly entitled *A Time for Anger*, Schaeffer (1982, p. 24) said that "secular humanism" is "at loggerheads with Christianity because it is a philosophy which holds that God is nonexistent or irrelevant to human affairs, and that man must choose or invent his own ethics; secular humanism makes man the measure of all things. This philosophy always seeks to exclude God from the discussion of moral issues."

The long list of current social ills provides the New Christian Right "proof" of the perfidy of secular humanists. Under the leadership of secular humanists, they argue, the nation has become militarily vulnerable, economically weaker, and socially more evil. The murder of babies is sanctioned, pornography is protected, the sanctity of the family is threatened by government intervention through many agencies, public practices of religion are curtailed, drug abuse is epidemic, divorce rates are climbing, and so forth.

"Moral sanity" is offered as an alternative to secular humanism. In this perspective, morality is a way of thinking about issues rather than the stand one takes on those issues. This "way" stresses contextual force, calling for a submission of one's own thinking to divinely ordained principles. The morality of one's acts derives from the fact that they were done as an expression of these principles. "Moral sanity" is exemplified in the story of Abraham, who was willing to kill his son as a human sacrifice—an act that seemed wrong to him and the deathknell of all of his hopes—in wide-eyed obedience to God's commands.

When acting morally, persons do not experience doubt or confusion, or worry much about the consequences of their actions. Because what they are doing is in obedience to God, they trust God to make sure that what God wants will be done. Even if the consequences of their acts seem "evil" or bizarre, or if they seem to be taking strange stands on issues—like advocating a strong nuclear military force, or protecting the rights of parents who abuse their children—they rest confident in the assurance that God knows what is going on and that they do right when they obey God's commands. Anything else would be trying to outthink God, and that is "moral insanity."

The contrast between religious neotraditionalism and modernistic communication is perhaps most sharply drawn in the controversy about the content of public education. In each instance, the modernists contended that "students should learn what is necessary to be 'citizen scientists' able to cope with a world filled with problems that science could solve. But this was the epitome of the humanist position—that people rather than gods or authorities were humanity's best hope" (Cole, 1983, p. 28). The New Christian Right, on the other hand, argued in favor of censoring unsavory materials in libraries, incorporating biblical teachings as an alternative to science in the curriculum, and explicitly emphasizing the Christian origins of American social institutions.

The practices of the New Christian Right now include television production, political activism, social welfare programs, sophisticated mass mail campaigns, and the formation of political and economic "publics." Will these practices be effective against modernity? Peter Berger (1979, p. 97) offered some wise counsel against premature predictions of the future. "It is only human to be exhilarated if one thinks one is riding on the crest of the future. All too often, however, such exhilaration gives way to the sobering recognition that what looked like a mighty wave of history was only a marginal eddy in the stream of events."

However, religious neotraditionalism has made a surprisingly strong showing in the latter third of the twentieth century, and I would be surprised if it were not one of the major forces for some time to come. "A new age that some call the 'postmodern' has begun to appear," Harvey Cox (1984, p. 20) observed. "No one is quite sure just what the postmodern era will be like, but one thing seems clear. Rather than an age of rampant secularization and religious decline, it appears to be more of an era of religious revival and the return of the sacral."

Nonreligious Neotraditionalists

Not all neotraditionlists are religious. Some share the disillusionment with modernity but do not find a return to Christianity (or Islamic fundamentalism, Buddhism, etc.) satisfactory. They treat a wide variety of practices or traditions as the embodiment of values that should be celebrated and defended from the encroachments of modernity.

Social practices with little (overt) functional significance can become the celebrated resources protected from risk. One such practice is the "debutante." Although outsiders to this tradition may find the "debut" of a young lady in society a curious spectacle whose time has passed, "to the intoxicated players, it is a ritual, a celebration of wealth, a familial rite, and an affirmation of social identity. What's more, after more than a decade of feminism and two decades of countercultural revolt and social upheaval, it offers a refuge from confusion. For qualified participants in search of validation in uncertain times, it provides the illusion of position and the solace of belonging" (*New York Times Magazine*, January 14, 1984, p. 28). Those at the pinnacle of the American social ladder remember a clearer, more orderly society in which there were clear rules for conduct and roles for persons. Whether or not such a society ever existed is irrelevant, its remembrance serves to illuminate the unsavory characteristics of the current situation. "Now nothing is clear anymore. Our present is miserable; our future is uncertain" said Amitai Etzioni (ibid.). "So the idea of a powerful Establishment, based on a solid set of rules, appeals to us."

Nordstrom (1980, p. 397) celebrated a "new spirituality" in the contemporary United States based on the practice of meditation rather than in the traditional forms of religion. The vocabulary and forms for this spirituality derive from Zen and Hindu meditation, martial arts, and reverence for a rich array of gurus.

Others find a sense of sacred duty in the protection of the environment. The ecology movement differs in content but parallels in form traditional religious activities. Greenpeace and the Sierra Club find meaning in the tides, whales, and baby seals beyond their instrumental purposes. Jacques Cousteau fills the role of a "secular saint" of ecology; Jacob Bronowski's *The Ascent of Man* (1973) and Carl Sagan's *Cosmos* (1980) use many of the same rhetorical devices as religious publications in a deliberate attempt to stimulate a sense of sacred wonder about their subject matter without relying on a traditional theology. Bronowski and Sagan may be contrasted with the public persona of the more modern, Faustian former Secretary of the Interior of the United States, James Watt, who outspokenly expressed his disdain for "useless" wilderness areas and his willingness to sell them to developers. Watt provoked instant, intense outrage that surprised him and ultimately cost him his job. Americans who were secular to the core felt that he was profaning something sacred. Interestingly enough, Watt's chief support came from conservative Christians, who—among other things—shared his belief that nature exists for humans to exploit.

The emphasis on "physical fitness" may be seen as a contemporary means to counter the secularizing effect of modernity. There are more than three hundred marathon (26 miles, 385 yards) races each year in the United States and more than fifteen thousand runners started the 1983 New York marathon. Why do they run? Sheehan (1984) explained that it is for the "experience," not for "fitness." His description of this "experience" uses language one might expect to find in the writings of religious mystics.

> The marathoner comes to be the total person running the total race.
>
> When I run a marathon, I put myself at the center of my life, the center of my universe. For these hours, I move past ideas of food and shelter and sexual fulfillment and other basic drives. I bring my life and its meaning down to this struggle, this supreme effort that I must make.
>
> The music of a marathon is a powerful martial strain, a tune of glory. It asks us to forsake pleasures, to discipline the body, to find courage, to renew faith, and to become one's own person utterly and completely. . . .
>
> The achievement is not the sole reason for running. There is also what goes on before the mastering of the challenge, what goes on while finding an additional purpose in life. . . .
>
> We who run are different from those who merely study us. We are out there experiencing what they are trying to put into words. We know what they are merely trying to know. They are seeking belief, while we already believe. Our difficulty is in expressing the whole truth of that experience, that knowledge, that belief.

Spectator sports are another secular surrogate for sacred practices. They provide something comparable to the pageantry of religious ceremony, the awe inspired by creation stories or symbols of transcendent power, or even the coordination enabled by common language and training. There is a quality of loyalty evoked in fans that goes beyond esthetic appreciation of athletic skills. The total emotional experience goes far beyond the game itself; there are symbols (the colors and emblems of the game), spectacles (parades, cheerleaders, mass activities), and authorities (coaches, judges). The Olympic Games utilize explicitly religious symbols stripped of religious meaning. The clearest example is the "eternal flame" carried from the site of one Olympic meeting to the next. The world cup in soccer elicits a response by fans that can only be deemed "holy": chanting, singing, imploring the deities/players, and so forth. American football serves the same function. In contrast to a confused and mundane secular world, football games "seem clear and occasionally noble: eleven men against eleven men, evenly matched between discernible boundaries, each side bound by the same rules, each side with a visible goal to reach and a great prize to gain. . . . The strategy is enormously complex and the execution brutally simple. The object is to dominate. The experience, for the viewers, is televised adrenalin. More Americans will watch next Sunday's game than attend church" (Harris, 1984, p. 14). Males in contemporary American society use football as a resource for coherence and coordination. Football metaphors are used in business, government, foreign policy, even social relationships: "we have to follow the game plan"; "nothing to do but fall back and punt"; "we were blind-sided on that one"; and "that was a nice bit of broken-field running."

The most explicit attempt to restore the sacredness lost by the practices of happy modernists is a particular way of doing science. Science is frequently seen by nonscientists as the greatest threat to all that is holy, "as a contaminator, a spoiler, a reducer, that makes life bleak and mechanical, robs it of color and joy, and imposes on it a spurious certainty" (Maslow, 1966, p. 138).

The general public may be pardoned for misunderstanding science, however, for scientists are notoriously poor in describing their practices and often deeply mystified by an obligatory management of awareness. Although scientists have a "religious" attitude toward honesty and truth, pay homage to their noble predecessors (footnotes are a formula of veneration), and experience "the occasional shudder of awe, of humility and smallness before the great mysteries [they deal] with" (ibid., p. 144), they are often shy about expressing these attitudes. Carefully culled from formal scientific reports, these sacred moments are not usually available for nonscientists to see. Often misunderstood and misunderstanding itself, scientific culture is characterized by an unnecessary and dysfunctional "taboo on tenderness."

The Logic of Interaction

When neotraditionalists communicate among themselves, they achieve coherence, coordination, and mystery without undue difficulty. In fact, their communication offers many of the virtues of ethnocentric communication (which it so closely resembles). It lends itself to elaboration, makes coordination easy by institutionalizing scripts for most occasions, and co-opts mystery.

However, neotraditional communication does not occur in the comforting confines of traditional society. A hostile response to what it perceives as the dangerous dysfunctions of modernistic communication, it frequently engages in interaction with happy modernists. Coordination in these interactions is difficult, and practices often devolve into reciprocated diatribe. The most characteristic acts of each challenge the basic assumptions of the other, and each side's attempts to explain its own position seem foolish when interpreted in the social reality of the other.

The heated controversy between "creationists" and "evolutionists" in the United States exemplifies this diatribe, in which the richness of both worldviews is constricted by the logic of interaction with each other.

Creationists argue that a literal reading of the biblical story of evolution is as well supported by the data as is the theory of evolution, and thus should be taught in the public schools with at least as much emphasis as is given to theories of evolution. Evolutionists can hardly believe that creationists are serious, for evolution is supported by "facts" about which there can be no argument: they "are clear and not disputed by any serious scientific worker" (Lewontin, 1983, p. xxiii). Lewontin suggested that Caucasians in the southern part of the United States have found creationism a means of demanding respect, for they have as a group been rendered powerless and oppressed. He turned to a patient explanation of the "fundamental contradiction between evolution and creationism," which forces one to choose between a world structured by "the regular operation of repeatable causes and their repeatable effects, operating roughly along the lines of known physical law" or one in which there are no regularities because miracles may happen at any time. "Creation," Lewontin argued (ibid., p. xxvi), "is defeated by human experience" because creationists, just like scientists, "live in a world dominated by regularity." A creationist "crosses seas not on foot but in machines, finds the pitcher empty when he has poured out its contents, and the cupboard bare when he has eaten the last of the loaf." The anticreationist argument continues by offering "science" as the means of overcoming the well-known problems of traditional society. Writing in the *Chronicle of Higher Education*, the happy modernist V. V. Raman (1984, p. 80) called for the application of science to both technical and nontechnical fields because it provides a mode of inquiry, an intellectual framework, a worldview, and a value system that may produce "a world where there is less dogmatism and greater mutual understanding."

I prefaced this discussion by saying that the logic of interaction produced something less than the best argument. The creationists' response is straightforward (although absolutely unconvincing to evolutionists).

Start with Lewontin's curious claim about "human experience" being the deathknell of creationism. Surely he knows that theories are underdetermined by "facts." Humans lived for thousands of years well acquainted with the "human experience" of wet feet, empty pitchers, and bare cupboards without discovering the theory of evolution. Further, those who constructed evolutionary theory (Wallace, Darwin) did so in a creative process not described in Lewontin's defense against creationists. Stung by the ascription of cultural inferiority, creationists claim that "evolution" is *only* a theory and that those who find any alternative theory unthinkable have made it into a religion. If so, they reason, it should be treated like any other religion. Raman's reasons for teaching science, they argue, are the same reasons they would cite for Bible studies.

And so it goes. My purpose is not to adjudicate or even describe fully this interminable public diatribe, but to offer it as an example of the constricting logic of interaction produced when neotraditionalists and happy modernists meet. The same logic (with different content, of course) is being played out in Muslim countries between modernizers and fundamentalists; in the People's Republic of China between doctrinaire communists and reformers.

These diatribes frustrate the participants because they feel that their opponents persistently miss the point, and they are far from eloquent, graceful, or beautiful. However, they comprise a significant part of contemporary public discourse, and the way they are handled will have great implications for the future of the world.

Wails

I am tempted to say that neotraditional communication results from a different linear punctuation of the sequence of events so prized by happy modernists, and wails by those who perceive the sequence as a loop with neither beginning nor end, and a strange loop at that. I think there is a lot to this characterization, but I am not accustomed to having things work out so neatly in real life.

It is certain that there is a group of persons whose persistent self-reflective stance alienates them from all the social roles and institutions to which they belong. Colin Wilson (1956) characterized them as "outsiders." They have difficulty achieving sufficient willing suspension of disbelief to give a "good reading" to the stories they know and to be sufficiently enmeshed in their practices.

"Outsiders" are puzzling to both ethnocentric and modernistic communicators. Human beings are, perhaps more than anything else, "joiners" or "game-players." Give human beings a patterned activity, and they will learn the rules and join the game, whether the game is language, business, or war. Usually, they refuse to participate only when they are deeply enmeshed in some other game whose rules preclude it. However, there are some who perceive the world in such a way that they do not feel a part of it.

In *John Bull's Other Island* (1956), George Bernard Shaw envisions a conversation between a "happy modernist" (Broadbent) and an "outsider" (Keegan):

Broadbent: I find the world quite good enough for me—rather a jolly place, in fact.

Keegan (looking at him with quiet wonder): You are satisfied?

Broadbent: As a reasonable man, yes, I see no evils in the world—except of course, natural evils—that cannot be remedied by freedom, self-government, and English institutions. I think so, not because I am an Englishman, but as a matter of common sense.

Keegan: You feel at home in the world then?

Broadbent: Of course. Don't you?

Keegan (from the very depths of his being): No.

Coordination, coherence, and mystery are difficult for outsiders. One available means of communication for them consists of "wails." Varying greatly in eloquence, these comprise laments about their predicament. Many wails are nonverbal. At least some suicides by young persons, some decisions to use drugs, some patterns of rebellious "acting out" seem to be "wails" prompted by the inability to give "good readings" to their stories.

William Barrett (1973, p. 364) gave one of the most eloquent "wails." "Civilization," he said, "was the necessary instrument for the psychological development of mankind out of the womb of the unconscious and the umbilical closeness to nature. That was our historical destiny. . . . It does not seem to have been intended to make us happier." Civilization requires many things of us and offers much to us. However, "wailers" like Barrett doubt the value of what it offers. For example, he cites the dysfunctional effects of technology and questions the possibility of "progress." This is of great significance, because technology is "the most adventurous, creative, and original part of our culture. There can hardly be any more striking symptom of loss of heart than when a civilization begins to doubt what it does best" (ibid.).

Dadaism is the clearest example of the wails of outsiders. Convinced that all stories were absurd, they produced deliberately absurd messages, such as a urinal exhibited as an art form. They wanted to expose the ultimate incoherency of the human condition, but they were interpreted as making the coherent statement that there is no coherence, and thus they failed (Bigsby, 1972). Perhaps in failing, the dadists proved their point.

Relativism

A more sanguine expression of an outsider's perspective is the affirmation that *any* set of stories is as good as any other. Many modern academicians unexpectedly found themselves relativists. The moral order of modernity taught them to put their resources at risk, and to engage in practices that systematically exposed them to novelty. As long as they could believe that successive revisions made them better and closer to the truth, they could feel confident that their "new" idea, whatever it was, was preferable to the "old." But incontrovertible evidence mounted to the effect that "new" was not necessarily better than "old," and that the attempt to change things often made them worse rather than better. They therefore retained powerful ways to say that one culture, for example, was "different" from another, but not to say that one was "better" or even preferable. They learned how to give an unlimited number of "readings" of a text, but became sensitive to the "problem" of privileging one reading over another. The only basis for making value judgments was as a matter of personal, private taste—and this was a bit embarrassing, for it fits the moral order of neither modernity nor traditional society.

A perceptive critic of modernity, Nietzsche saw clearly that modernity led to disillusionment with any external criterion and argued that a new moral order needs to be constructed in which only the "self" remains as a judgmental anchor. The practices of modernity would produce, he believed, an "overman" or "great spirit." This type of person would follow the performance demands of his own will, not that of fitting into the predetermined occasions of some traditional society or even a persistent pursuit of truth while shackled to a method. The moral order of such selves stresses a persistent pursuit of individual freedom at the price of relentless skepticism. "Great spirits are skeptics," he wrote. "Men of conviction are not worth the least consideration in fundamental questions of value or disvalue. Convictions are prisons. . . . Freedom from all kinds of convictions, to be able to see freely, is part of strength" (quoted in Kaufmann, 1980, p. 126).

This is not exactly what has developed. In the United States, those who reached adulthood during the 1960s and 1970s have been referred to as the "me-generation" because their value systems seem to express only their own interests. The moral decision-making process of this generation has been caricatured as "if you like it, do it" or "whatever turns you on." A concomitant part of that ethic is an inability to judge the relative values of different ways of life. As an ethical maxim, "different strokes for different folks" is an explicit expression of thoroughgoing relativism, not the emergence of a transcendent moral order as Nietzsche envisioned.

Relativism *seems* ultimately tolerant of other persons and ways of life, but it is not. It is at least *heard* as an adamant statement that no tradition is privileged, and that those who are satisfactorily enmeshed in a tradition are deluded. As relativism "plays out" in interactions with others over major segments of the human life cycle, it encounters/engenders predictable difficulties.

The ability to coordinate with others is limited by the relativist's detachment from any single standard. The most intricate forms of coordination occur when persons can anticipate each other's acts well enough to predict long sequences. One takes "risks" in conversation—as in acrobatics—when one knows that the other is faithful, constant, and ready to "cover" when what they do is ill-advised. Without such trust, conversations are more cautious and tend to repeat rather simple patterns. This raises important questions about the ability of outsiders to achieve coordination. On what basis can others depend on or trust one who explicitly denies the existence of any dependable or trustworthy set of stories or practices?

The ability to achieve coherence and mystery is also limited. There is a kind of "rush," a surge of excitement tantamount to an "awakening" when one suspends belief and is liberated from a particular language game. But this technology of liberation is, in an ironic sense, too powerful: it is capable of liberating anyone who persistently uses it from *any* language game—including the language game of liberation from language games. The suspension of belief—if too thorough—confronts the spectre of nihilism, that faceless, nontheological devil that crops up again and again in the literature of the twentieth century. Nihilism is less the *doctrine* that nothing exists than a *sensation* that one has nothing on which to rely; a free-floating disorientation based on a distrust of all symbolic systems. Hermann Hesse's character Joseph expressed the outsider's critique of modernity well:

"Oh, if only it were possible to find understanding," Joseph exclaimed. "If only there were a dogma to believe in. Everything is contradictory, everything tangential; there are no certainties anywhere. Everything can be interpreted one way and then again in the opposite sense. The whole of world history can be explained as development and progress and can also be seen as nothing but decadence and meaninglessness. Isn't there any truth? Is there no real and valid doctrine?" [Hesse, 1943/1969, p. 69].

The condition of "outsiders," I believe, is a natural response to modernity for those who understand it sufficiently well. However, wails and relativism afford no form of communication adequate to achieve coordination, coherence, and mystery. As such, they should be seen as a transition to some other way of being human rather than viable patterns in themselves.

9.
Cosmopolitan Communication

Like all other forms of communication, "cosmopolitan" is a means of achieving coordination, coherence, and mystery within the constraints imposed by the "facts of life" and in response to particular social and material conditions. Its distinctive features derive from giving primacy to coordination rather than coherence, and from its unusual means of achieving mystery.

Again, like all other forms of communication, "cosmopolitan" consists of practices that—however they originated—(re)construct and express resources. Successive iterations of this process comprise the institutions and "world" of a unique way of being human. Unlike the other forms of communication discussed in this book, cosmopolitan has not (yet) been a dominant influence in any large society. Thus the shape of the institutions it constructs and the nature of the way of being human it permits are apparent more in hints, examples, and promises than in the history of a distinctive type of society. The qualities of those hints and promises, however, are sufficiently intriguing to warrant careful consideration of such examples as can be found.

The human condition emerges from an inherent tension between coordination and coherence/mystery. This tension originates in the duality of the human being as dreamer and actor; as a hermeneutic being who envisions unworldly vistas and inhuman entities—gods, ghosts, and aliens from outer space—and at the same time an old primate whose hands, arms, and social organization are shaped to climb, run, and mate. No adequate understanding of communication (or of any other aspect of the human condition) can be achieved if this tension is not respected. In the stories we tell, we can transcend the fact that we are incarnate, a physical body inextricably linked to the rude, brute facts of the physical world. In these stories, we may have godlike powers, superhuman intelligence, and immortality; we populate and organize the world as we wish. However, these stories are tempered (and sometimes spurred!) by our interactions with others, where we usually find ourselves involved in patterns/relationships/episodes not of our choosing, sometimes beyond our comprehension, and often contrary to our intentions.

This tension between coordination and coherence/mystery cannot be "solved," only dealt with more or less successfully. The concept of "eloquence" helps describe several ways of coping with it. In its most general sense, eloquence refers to the grace/skill/ smoothness/sophistication of a performance. The opposites of eloquence include clumsy, awkward, hesitant, unskilled, or inappropriate performances. Eloquence refers to the extent to which the potentials of a given system (e.g., a language) are utilized in order to achieve a purpose. An inelegant statement, for example, does not utilize the power or subtlety of the resources available. If the purpose is to give precise directions, then "proceed north on Elm Street for 1.2 miles, then turn right at the intersection with North Maple" is more eloquent than "go along here for a ways then turn right; you can't miss it."

If eloquence is the utilization of what a system allows, then the nature of systems in which persons act shapes the form of eloquence. Eloquent performance differs among primitive, traditional, and modern societies in ways that express the distinctive character- istics of each. However, a common feature distinguishes the eloquence in monocultural, ethnocentric, and modernistic communication from cosmopolitan. All three make coher- ence primary; or, better said, they strive to achieve coordination *through* coherence and mystery. Given an irreducible conflict, they are willing to let coordination suffer. In vastly different ways, of course, all three say, "if we can coordinate within the boundaries of our stories, fine; if not, we will protect our stories at whatever cost to our ability to coordinate." "Rhetorical eloquence" thus becomes the sophisticated exploitation of the potential means for achieving coherence and mystery.

In monocultural communication, incredibly rich stories are set against the de facto denial of the humanness of other groups (or the existence of other groups of humans). Coordination with other groups is at best unimportant. For example, the BaMubuti of the Ituri forest have worked out elaborate ways of interacting with the villagers who live near the forest, but the villagers are unimportant because they are outside of and do not pertain to the forest that is for them simultaneously home, provider, and deity (Turnbull, 1961).

In ethnocentric communication, elaborate material cultures and sophisticated sto- ries are buttressed by well-known "scripts" for engaging with nonnatives. Coordinating with nonnatives is important only to the extent that it achieves the purposes and reconstructs the resources of whatever group is called "us." For example, the event that Indians call the "First War for Independence," the British call the "Indian Mutiny." Each side was willing to fight (a pattern of troubled coordination) in order to protect its own stories, and each interprets the undesirable events as the other's fault.

Modernistic communication blatantly subordinates the possibility of coordination in specific instances to the goal of protecting the story of a relentless quest for "progress" in which whatever now exists must yield to that which is new. A Norman Rockwell painting (which I call "Development") makes the point. On one side of a tattered "home plate" of a sandlot baseball field stands an indignant little boy with bat and ball; on the other side, backed by a burly construction worker and a bulldozer, stands an architect holding the blueprints for a new building. There is little doubt about who will win the argument, and troubled patterns of coordination are the price willingly paid for "progress."

Primitive rituals, traditional colonialism, and modern scientific research practices are similar in that each achieves eloquence by exploiting the potential for coherence and mystery within their stories. In sharp contrast, cosmopolitan communication seeks eloquence by elaborating the potential for coordination. This calls for a unique form of eloquence, which I call "social eloquence" to distinguish it from "rhetorical eloquence."

Cosmopolitan communication results from a commitment to find ways of achieving coordination without (1) denying the existence or humanity of "other" ways of achieving coherence and mystery, as monocultural communication does; (2) deprecating or opposing "other" ways of achieving coherence and mystery, as ethnocentric communication does; or (3) being committed to a perpetual process of changing one's own way of achieving coherence and mystery, as modernistic communication does. When performed well—with high levels of social eloquence—cosmopolitan communication enables coordination among groups with different, even incommensurate, social realities. Unlike other forms of communication, it is particularly sensitive to the unintended consequences of practices and to the nonsummative nature of the logic of interaction. Social eloquence exploits resources, enabling the differentiation of what is said from what is meant, of what is meant from what is heard, and of resources expressed from those (re)constructed.

The shift to an emphasis on coordination rather than coherence and mystery occurred as a response to particular social and material conditions. At least three conditions may be cited as the impetus toward cosmopolitan communication: democratization, the communication revolution, and disillusionment with modernity.

Particularly in the West, the democratization that began in the Enlightenment was realized after World War I. Rigid patterns of class distinctions softened, the middle class expanded in size and in influence, and successive waves of reforms brought new groups into the political/cultural/social mainstream of their societies. Nowhere completely, but almost everywhere more than before 1918, it became unfashionable (and often illegal) to discriminate against minority nationalities, women, racial groups, or men who lacked aristocratic pedigrees; previously private property has been opened to public use; and matters of state are at least nominally decided by popular vote.

The unintended consequence of democratization was to enfranchise successive waves of hitherto "marginal" groups. "Marginal" persons always have a different perspective on the symbols and practices of a culture than do the dominant class, and usually this perspective is richer and more accurate. The dominant class is always subject to certain mystifications because for its members the status quo is a "given" within which they move relatively unimpeded. Further, elites have disproportionate access to the means of producing cultural symbols, so that if they do not "fit in" to the established patterns, they have opportunity to change these patterns themselves. The mystifications of the elite are very apparent to persons on the margins of society, or subordinate groups within it, because they are frequently impeded in efforts to move "naturally" within society and because (some/most of) the dominant cultural symbols of society are alien to them. Marginals or oppressed persons often come to have a sophisticated, two-leveled perception of society in which their own reality is clearly distinguished from that of—for example—the king, the church, the "white male system," or "the man."

The two-leveled perception of the social order characteristic of marginals resembles that of ethnocentric communication's differentiation of "natives" and "nonnatives," but with an important difference. The discussion of ethnocentric communication in chapter 6, without calling attention to the fact, took the perspective of a socially dominant person (e.g., the colonist) or of a peer in social interaction. For such persons, those who are not natives may be subjugated, ignored, attacked, and so on. But what of subordinated persons who cannot avoid interacting with the dominant group and have no hope of successfully opposing that group? Some internalize the value structures of the dominant group, of course. American blacks call this "tomming" (after the character in *Uncle Tom's*

Cabin) and they who do it "oreos" (after a cookie in which a white center is sandwiched between chocolate wafers). Others, however, develop a rich array of methods for achieving coordination with asymmetrical coherence, in which the participant from the "dominant" group is deliberately led to perceive the interaction in one way, whereas the subordinate participant perceives it in quite another (Stanback and Pearce, 1981).

As the various marginal or previously subordinated groups were included in the mainstream, they brought new and richer perspectives of the social order, and they comprised a political polity in which a tacit reliance on a shared history or faith no longer provided the basis of coordination through coherence. In fin de siècle Vienna, coordination broke down as unifying traditions were systematically undercut by the efforts of artists and theorists (Johnston, 1972). A contemporary analysis of American culture refers to the ferment in the 1960s and 1970s as the "third disestablishment" of religion. In this period, Wade Clark Roof and William McKinney (1987) argued, the "Protestant-Catholic-Jewish" hegemony, which had provided a shared "Judeo-Christian heritage," was disrupted, undercutting the traditional American basis for achieving coordination and throwing American society into a frightening search for a means of achieving conjoint enactments of its favorite stories. The establishment of "new nations" in the aftermath of European empires threw together many "nations" into single "states" that must learn to coordinate without consensus (von Vorys, 1975).

At the same time that new groups were being admitted to the mainstream, the "communication revolution" explosively increased the means of producing cultural symbols. Through newly inexpensive books, a dramatic increase in literacy, the proliferation of broadcast media, recordings and direct-mail technology, many newly enfranchised groups were able to gain a hearing. I believe it no coincidence that European Jews have made disproportionate contributions to the humanities and social sciences, that it was a woman who noticed differences in the moral orders characteristic of men and women, and that this book about qualitatively different forms of communication is written by a white, Protestant, southern male trying to make a career in New England academia. All these are "marginals."

There is a second effect of the communication revolution: peoples that previously might have remained oblivious to each other or that comfortably ignored each other are recurrently forced to coordinate with those whose culture, traditions, purposes, and ways of life are exotically foreign. Mass communication reminds us of what is going on in far-flung parts of the world; political interdependency makes Johannesburg, the Persian Gulf, Seoul, Buenos Aires, and Washington part of the same community; public transportation makes Managua, Bangkok, Geneva, and Cairo, so far apart in so many ways, geographically contiguous.

Finally, the disillusionment with modernity described in chapters 7 and 8 undercuts contemporary confidence in coherence and mystery as a viable basis for coordination. Modernistic communication, with its relentless pursuit of novelty, is more a threat to any established pattern of coordination than a viable means of attaining it. Believing that the threat of nuclear war, the deterioration of the global ecology, and the requisites of a world economy demand coordination, many persons have turned their attention to ways of achieving coordination per se rather than as a product of coherence and mystery.

These three factors combine to produce the conviction that no degree of "rhetorical eloquence" will suffice as a form of communication adequate for the contemporary period. The content of existing stories is challenged by the emergence of previously marginal or subordinated groups. The possibility of any set of stories serving as an adequate basis for coordination has been thrown into question as part of the disillusionment with modernity. The necessity for coordination has been made overwhelmingly clear by the history of this century. The result is a set of social and material conditions that call for a way of communicating unlike any of those based on "rhetorical eloquence." They demand "social eloquence."

Social eloquence exploits the potential of symbolic systems to achieve coordination among incommensurate social realities without denying their differences. It consists of a willingness and ability to construct ways of comparing and thus rendering rational the differences among the stories and practices of various social realities. It is a part of "cosmopolitan communication"—itself a response to the disillusions of modernity.

Examples of Cosmopolitan Communication

None of the following examples of cosmopolitan communication is fully satisfactory. In part, this is due to the fact that cosmopolitan communication has yet to be institutionalized in the same way that the other forms of communication have. Cosmopolitan communication is not so much new as newly recognized as necessary. Probably occurring in every culture, it has often been overlooked by opinion-makers because it was a covert strategy employed against them by subordinated groups in their society, or thought posthumously to be the special province of saints and sages. In the past honored more in praise than in practice, the characteristics of cosmopolitan communication are only now appearing even to hard-eyed strategists as necessary virtues rather than virtuous luxuries or eccentricities.

Interpretive/Critical Research

"Scientific research" was cited as an example of modernistic communication. Of course, that discussion was limited only to one type of scientific research, known as the hypothetico-deductive model. In this type of work, a hypothesis is deduced from some theoretical framework, an experiment is performed that will disconfirm the hypothesis if it is indeed false, and if this rigorous attempt to disprove the hypothesis fails, it is accepted as provisionally true.

For the last hundred years, there has been a debate about whether this is the only model of scientific research (it seems clear by now that it is not), whether the scientific study of humankind requires a different model (it seems clear that it does), and whether the use of this other procedure for studying humankind deserves to be called "science" (after all this, who cares?).

Instead of trying to prove the truth/falsity of the *scientist's* hypothesis, interpretive/ critical research attempts to understand what the *subjects* are doing and to create the necessary conditions for improved communication among them and between them and the researcher. Researchers describe the intentions and purposes of the persons they study, uncover the often implicit rules they follow, and articulate the larger patterns they fit into. Such studies are intended to "make possible communication between [persons] where none existed before, or where, if it did exist, such communication was distorted" (Fay, 1975, p. 81).

There are many forms of interpretive/critical research. The one I prefer follows six steps. *First, select an interesting set of practices.* Usually these force themselves on the researcher's attention because they deal with important issues, they cause pain to some or all of the participants, or they have some unusual feature (such as the compulsion to participate in unwanted patterns). Given some inherent interest, the research is feasible if there is a sequence of events in which two or more parties interpret and respond to each others' actions, and if the stories each party tells are accessible.

One such set of practices is the interaction between the New Christian Right (NCR) and those they call "secular humanists" in the United States. During the 1960s and 1970s, a great deal of social legislation was passed, most of it sponsored by the more liberal segment of American politics. During this period, many Christian conservatives felt disenfranchised and (correctly) perceived themselves as dismissed as politically impotent anachronisms. Alarmed, many of them organized, deliberately adopted the political techniques used by the liberals, and entered the 1980 campaign. They were widely believed to have contributed the deciding margin in as many as a third of the elections of members of Congress, where several well-known liberal incumbants were defeated, and to have given Ronald Reagan much of his margin of victory in the presidential contest. This event shocked liberals, flabbergasted sociologists of religion in modern society, and, I suspect, surprised the NCR. It also set off an explosive chain of events.

Second, describe the sequence of events. It might appear easy to construct a timeline identifying the events in a particular interaction, but it is not. Whatever label you choose to describe each act in a sequence carries with it a "halo" of interpretation. Often, any label acceptable to one group will be unacceptable to the other, and you may have to do a double-entry description, indicating how the "same" event is perceived differently by each participant. Another problem focuses on punctuating "cause" and "effects" and the judgment of the relative importance of particular events. One person may treat as "critical" an event that the other does not even recognize. Participants may even sharply disagree about where to punctuate the "beginning" and "end" of the sequence of acts.

The difficulty in constructing a "neutral" sequence of events is not just a research problem; it is the source of the value of doing this kind of research. After struggling with the description of sequences of events just a few times, one develops a profound appreciation for the inherent tension between coordination and coherence. The solution to the problem is not found in the development of a better research instrument but in an increased sensitivity and sophistication in the researcher.

The NCR differs considerably from secular humanists in their interpreting events during the early 1980s. For example, the NCR accused secular humanists of rewriting the history of the United States to obscure the extent to which it was consciously built on Christian principles; secular humanists accused the NCR of profoundly misunderstanding and imperilling democratic procedures. Cutting through all of this confused charge and countercharge requires both effort and judgment, the latter based on a detailed knowledge of the "world" of both/all participants and a trained capacity to detect, describe, and compare their logics of meaning and action.

Third, learn to speak "like a native" in both groups. Start with the group with which you have least sympathy, and the aspect of the discourse that you find most foreign or perplexing. Work at understanding that discourse until you can use it the way they do. For example, the NCR invented the term "secular humanists" and accused them of "moral insanity." This seemed a perplexing set of terms, for many of the "secular humanists" were, by their own lights, deeply religious persons and considered themselves to be the vanguard of moral reasoning in their society. Evidently, the NCR meant something special by these terms, and one cannot hope to understand their support for a strong nuclear deterrent or opposition to abortion—for example—without interpreting their politics in the context of their own stories.

The criterion for knowing when you have achieved sufficient understanding of the worldview of the group you are studying is simple. When you know its vocabulary and how to use it, know its moral code and can make appropriate evaluations, and know when and how to give explanations, apologies, and excuses *so that the natives hear you talking as they do.* Then you can rest content that you understand them.

When you come to understand those aspects of their world that seem most foreign, you will discover that you had misunderstood much of what seemed easily comprehensible. Within the worldview of various groups, words and actions often mean something quite different from what you would expect. We usually underestimate the "otherness" of other persons, and are separated from them by the use of a common language.

Consider the term "moral." The NCR accusation of "moral insanity" makes perfect sense within its concept of morality, but means something quite different from what secular humanists assumed it meant. In the NCR worldview, "God" is the highest context, and under God everything has a moral dimension. There is a sharp division between "morality" and "immorality." That which is moral is so because it conforms to God's will as expressed through revelation; to act morally is to deduce from revealed truth what is right and then to do it. Moral problems do not involve determining what is right and wrong, but in summoning sufficient courage or faith to do what is clearly right. Immorality is anything that has not been subjected to God's will. Secular humanists are morally insane because they keep trying to figure out *for themselves* what is right and wrong. This usurps God's rightful role as expert and amounts to acting not only blasphemously but foolishly. God's truth exceeds human capabilities; humans are inherently incapable of knowing enough to make decisions about what is right and wrong. The very "progress" of science is cited as proof: the data on which a secular humanist bases a decision are surely to be revised as a result of next week's research. The succession of scientific "paradigms" shows the inability of science to provide a permanent, unquestionable foundation for policy decisions.

For members of the NCR, "morality" is closely linked to "honor." Failure to subordinate one's judgment to God's revealed truth is not only foolish, it is shameful. However, they have recently shifted the arena in which morality/honor is played out. Prior to 1979, most leaders of conservative Christian groups in the United States were concerned with "private" morality. Seeing society as primarily an opportunity for souls to be saved, a testing ground for admission to a better and more important world to come, they strongly urged individuals to "get right with God," but presumed that society as a whole would continue in sin until ended by triumphant divine intervention. As a result, private "good works" were an important manifestation of their religious experience but matters of large-scale social policy and political institutions were irrelevant to their main mission. They were scandalized when, during the turbulent 1960s, many liberal clergymen unabashedly used their churches as vehicles to lobby for social legislation and gave theological endorsement to political activism.

Culminating in a meeting of the Religious Roundtable in Dallas, Texas, in 1979, many conservative Christian leaders became convinced that they had to take seriously the morality of the social order. This "new" focus of the NCR was well expressed in Jerry Falwell's rationale for forming the Moral Majority as a special-interest political action group. It is God's will, he declared, that the gospel shall be preached throughout the world, and God has always used the affairs of nations as instruments of the divine will. In these last days before God's final intervention in human history, when God will establish a heavenly kingdom, the United States has been raised up as a base for worldwide evangelism. Founded by Christians for the purpose of securing freedom to worship, the United States provides political liberties (enabling evangelists to preach) and a high-tech, prosperous economy (enabling them to disseminate their teachings widely). Since the early 1960s, however, a small cabal of "secular humanists" has assumed key posts in the United States, and made "morally insane" decisions that restrict religious freedom (e.g., prohibiting organized prayers in public schools), condoned evil (e.g., the murder of babies in abortion clinics), and threatened civil liberties and prosperity (e.g., by weakening national defense against atheistic communism). We have little to fear from nuclear war with the Soviet Union, Falwell believes, but we have much to fear from publicly condoned immorality. If God decides that the United States is not a fit instrument of the divine will, we will surely perish. Given this scenario, honor, reason, and duty combine to compel effective political action.

Those whom the NCR calls "secular humanists" also link "morality" and "honor." However, their notion of morality, expressed in essays in the *American Humanists* or the several "Humanist Manifestoes," endorses modernistic communication in contrast to the NCR neotraditionalism. For them, morality is a relentless pursuit of ways and means to improve the human condition, in which attention is given to the *effects* of social policies rather than to the *reasons* for them, and it is presumed that various beliefs about what is good and bad will be periodically revised on the basis of facts. This process makes sense because humans are somehow entrusted with guiding their own social structures. Either alone in the universe or under a paternal divine observation, it is shameful to allow evil to occur without doing something about it.

These are very different notions of morality, both of which are inextricably linked to honor. Having come this far in the study of these groups, some researchers may no longer be able to sustain a willing suspension of belief. Their *own* code of honor may compel them to join one group or set themselves to persuade (educate, force, etc.) the other to see the error of their ways. In given situations, this response may be the "right" one but it is ethnocentric, *not cosmopolitan*, communication by the researcher. In other cases, the researcher may well decide to determine, by analysis of appropriate data, which of these is the "better" concept of morality. If so, this is modernistic, *not cosmopolitan*, communication by the researcher. Cosmopolitan communication, at this point, focuses on the patterns produced when these groups interact with each other, with a commitment to achieving as much as possible of the potential for coordination.

Fourth, describe the emerging logic of interaction. In most cases, it is safe to assume that the stories of each group (which you learned in step 3) are richer, more elegant, and capable of more rhetorical eloquence than those seen in the interaction between them. The moral orders of various groups are often opaque to one another; persons who communicate eloquently within their own group may have little or nothing to say to each other that the other can hear. The most cherished or persuasive arguments within each person's worldview are profaned and trivialized when interpreted and evaluated according to the standards of another.

It is also safe to assume that the logic of interaction always differs to some extent from what any participant intended. The interaction between secular humanists and the NCR is described in Figure 9–1. Read through the figure in a serpentine manner starting from upper left to lower left, one step to the right, then from bottom to top, another step to the right, then top to bottom, and so on. Each participating group lives in its own world, comprised of stories about self, community, the cosmos, and the nature of answers to questions like these. Each expresses those stories by actions that then enter the other participant's world as interpreted and evaluated by alien criteria. Each feels that the other's action requires a response, this response elicits a reaction from the other, and soon both are quite far away from what they intended to be doing.

As long as conservative Christians confined themselves to personal evangelism, secular humanists dismissed them as harmless anachronisms. But when they entered politics, and did so with undeniable effectiveness, the secular humanists were appalled. The political stances taken by the NCR were dramatically opposed to the "advances" on which secular humanists prided themselves as having achieved, and the NCR explanations of its positions sounded like the worst sort of medieval superstition and irresponsibility. Aghast that such an element was a part of contemporary discourse, they responded with a mixture of denunciations ("the least intelligent, the least sophisticated among us . . ."), lectures about the proper role of religion and politics, and dire warnings that NCR activities were subverting democratic procedures (by enlisting God for partisan purposes).

This response by secular humanists, to say the least, did not validate the NCR feeling that it was courageously accepting a new level of social responsibility. It continued its political activity and counterattacked. NCR denounced secular humanists as demonstrably poor architects of public policy (citing a long list of social problems as proof), deeply mystified about their own beliefs (so deeply enmeshed are they, the NCR claimed, that secular humanists did not even recognize their beliefs as a particular set that differed from others, and did not understand that "secular humanism" is a religion), and hypocritical in their defense of democratic practices ("after all," the NCR leaders protested, "we learned all our political strategies from you liberals").

Note how quickly conflicts of this kind become self-sustaining. Each side can become fully occupied with opposing the other and denouncing the nature of the other's response, so that, if the original problem were to disappear, neither would notice or care.

Fifth, describe the interaction in the context of the resources of all participants as a system. By this point, the interpretive/critical researcher has a unique knowledge, exceeding that of the participants. This is not "expert" knowledge of some principle or information outside the system. That is, the researcher knows no "laws" of human interaction or inexorable process of historical materialism that enables her or him to "correct" the participants' own understanding of what is happening. However, the researcher has by now engaged in a disciplined inquiry that makes him or her aware of information available within the system to some participants but not others. The most useful forms of information are those aspects of each participants' social reality that are not and cannot be expressed in the interaction, and those aspects of the participants' social realities that are outside their awareness. On the basis of this knowledge, and if the researcher communicates in a cosmopolitan manner, he or she can construct a more complete picture of the interaction than can the participants.

Further, the researcher can make connections among aspects of the interaction that

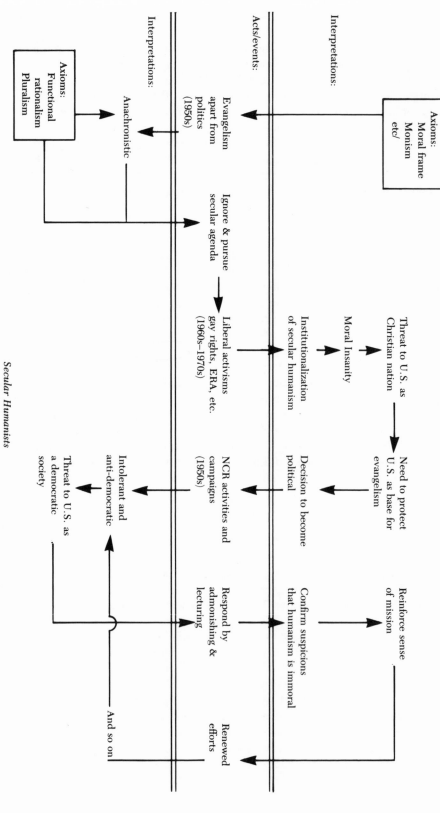

New Christian Right

Axioms:
Moral frame
Monism
etc/

Interpretations:

Acts/events:

Threat to U.S. as
Christian nation —— Need to protect
U.S. as base for
evangelism

Moral Insanity

Institutionalization
of secular humanism

Decision to become
political

Reinforce sense
of mission

Confirm suspicions
that humanism is immoral

NCR activities and
campaigns
(1950s)

Respond by
admonishing &
lecturing

Renewed
efforts

And so on

Interpretations:

Anachronistic

Evangelism
apart from
politics
(1950s)

Ignore & pursue
secular agenda

Liberal activisms
gay rights, ERA, etc.
(1960s–1970s)

Intolerant and
anti-democratic

Threat to U.S. as
a democratic
society

Axioms:
Functional
rationalism
Pluralism

Secular Humanists

Figure 9–1. Interaction between the new Christian right and secular humanists.

are not available to participants. The participants have a vested interest in a particular punctuation of the sequence of events, which brings with it a sensitivity to some connections and an inability to see others. The researcher, on the other hand, must flip between the punctuations of the participants, and should systematically impose a wide range of other punctuations.

On this basis, the researcher can begin to label the interaction as a whole. For example, the secular humanist—New Christian Right interaction between 1979 and late 1983 is appropriately identified as "reciprocated diatribe" (Pearce, Littlejohn, and Alexander, 1987). Each act by each participant elicited a louder, more shrill, and less informative response from the other; the interaction was quickly reduced to name-calling with a lot of emotion.

A particular event in late 1983 marked the beginning of a change: Senator Edward Kennedy, the quintessential secular humanist, presented a speech entitled "Tolerance and Truth" in the very stronghold of the NCR, Liberty Baptist College. Whether this speech was a response to violent acts committed as part of this interaction (a wave of bombings of abortion clinics) or of an accident (Kennedy was mistakenly sent a card identifying him as a member of the Moral Majority and called to ask if he should return it) is unimportant. Kennedy used the event to propose a "contract for civility" between himself and his host, Rev. Jerry Falwell. His task was less to convince Falwell that a more civil pattern of interaction was desirable (Falwell had been quick to denounce the abortion clinic bombers) than to demonstrate that it was possible. In a carefully crafted speech, he showed Falwell that it was possible for them to disagree with each other and to continue to command the respect of their own followers but to do so in a form of discourse that conspicuously displayed toleration of each other (Branham and Pearce, 1987).

Falwell accepted the contract. In the next several years, he and Kennedy exchanged visits in each others' homes, made a series of joint appearances (Cal Thomas, Director of Communications for the Moral Majority, quipped that they had become "the traveling Odd Couple"), and introduced a new level of civility in the interaction.

(6)   *Finally, assess the possibilities for critique and intervention.* The process of conducting interpretive/critical research affects the researcher. By learning to speak like a native of several social realities and by deliberately switching from one punctuation of an interaction to another, the researcher deliberately forfeits the comfort of deep enmeshment for the virtues of a willing suspension of belief. Peter Berger (1961, pp. 10–11) called "alternation" the experience of seeing the world from several perspectives, each of which reveals it as very differently composed. Invoking the image of a theater in which the set may appear quite different, depending on which sets of lights and filters are switched on, he described a sensation of intellectual vertigo. "Once the apparatus of switches has been perceived, the stage never quite loses its precarious character. Somewhere, even if just under the threshold of everyday thinking, remains the memory of metamorphosis, of masks and cloaks, of the artistry behind the settings of the stage" (Berger, 1961, p. 19).

It is this "memory of metamorphosis" that enables the willing suspension of belief required for cosmopolitan communication. Having studied the pattern of interaction, many researchers will decide that they must join it, lending their energies to the support or opposition of one side or another. In this way human beings have throughout their history persuaded themselves that "this" battle must be fought; that "this" foe is sufficiently despicable that all available energies should be mobilized; that "this" cause is the path of honor. Such decisions, however, mean engaging in some form of communication other than cosmopolitan. From the perspective of cosmopolitan communication, they risk perpetuating the *pattern* of the interaction even if they alter the relative position of some of the components. To add one's own denunciations of the NCR or *exposé* of the hypocrisy of the secular humanists is a homeostatic move; if the pattern is a reciprocated diatribe, this involvement is likely to intensify the diatribe, not change its form.

A cosmopolitan response focuses on the form of coordination, asking whether more desirable patterns of interactions are feasible, given the social realities of these groups. If so, then there is a wide array of available intervention procedures that do not involve becoming a part of the pattern. Some of these intervention procedures are described below; for the moment, consider "translation."

In my study of the secular humanist–New Christian Right interaction, I have found little reason to believe that the leading protagonists for either side understand that those of the other side are acting honorably *within their own logic of meaning and action*. And if they are *aware* of the other's code of honor, their public utterances contain no *expression* of that awareness, and thus each side feels dishonored and misunderstood by the other. No matter how rhetorically effective within one's own group, calling other persons "morally insane" or "the least intelligent among us" is not socially eloquent. One intervention is simply the addition of a more socially eloquent vocabulary to the interaction, and a vehicle for this is a particular notion of "translation."

Translation is usually understood as the substitution of words in one language for those in another. However, experienced translators know that a literal rewording of what is said in one language often makes no sense in another. Translation requires finding a way of saying in one language what has been said in another. This sometimes requires enriching the language so as to make it possible to say something new.

An ethnographer, Clifford Geertz sometimes describes his work as translating the meanings and symbols of one culture into another (Plate 9–1). When done successfully, it enables very different groups to understand each other's motives, reasons, and meanings. "Translation," he says, "is not simply a recasting of others' ways of putting things in terms of our own ways of putting them (that is the kind in which things get lost), but displaying the logic of their ways of putting them in the locutions of ours; a conception which again brings it rather closer to what a critic does to illumine a poem than what an astronomer does to account for a star" (Geertz, 1983, p. 10).

A translation of the interaction between the NCR and secular humanists is not simply a matter of saying to the other what each means; it is a process of getting both to use a more socially eloquent vocabulary so that they can understand each other. The effects of social eloquence are less marked on the *listener* than on the *speaker*. By using a different, more socially eloquent language to express one's *own* position, one becomes more able to hear and understand what *others* are saying. Translation is thus a transformative, as much as it is an interpretive, process. In the paragraphs above, I noted that the researcher might at several stages feel compelled to become involved in the interaction, and I claimed that this meant that they were engaging in something other than cosmopolitan communication. I want now to stress the fact that cosmopolitan communication is distinguished by the *place* and *manner* in which it intervenes in patterns of interactions, not by being uninvolved in some detached intellectual "ivory tower."

Plate 9–1.   Who's observing whom: Reflexivity in cosmopolitan communication.
Photograph by Martha G. Tyler.

Najagneq, the Inuit Shaman

Primitive society clearly differentiates shamans from other persons. The shamans, among other things, are the custodians of the mysteries; guardians of the myths by which the tribe achieves coherence and mystery. In primitive society, monocultural communication is appropriately practiced by those who are not shamans, but what form of communication is appropriate for the shamans themselves? How do they communicate with their fellows? At least one story suggests that they resolve the tension between coordination and coherence and mystery by focusing on coordination. That is, shamans tell the majority what they need/want to hear, not what they really believe.

Knud Rasmussen, leader of the fifth Danish Thule expedition, which traveled from Greenland to Alaska between 1921 and 1924, interviewed a number of Inuit shamans. All told remarkable stories of magic and spirits. One of them, Najagneq, was imprisoned in Nome for a year for killing several men from his community. When his villagers arrived to testify at his trial, he told them that the white men had already killed him ten times, but that he had ten white horses as "helping spirits," and by sacrificing them he remained alive. According to Rasmussen, Najagneq was quite aware that what he told the villagers was not factually accurate. However, he was not being simply deceitful but alluding to a "higher" truth. He believed deeply in "a power we call Sila, one that cannot be explained in so many words. A strong spirit, the upholder of the universe, of the weather, in fact all life on earth—so mighty that his speech to man comes not through ordinary words, but through storms, snowfall, rain showers, the tempests of the sea, through all the forces that man fears" (Campbell, 1959, p. 53).

Joseph Campbell's interpretation of the shamans' position is that they can produce "as profound a statement concerning the relationship of man to the mystery of his being as any that will be found in the annals of the higher religions," but that they seldom choose to do so when talking to their nonshaman compatriots. For the mundane members of their society, shamans are capable of "wantonly producing paradies of [their] mythology to intimidate and impress [their] simpler fellows" (ibid., pp. 54–55).

This form of communication must be evaluated in its social context, and I do not suggest that an imitation of it comprises cosmopolitan communication in the contemporary period. However, it does illustrate communication that focuses on coordination rather than coherence. Apparently, shamans were entitled to just the amount of respect they could generate. Given the fact that they could not invite nonshamans to share the mysteries, how else were they to proceed? Campbell (1959, p. 462) declared that the "whole point and mystery" of the study of myths is to see that, in the hands of the shaman, myths functioned simultaneously at two levels. As a "way," they disengaged the shaman "from his local, historical conditions and [led] him toward some kind of ineffable experience." As an "ethnic idea," on the other hand, they bound him "to his families' system of historically conditioned sentiments, activities, and beliefs."

The "Milan Method" of Family Therapy

Therapists specialize in intervening in patterns of coordination that their clients find distressing. A team of family therapists in Milan, Italy, developed a method of intervention that exemplifies cosmopolitan communication.

Therapists using the "Milan method" assume that families consist of systems that evolve according to their own logic. Sometimes this evolution gets "stuck" in a pattern that causes one or more members pain, and sometimes these families seek (or are referred to) therapy. The therapists' role is to help the family get past the "stuck place" so that the natural evolution of the family can continue. They describe their method as involving circularity, neutrality, and hypothesizing (Selvini-Palazzoli et al., 1980).

Hypothesizing denotes the process of making connections among aspects of the stories the family tells and the acts they perform. The therapists engage in what they describe as an "orgy of hypothesizing" in which one story after another is constructed, each suggesting different patterns of connections. The stories they take most seriously treat the "symptom" (that is, that which the clients complain about) as a "message" in the context of an interpersonal pattern. Rather than "having" problems, clients are heard as "presenting" problems to the team when they say, for instance, "I'm depressed." If patients "have" problems, the obvious question is to ask "Why are you depressed?" but this query, the Milan team suggests, leads in unproductive directions because it initiates discourse using a vocabulary of "causes" rather than one that focuses on the pattern of coordination within a family. Assuming that depression (or any other problem) occurs in the context of coordinated actions with other persons, they insist that the whole family participate in the therapy. Further, assuming that depression is a message, they ask "To whom does the client show depression?" as well as how and when this "showing" occurs. Finally, assuming that the coordinated patterns are produced by a nonsummative logic of interaction, they ask questions about who else is involved in the interpersonal construction of depression. For example: "If father were no longer depressed who would be first to notice, mother, son, or daughter?" and "Who would be most affected if father no longer showed depression?"

The hypotheses themselves treat the symptom as a purposive message about the nature of the family system, often "positively connoting" the symptom by claiming that it serves an important function for the family. Father's depression, they might say, gives the children an opportunity to repay their parents for all the nurturing they received from them; or father is concerned that the family is coming apart with everyone getting involved in their own circle of friends, so he generously offers himself as a problem to bring their attention back to the family. As part of their therapeutic injunction, therapists might praise father for carrying the burden of keeping the family together, but warn that at some future time, which only he will determine, it will be time for someone else in the family to assume the responsibility, relieving father of the need to show depression.

Circularity is a form of questioning that leads members of the family to make connections they previously had not perceived, and to reframe their perceptions of particular acts. One result of circular questioning is to reduce the strength of contextual and prefigurative forces by suggesting that practical and reflexive forces are involved. For example, a daughter might be asked, "Which of your parents would be most upset if they quit quarreling so much?" The answer at least opens the possibility that members of the family have vested interests in retaining the "problem," and that some members may have a stronger interest than others.

A second result of circular questioning is to put persons in an "observer" position with respect to their own actions. This is done by asking one person to describe a second's perception of a third. Listening to other members of the family describe you introduces a "third-person" perspective that carries with it a different set of rights and duties. In the "first-person" orientation—that is, if the therapist asked *you* if you love your mother—you have the right to ascribe whatever emotion that you want; it does not make sense for the therapists to follow up with "How do you know?" But if someone else is asked if you love your mother, they cannot claim immediate knowledge; it does make sense to ask them "How do you know?" and to require them to offer "proof." Being placed in a "third-person" perspective to one's own stories breaks up the willing suspension of disbelief.

Neutrality is an operating principle, a reminder to the therapists that the family is a powerful, complex system that protects itself by co-opting intruders into its own pattern. Therapists expect various family members to try to engage them in a coalition, securing their aid "against" the others; they dread losing their neutrality because then all their energies merely strengthen the pattern rather than intervene in it. The Milan team describes therapists who lose their neutrality as "Dr. Homeostat." Note that neutrality is not an attempt to remain uninvolved with the family, but a deliberate attempt to maintain a stance from which therapists can intervene by changing the *pattern* of coordination, not just the place of the components of the system *within* that pattern. Milan therapists work as teams, using their enmeshment with co-therapists as a means to resist being enmeshed in the family (Cronen, Pearce, and Tomm, 1985).

The Hill Adolescent Center

A part of the Tri-County Youth Programs, Inc., the Ralph C. Elizabeth Goldsmith Hill Adolescent Center is located in Northampton, Massachusetts. The following report is based on observations conducted over a three-month period in 1983, made possible by Dr. Stephen Bengis, at that time director of the center. Quotations in this section are from my fieldnotes and present the vocabulary used by the staff and "young adults" in the center.

The center is a residential and educational program for severely disturbed adolescents (13–22 years old). It has some features of a jail, in that all participants are subjected to 24-hour surveillance, and some features of a hospital, in that all participants are defined as requiring some form of intervention. However, personal surveillance is used for restraint instead of steel bars or brick walls, and the staff explicitly repudiates what they call "the medical model" of treatment. All participants in the program have "a history of failure" in other placements (schools, group homes, foster care), which is attributed to having "learned negative behaviors for survival purposes in destructive environments." They are treated by enmeshing them in an environment in which they can be "reeducated" to learn behaviors that will allow them to reintegrate into their communities. Inappropriate and destructive behavior is viewed as "maladaptive" rather than "sick."

The staff helps the adolescents to frame their experiences in terms of a sacred story similar to Joseph Campbell's (1949) notion of the monomyth. This story enables them to confront the facts of their history without trauma, to see themselves as empowered, and to integrate themselves into the program. The essential elements of the story are general enough to fit the experience of all clients. Individuals are urged to adapt their own story into its narrative theme.

1. The adolescents are multiply handicapped. Almost all have been destructively abused and virtually none have had the benefits of the "creative mediation" between themselves and the world that is necessary for them to develop the concepts they need

to participate in social systems. Their individual forms of "acting out"—arson, running away from home, assault, self-destructive acts—are reasonable and adaptive survival mechanisms in their own life histories although they are strikingly inappropriate in the larger social context. Repetition of those forms of "acting out" in a more nourishing environment such as the Hill Center is seen as a request for help, not as rebellion or a symptom of sickness.

2. The Hill Center constitutes an environment in which such requests can be recognized and honored. As such, it is a refuge from the ordinary world in which failure had been experienced, in which the adolescents may gain the resources they need to reemerge into the outer world and perform acceptably. This process is an arduous one, in which the adolescents must come to grips with their own selves and undergo a radical transformation.

The structure of what the staff calls a "sanity-producing environment" is constructed around "anchor points" for behavior. The adolescent is assigned certain tasks and certain limits on the range of permissible behavior. Often these anchor points are arbitrary; the fact of structure is more important than the content of the behavior. At issue is the adolescent's ability to recognize and work within a set of constraints. If an anchor point is exceeded, the adolescent is confronted. In one instance, an adolescent who went to an off-limits room in the school was accosted by three staff members who displayed their anger, outrage, and sense of betrayal. They accused him of lying, demanded an explanation of why he lied, and insisted on an acknowledgment of his guilt. By selecting trivial events and emotionally-neutral situations as anchors, the adolescents are allowed to practice self-control in areas of their life in which they are not heavily conflicted, thus gaining a sense of empowerment and success in acting in a social system. Such anchors also allow them to ask for help by "acting out" in ways that are minimally harmful to themselves and to others.

More serious breaches of the social order elicit a "hold." The staff throw an offending adolescent to the floor and hold him or her down until they quit struggling. As learning goes on, the hold becomes progressively symbolic and internalized. Instead of a multiperson pile, it becomes a single touch, then a word, and finally an internalized restraint. The physical aspect of the hold has dual purposes. In addition to restraint, it provides contact, which, coupled with talk, reassures the adolescent of the concern and caring of the staff.

Another part of this structure is summarized in the maxim "there is no bottom line," which is understood to mean that no action is sufficiently horrible to merit instant dismissal from the program. Dismissal is a genuine threat, for it generally means being sent to a more confining institution, such as a mental hospital (conspicuously located across the street from the residence) or to a jail. Because there is no "bottom line," even grossly antisocial behavior is disempowered. As the adolescents progress, they are sometimes questioned about the absence of their "acting out" behaviors, and encouraged—in a context of community and understanding—to "pretend" to do the acts that got them into trouble. This pretense, of course, radically redefines the meaning of those acts, and is the occasion for a great deal of shared mirth.

Another aspect of the structure of the system is the presumed intentionality of all actions. The adolescents are consistently told that the consequence of their actions is their intention. If something is broken during play, the adolescent is accused of intending to break it. Although the staff does not perceive these attributions of intentionality as necessarily true, they use it as a means of structuring a way of thinking that features taking responsibility and making choices. At first, the staff imposes a "superstructure" of intentionality by confronting the adolescents with the consequences of their acts and demanding an articulation of why they did what they did. These confrontations are both physical and verbal: holds are used to require the adolescents to articulate an acceptable rationale for their actions. As they internalize this logic, the adolescents restrain themselves before they act, and thus gain power and the ability to choose among an array of options.

3. The final form of the story, of course, celebrates the triumphant return of the reborn heroes into the situation that had previously bested them. For the Hill Center, this means that the person is able to live in normal society without requiring institutionalization. It also means that the adolescents, because of their struggles, become very "interesting" persons. In fact, the staff frequently complain that the quality of their interaction with persons outside the program is superficial and unsatisfactory in comparison with the nature of the interactions they have had with staffers and adolescents in the program.

The Hill Center attempts to create the possibility for coordination by providing structure. Cronen, Pearce, and Tomm (1985) argue that there are two types of confusion. One type is tightly structured but twisted in some way so that things do not turn out the way they were intended; a "strange loop" or some form of dilemma or paradox embodies this form of confusion. The other type of confusion is a jumble, the absence of any kind of order. Either type of confusion makes coordination difficult.

The problem confronting the adolescents, as envisioned by the staff of the Hill Center, is the latter kind of confusion. The adolescents do not know their own moral order sufficiently well to recognize how it is savaging them; they do not know the moral order of the larger society sufficiently well to coordinate with it; and the particular patterns of acting out that they have learned as survival mechanisms are dysfunctional in that larger society. The Hill Center does not attempt to lead the adolescents to embrace the moral order of the larger society. On the contrary, they celebrate themselves and the institute as the "best of a middle-class counter-culture"; they disempower rather than forbid or denounce self-destructive or antisocial behaviors. The structuring processes are designed to promote an unusual amount of self-awareness leading to an ability to control one's impulses, to choose among a repertoire of behaviors, and to understand the necessity of working within constraints in order to remain a part of a social community.

The Kaleidoscope Project

The Kaleidoscope Project attempts to create the conditions for cosmopolitan communication in public confrontations about controversial topics. The "Campus Kaleidoscope" program was an initiative taken in 1985 by the National Council of Christians and Jews to promote public discourse about important topics on college campuses. At the University of Massachusetts this program was specifically tailored according to the concept of social eloquence.

The quality of public discourse about controversial issues is widely criticized. In some places, persons engage in a coordinated avoidance of controversy and call it tolerance or civility. In others, substantive differences are buried beneath the use of a

common language. In yet others, differences produce acrimonious, unproductive diatribes. Kaleidoscope sessions were envisioned as serving either of two functions: providing showcases for persons who already employ social eloquence or constituting interven-
tions in "normal" discourse, enabling the evolution of cosmopolitan communication.

Considerable work is done before and during Kaleidoscope sessions to "reframe"
expectations about the event. In contrast to the well-known form of "debate," in which
the agenda is to decide "which of these rhetorically eloquent speakers has the correct
position about the topic?," Kaleidoscope sessions address the question "How can two
reasonable persons come to hold such different positions about the topic?" Where debate
leads to a vocabulary of contentions, proof, and rebuttals, Kaleidoscope sessions employ
vocabularies featuring autobiographical descriptions, reflective probing of one's own
assumptions, and questions about the other's history and assumptions. When a Kaleidoscope session has worked well, the speakers are no less committed to their own position
than before, but have a different, more accepting relationship with each other; a "good"
Kaleidoscope session might leave the audience more confused than it was, having seen
that there is a reasonable defense for the side of the issue that opposes their own position.

Social eloquence is not easily produced. The Kaleidoscope format is very intrusive.
It is prefaced by a clear statement that this is a special event; the speakers are periodically
sent to the back of the room to hear their position talked about in their presence; and
the chairperson takes a strong role in modeling appropriate questions and intervening
when inappropriate discourse occurs. For example, if an audience member asks "How
can you say anything that stupid?" the chairperson will rephrase the question like this:
"The questioner believes what you say is stupid. Why do you suppose he thinks that?"
Or, "Did you ever think that what is now your present position was stupid? If so, what
was it that made you change your mind?"

Practicing Cosmopolitan Communication

Some of the intervention techniques themselves do not look very much like social
eloquence, and should be judged as tools that make social eloquence possible rather
than social eloquence itself. For example, Najagneq's disregard for facticity, the forceful
"holds" at the Hill Center, the Milan therapists' refusal to "help" the "designated patient"
or to accept a family's own story about its "problem," the interruption of a passionate
speech by the chairperson of a Kaleidoscope session with a demand to rephrase or
be silent; and the delicate dances performed by interpretive/critical researchers who
alternately move "inside" and "outside" the worldview of the groups they study—all
these are ways of making more socially eloquent coordination possible.

Cosmopolitan communication resembles monocultural communication in many
ways. Like monocultural communicators, cosmopolitans treat others like natives and do
not put their resources at risk. They differ from monocultural communicators both in
the *content* of the resources that define what it means to be a "native," by the *emphasis*
on achieving coordination through social eloquence rather than by consensus in the
stories told to achieve coherence and mystery, and by the degree of *mindfulness* about
communication per se.

The intellectual grounding for this mindfulness lies in the profound, widespread
sense that a watershed of some sorts has been passed in the twentieth century. There is

much less agreement about the nature of that watershed than recognition that something epochal has happened. Some find their favorite expressions of the nature of this watershed in the "new physics," which has undercut the past to the extent that Niels Bohr has said, "anyone who is not shocked by quantum physics doesn't understand quantum physics" (quoted by Gribbon, 1984). Others are more at home in the "new paradigm" in social theory, which stresses the constructed nature of the events and objects of the social world and the open-endedness, nonsummativity, and nonpredictability of the process by which they are constructed. Still others are more comfortable in the self-reflexive critiques of the "new criticism" in the humanities, which identifies every "decoding" as yet another "encoding," which will, in turn, be decoded by other encodings, and so on.

Each of these intellectual traditions converges on a unique mindfulness of the processes by which groups construct their own stories; an awareness of the differences among these stories; and a sensitivity to the problems of coordination by persons who are attempting to collaboratively produce different stories. Aware that there are no neutral procedures for adjudicating the differences among the stories told by various groups, the attention of cosmopolitan communicators turns to the possibility of coordinating among them.

The problem is clarified by the set of terms first introduced in chapter 2. If two sets of stories are *compatible*, then they can be reduced to agreement or disagreement about the same set of issues. For example, both may organize their myths around the story of a hero, and even if they disagree about whether it was Achilles or Hector who was the most heroic figure in the Trojan War, their differences may be adjudicated by rhetorical eloquence. If, however, two sets of stories differ not only in their judgments about issues but also about the issues they find relevant, they are *incommensurate*. No amount of rhetorical eloquence attesting to the heroic virtues of Achilles will suffice to endear him to a culture that honors sensitivity and altruism rather than martial skills. By contrasting martial skills with altruism, incommensurate stories are made *comparable*. If two sets of stories differ so much that the differences between them cannot even be described, they are *incomparable*. If we meet sentient aliens who taste colors and communicate telepathically, their stories and ours may well be incomparable.

In my judgment, all human stories are *potentially* comparable even if they are, and will probably remain, incommensurate. In practice, this means that cosmopolitan communicators take their own and others' beliefs very seriously, they work to make them comparable, but they do not expect or attempt to make them commensurate.

This vocabulary enables a comparison of three practices. *Rhetorical eloquence* names the practices that assume that a conflict is among ultimately compatible social realities. They consist in various ways in which some common standard is identified and then appealed to for the adjudication of a conflict. *Social eloquence* names the practices that assume that a conflict is among comparable but incommensurate social realities. These practices facilitate coordination without (necessarily) agreement among the participants. *Intervention techniques* name the practices that disrupt various patterns of communication that are judged undesirable and create the conditions in which other forms of communication may occur.

 The practices of cosmopolitan communication may be best described by comparing it with Sally Freeman's (personal communication) characterization of the "normal development" of conflicts in contemporary society:

1. *The conflict begins.*   Assume that a conflict occurs because two or more persons cannot coordinate to produce a mutually acceptable set of events and objects, and that the reason why they cannot derives from the incommensurability of the stories they tell. However, the disputants think the conflict is about, say, who "owns" the event/objects or who should be credited for purchasing them. As a result, they act as "foundationalists," assuming that their stories are compatible, if only they can get beneath their apparent differences.

To "resolve" their conflict, they employ ever more strenuous efforts in rhetorical eloquence, attempting to express themselves clearly, display the rigor with which their thinking and action adhere to the premises of the (presumably shared) moral order, and explain why the other person(s) should agree with them. A ridiculous example of this reliance on rhetorical eloquence is presented by an American tourist in a non-English speaking country who, having determined that no one understood what he said, repeats his statement in louder and slower English, as if that addressed the real problem.

2. *The disputants are disappointed.*   If the conflict is really between incommensurate stories, then rhetorical eloquence will exacerbate rather than resolve it. As each articulates (with progressively more stylistic flourishes, data, and passion) the reasoning contained in their own stories, each in fact *weakens* their case in the hearing of the other. The result is that each has invested a good bit of energy in rhetorical eloquence, but the other remains unconvinced.

Assume that the disputants are caring, sincere persons. (If they are not, proceed directly to Step 5.) Generously, all assume that it was their fault that the others were not persuaded. "If only," the argument goes, "I had been more eloquent, then they would have understood me; and if they had understood me, of course they would have agreed with me."

3. *The disputants try harder.*   Given this analysis of the situation, the prescription is for "more" rhetorical eloquence (or is it "more eloquent" rhetoric?). Plato posed the question of what else was legitimate if the truth was insufficient to persuade a given audience. His modern counterparts, confronting an audience insufficiently responsive to the original display of rhetorical eloquence, have sought the advice of advertising companies, submitted to assertiveness training, hired highly credible spokespersons, and performed symbolic acts of charity, purity, or loyalty.

4. *The disputants get frustrated.*   If the conflict is between incommensurate social realities, then "more" rhetorical eloquence will not suffice to achieve coordination. In fact, the sincere attempt to persuade the other is likely to be counterproductive for two reasons. First, the more clearly they articulate their own position, *if the worldviews are incommensurate*, the less credible each appears to the other. Second, the disputants will eventually reach a point where the amount of energy they have spent unsuccessfully to persuade the other seems wasted. In many cases, the other is blamed for obstinate refusal to be convinced by such eloquent argumentation. The result is a growing resentment of the other coupled with a deepening enmeshment in one's own position.

Examples of this stage in the conflict are all too common. The Iranians will continue their war against Iraq, Foreign Minister Tarik Azis said, because they are led by the mullahs, and "The Iranian clergy are like the dinosaurs coming up from the basement of history; they will never stop until they are wiped out" (*New York Times*, October 4, 1987, page E 1).

5. *A stable pattern of conflict is produced.*   The pattern replaces rhetorical elo-

quence with some means of combating or fending off the other. A full vocabulary of such forms remains to be developed; however, such a vocabulary must include "diatribe" and "domination." Depending on the civility of participants, steps 2–4 may be completed quickly or indefinitely prolonged. However, in most instances in which coordination is impossible between incommensurate social realities, the disputants will reach a point where they correctly recognize that further rhetorical eloquence seems fruitless. Then, if they have roughly equivalent power, reciprocated diatribe will occur, as each criticizes the other. If their power is unequal, the more powerful will use the ballot box, distribution of economic resources, military force, moral suasion, or something to dominate the other; the less powerful will either submit, subvert, sullenly resist, or revolt.

6. *The pattern (diatribe or domination) goes on.*   Once these patterns are put into place, they are self-confirming, reconstituting themselves in practice. As the pattern unfolds, the disputants become more convinced that they correctly perceive the other as perverse, untrustworthy, wrong-headed, ill-mannered, greedy, lecherous, insensitive, narrow-minded, egotistical, or evil. This perception, of course, leads to the belief that there is nothing to be done with the others but to oppose them, instruct them, eliminate them, remove them from sources of power, and isolate them from children and other groups vulnerable to their invidious influence. A grisly "final solution" to the problem can be contemplated in the comfort of a strong prefigurative and contextual logic: "we have to do it; everything else has failed, and honor demands that we do something."

7. *The pattern is sometimes transformed.*   Not always or even usually, a series of events may occur in which the pattern is fundamentally altered. It is difficult to transform a well-established pattern of domination or diatribe. Socially eloquent practices are often co-opted into the system; this is the risk recognized by the Milan team and countered by practices designed to achieve neutrality. If a would-be intervention agent tells the participants of a diatribe that their communication pattern is a poor one, this comment is likely to be heard as a *part* of the pattern (one more insult) rather than a *description* of it. An intervention agent who wishes to oppose a pattern of domination faces the difficult task of *changing* the pattern without simply *becoming a part* of it. Anything done to aid the oppressed or humble the mighty lends itself to interpretation as a bid for power (thus replacing the dominant party without changing the pattern) rather than an attempt to create a different pattern.

Unfortunately, undesirable patterns of communication are not always improved by mere contact with more desirable ones. The Roman soldier who burst into the laboratory of the great Greek scientist Archimedes was neither illuminated nor educated by the experience, and Archimedes died. In much the same way, social eloquence seems delicate, too frail to survive the rough and tumble of diatribe and domination. The characteristics of social eloquence—the virtues of cosmopolitan communication—appear to be naïve weaknesses from the perspective of those deeply enmeshed in a struggle for domination or in a pattern of diatribe.

To create the conditions in which social eloquence can be practiced effectively and in which cosmopolitan communication can reconstruct itself, the hegemony of diatribe or domination must be broken. Intervention strategies that themselves do not resemble social eloquence are sometimes necessary for social eloquence to occur.

Regardless of the *means* of intervention, the necessary *effect* in transforming diatribe and domination to cosmopolitan communication consists in a reconceptualization of the difference between the conflicted social orders. If that difference is seen as "incomparable," then it correctly follows that no rational discourse is possible, and the only available means for achieving coordination is the exercise of power. However, social eloquence is based on the assumption that although most conflicts occur between "incommensurate" social realities, all social realities are *potentially* comparable.

Assume that there is a conflict based on differences of opinion, belief, or moral judgment. Assume further that this conflict does not yield to the ministrations of as much rhetorical eloquence as each disputant was willing or able to supply. What should happen now?

If the conflict is perceived as *incomparable*, then no further attempt to understand and be understood is appropriate. Each side should, as humanely as possible, destroy or render ineffective the other.

However, if the conflict is perceived as *incommensurate but potentially comparable*, then a different agenda is implied. Participants should set themselves to the task of creating the possibility for comparability without (necessarily) changing their own positions. This task is an impressively complex one; it involves understanding the other, making oneself understandable by the other, and creating, if necessary, a new vocabulary in which "translations" can occur.

The resources of cosmopolitan communication are not put at risk, because these stories describe a diverse array of stories. The discovery that others achieve coherence and mystery by using different stories triggers a moral imperative to understand and appreciate those differences rather than a crisis of confidence or a moral imperative to defend orthodoxy. These resources create a different vision of the good, a different moral code, and different practices that have been widely institutionalized in any society. How can cosmopolitan communication be institutionalized? What heroic models can it offer? What visions of good and evil harness the passions of its practitioners?

Many of the sorriest moments in the history of traditional societies have witnessed the institutionalization of the "right" set of beliefs and practices against the supposed threats of heretics. The development of European science was retarded by clerical heresy-hunters; the isolation of prerevolutionary Russia was in part to protect the Russian Orthodox Church from contamination; public education was long opposed by the Catholic Church because it promoted "free thinking"; Spanish colonialism was legitimated by its purpose to spread the universal faith; and major waves of emigration from Europe were caused by the desire to escape religious persecution; etc.

In modern society, the recognition of difference triggers a moral imperative to ascertain the truth of the matter. Pursuit of this code of honor has led to the impressive series of social, technical, and political "advancements" that have characterized the last two centuries. However, another effect has been to subvert existing institutions, even those it built. I believe that this frantic pace of creation and destruction cannot last for long. The institutionalization of cosmopolitan communication, if it occurs, will take a form not yet apparent.

In traditional society, the virtuous ideal is the devout defender of the faith, whether "the faith" is invested in the person of the king or the Word of God; in modern society, the vision is profoundly ambivalent. On one side is the manager, the executive, and the television celebrity; on the other, the rebel, revolutionary, or reformer provides the example of virtue. But what is the model for a cosmopolitan communicator in contemporary society? I believe that the example is still evolving; we have not yet produced a full-fledged model to be celebrated in song and story, and imitated by the young. First approximations of such a model include psychological therapists, mediators, and states-men (as sharply differentiated from "politicians"), but I suspect that new cultural catego-ries will emerge as the resources of cosmopolitan communication are more prominently expressed and (re)constructed. Analyses of "popular culture" (novels, movies, songs and singers, advertisements, television) are a useful source of information about the emergence of these models, although my reading of these materials at the moment finds a distressing persistence of models appropriate for traditional and modern societies.

Cosmopolitan communicators treat each other as natives, not because they *share* the same resources but because they are similarly *shaped by* their own "local" resources and practices. The emphasis on coordination directs attention to the processes by which persons come to tell stories and engage in practices in addition to the content of those stories and practices, and it is in their shared participation in this *process* that all humans are "natives." The moral imperative to make incommensurate resources comparable and to find ways of coordinating without necessarily agreeing stems from the recognition that no matter how far persons are separated by the content of their resources and practices, they are united in the process of being shaped by the continuing process of expressing and (re)constructing resources in practices—that is, the fact that we all live *in* communication.

There are many textbooks for rhetorical eloquence, naming the techniques for effective persuasion and giving good advice about when they are most appropriate. In contrast, the study of social eloquence is vastly underdeveloped. We know far more about polemics and persuasion than about facilitation, enabling, and coordination. How-ever, there is an expanding expertise about various aspects of social eloquence, clearly showing that it is not simply a passive process of letting other persons have their way, nor a relativistic belief that all stories and all practices are equally right. Rather, it is an assertive process that seeks to transform (rather than oppose) unsatisfactory practices and co-opt (rather than eliminate or defeat) other persons. The examples cited in the previous section show that there are powerful intervention procedures consistent with a set of resources that stand in marked contrast to those of traditional or modern society.

Resources for Cosmopolitan Communication

The resources required for cosmopolitan communication differ from those of moder-nity and traditional Western society in their construction of truth, time, self, and society. In practice, these resources are not put "at risk," but they tend to incorporate rather than deny the validity of alternative stories.

Truth

The practices that dominated the Western tradition expressed "the basic conviction that there is or must be some permanent, ahistorical matrix or framework to which we can ultimately appeal in determining the nature of rationality, knowledge, truth, reality, goodness, or rightness" (R. Bernstein, 1983, p. 8). Modernity did not fundamentally change this belief. Its revolution consisted primarily in the substitution of some *future* state of knowledge to be achieved by human endeavor in place of some *past* state of knowledge received from some nonhuman agency. The notion that there *must be* some ultimate perspective to which any merely local knowledge claim must appeal remained intact.

Even some of the most thoughtful critics of commonsense views of communication fantasize forms of communication that will finally allow us all to *understand* and *agree* with each other. Matson and Montagu (1967, pp. 3, 6) characterize the view of human communication as "dialogue" as the "third revolution" in communication theory. A dialogic approach to communication, they argue, assumes that "the end of human communication is not to *command* but to *commune*; and that knowledge of the highest order . . . is to be sought and found not through detachment but through connection, not by objectivity but by intersubjectivity, not in a state of estranged aloofness but in something resembling an act of love." They approvingly cite Jaspers' (1960) concept of "authentic" communication as "a mutual struggle for *common ground* between two distinct and inviolable identities" [italics added]. In much the same frame of mind, a popular manual for negotiating conflicts, *Getting to Yes* (Urrey and Fisher, 1983) focuses on the identification of *common interests* that presumably lie beneath *conflicting positions*. In an appeal for "the civilization of dialogue," Robert M. Hutchins (cited by Matson and Montagu, 1967, p. v) said:

> The only civilization we can hope for, because the world must unite or be blown to bits . . . requires a common language and a common stock of ideas. It assumes that every man has reason and that every man can use it. It preserves to everyman his independent judgment and, since it does so, it deprives any man or group of men of the privilege of forcing their judgment upon any other man or group of men.

Such expressions of compulsory toleration based on underlying commonalities contain hidden tyrannies. For all his virtues, Hutchins disenfranchises most of the human species—those who are not "men" and all those men who do not accept the Cartesian concept of self ("to every man his independent judgment"), which Geertz (1983, pp. 73–93) shows to be deeply embedded in American "common sense" but totally alien to the implicit theories of self in contemporary Bali and Morocco. So what are Balinese and Moroccans to do? Must they accept the Cartesian concept of self before joining the "dialogue" in "the only civilization we can hope for"? If so, how is this anything but an exercise of "the privilege of forcing [his] judgment" on others, both men and women?

Hutchins provides a useful example precisely because he manifestly has no such imperialistic, chauvinistic intentions. Rather, it is the persistent search for "common interests" or "common ground" or "intersubjectivity" that inevitably leads to just these sorts of unwanted results. If the social realities/moral orders developed by various cultures are incommensurate, there is no set of neutral standards by which they can be ultimately shown to be "the same" (R. Bernstein, 1983, pp. 92–93). Even if such a set of standards existed somewhere, it is inaccessible to us because, formed as we are by enculturation in a particular local system, we cannot know other cultures as a native knows them. The pursuit of an ultimate truth to which all local expressions can be related, or even a commonality in the assumptions of various cultures, presupposes a concept of truth inimical to cosmopolitan communication.

Cosmopolitan communicators assume either of two notions about "ultimate" truth. They may feel that there is no *one* truth. Rather, there are plural truths, each deriving from a historical tradition (this is MacIntyre's position [1981]). Alternatively, they may believe that ultimate truth is "one" but has many faces. That is, "truth" is ineffable, and there are multiple, contradictory, valid expressions of it. The latter is the more commonly encountered story.

The Greek philosopher Heraclitus believed that reality is unitary, but humans experience it as opposites. In the twentieth century, the physicist Niels Bohr articulated the same concept as the "principle of complementarity." Reality can be expressed, he said, only by a set of simultaneous, contradictory, and clear statements. "The apparently paradoxical, contradictory accounts should not divert our attention from the essential wholeness" (Holton, 1970, p. 1018). Recognizing that this position scandalized those who believe that there is *a* truth, Bohr argued that those offended by his principle are merely responding to a learned tendency, a "habit of [not] accepting basic dualities without straining for their mutual dissolution or reduction. Indeed, we tend to be first of all reductionists, perhaps partly because our early intellectual heroes have been men in the tradition of Mach and Freud, rather than Kirkegaard and James" (ibid., p. 1049).

Both of these concepts of truth view the beliefs of any given culture, no matter how passionately held or forcefully asserted, as merely one among many inadequate ways of trying to tell the untellable. The fact that they are inadequate, however, does not mean that they are "wrong," because no "right" set of beliefs exists. In fact, the simultaneous expression of multiple contradictory stories is more adequate than any one story alone:

> The nature of reality is intrinsically and ultimately hidden from any finite exploration. . . . Reality is ultimately problematical, not contingently so, for to grasp and formulate it, even as a set of questions, is to fragmentize it. The best we can hope to do is catch partisan glimpses. . . . If we cannot hope ever to be perfectly right, we can perhaps find both enlightenment and refreshment by changing, from time to time, our ways of being wrong [Wheelwright, 1962, pp. 177–78].

This view of truth enables a "largeness of mind" that Geertz (1983, p. 16) described as both difficult and essential:

> To see ourselves as others see us can be eye-opening.
> To see others as sharing a nature with ourselves is the merest decency.
> But the far more difficult achievement is that of seeing ourselves amongst others; as a local example of the forms human life has locally taken,
> > —a case among cases,
> > —a world among worlds.
> Without this largeness of mind,
> > —objectivity is self-congratulation, and
> > —tolerance is a sham [adapted].

Cosmopolitan communicators know that their stories are unique to their group, and that other groups tell other stories. But they operate under the assumption that their own stories are legitimate, just as are those of the other groups. In fact, some forms of cosmopolitan communication are explicit attempts to preserve and protect "alien" stories, not for pragmatic purposes, but because "humanity" is enriched by including many diverse local stories.

The resources of a cosmopolitan communicator are neither automatically sheltered from the risk of change when brought into contact with another set of stories, nor are they automatically placed at risk. By defining one's own resources as "local"—just as everyone else's resources are "local"—the cosmopolitan communicator can find coherence in a world in which many incommensurate stories are told and incompatible practices are performed. This tolerance for difference liberates cosmopolitan communicators to care about and take steps to find out about worldviews other than their own. They are free to go beyond assuming that they know what others mean by what they say; they are led to practices that often surprise them by showing that their understanding of other local stories is wrong.

Time

Cosmopolitan communication expresses and creates a concept of time as a historical coevolutionary process that generates and then unfolds on the basis of its own logic of meaning and action. This stands in contrast to other concepts, such as static, linear, or cyclical.

Born "unfinished," human beings are shaped by the practices and stories of their cultures. The local differences among these stories make all of us "localites." The "facts of life" that all humans confront *underdetermine* the stories that can be told to make them coherent and to facilitate coordination and mystery. There are multiple and incommensurate ways of accounting for these facts of life, and it is largely an "accident"— not the result of a "law" or some "necessity"—that one set of stories is told in one locality and some other in another.

This notion of time as mutable history rather than causal sequence prevents cosmopolitan communicators from putting their resources at risk in one sense, but increases the precariousness of resources in another sense. Simple "news of difference" is not a reason to risk one's resources. However, news that one's own resources are destroying the stories and practices of other local cultures might well imperil those resources. More so than any other form of communication, the resources of cosmopolitanism are sensitive to information about unintended consequences of its own practices. For example, Herbert Schiller has shown that the normal practices of capitalist economy, when linked to the technology of global communications, have the effect of undermining the local stories of many non-Western nations and of perpetuating very much the same pattern of international economic relationships that was established during the period of European colonialism:

> Today, multinational corporations are the global organizers of the world economy; and information and communications are vital components in the system of administration and control. Communication, it needs to be said, includes much more than messages and the recognizable circuits through which the messages flow. It defines social reality and thus influences the organization of work, the character of technology, the curriculum of the educational system, formal and informal, and the use of "free" time—actually, the basic social arrangements of living. It is a measure of the effectiveness of the control processes that recognition of their existence is only now beginning to be appreciated and understood beyond a tiny, informed circle [Schiller, 1976, p. 3].

Such discoveries do put cosmopolitan communicators' resources "at risk."

Self

Cosmopolitan communication expresses and creates a distinctive concept of self. In one sense, others are treated like natives. All persons are seen as similarly confronting much the same facts of life; as attempting to achieve coherence, coordination, and mystery; as shaped by their local cultures; and as enmeshed—to a greater or lesser degree—in the historical development of the logics of meaning and action of particular social systems. In another sense, cosmopolitan communicators treat others as nonnatives. They are seen as inhabiting very different social worlds, with different moral orders and differing understandings of the facts of life. These differences are treated as real, legitimate, and (usually) valid ways of being human, even if they present an opaque face to one's own social world.

In *Personal Being*, Rom Harré (1984, pp. 75–111) argues that "self" is a social construction, a "theory" that the members of particular societies learn to accept. The practices and stories of one society teach persons that they are indomitable individuals whose personal freedom is the ultimate value; the resources of another society teach persons that they belong to the party or the state, and that the primary value is duty. Clearly these are very different concepts of self, and coordination between individuals from these societies is difficult. But at another level, the individuals in both societies are formed in the same way, through processes of storytelling and enmeshment in social practices.

Geertz (1983, p. 16) acknowledges the difficulty "in coming to grips with the diversity of the ways human beings construct their lives in the act of leading them." He warned of the twin perils of:

> overinterpretation and underinterpretation, reading more into things than reason permits and less into them than it demands. Where the first sort of mistake, telling stories about people only a professor can believe, has been much noted and more than a bit exaggerated, the second, reducing people to ordinary chaps out, like the rest of us, for money, sex, status, and power, never mind anyway when push comes to shove, has been much less so. But the one is as mischievous as the other. We are surrounded . . . neither by Martians nor by less well got-up editions of ourselves; a proposition that holds no matter what "we"—American ethnographers, Moroccan judges, Javanese metaphysicians, or Balinese dancers—we start from.

Society

The "discovery of communication" has, among other things, subverted our confidence in the "reality" of the events and objects of the social world. What appears solid, objective, imposingly factual is shown to be instead fabricated, the product of human activity. Kings, economic systems, power and prestige are not "found" things comprised of their attributes; but "made" things constituted by the work of persons attempting collaboratively to call into being their stories of truth, honor, and dignity. Further, this process is inherently corrigible, often producing events and objects that none of the participants expected or wanted.

Because it has not been institutionalized in any enduring society, cosmopolitan communication has not been practiced enough to generate a set of resources that can be compared to those of modernity or any of the traditional societies. As a result, these characterizations of the resources of cosmopolitan communicators (truth, time, self, and society) should be taken as reasonable inferences on the basis of such examples of cosmopolitan communication practices as are available. However, I believe that a society (re)constructed by cosmopolitan communication will be uniquely self-conscious, and will have a unique concept of itself.

The illusion that has fueled most of human history is that society consists of military might, political institutions, economic systems, artifacts, human rights, and the like. The vocabulary of social action constitutes its epistemology: revolutions are conducted to "gain possession" of the events and objects in society; strenuous efforts are made to "find a place in" the power structure; war is waged to "protect" human rights or an economic system. All of this reifies *products* of social action at the price of obscuring the *practices* that (re)produce the events and objects of the social world.

On the contrary, society consists of stories and skills. The level of technological development, form of economy, network of power relationships, and so on, exert a *shaping* but *not determining* influence on practices. Lives of dignity and honor can be and have been lived in a wide variety of political, economic, and technological circumstances. Contemporary society consists of an open-ended, multilayered texture of stories, many of which are contradictory and incommensurate with each other, from which individuals appropriate that which enables them to achieve coordination, coherence, and mystery. The skill with which individuals appropriate these stories varies, of course, and is directly related to the content of the stories that they appropriate. Some stories instruct their readers to appropriate them with resources not at risk and to treat others as natives; others do not. The differences in these skills, and the way they are exercised, constitute "forms of communication"; and the clusters of events and objects produced by the practice of each of these forms of communication comprise various "ways of being human."

The implications of this concept of society for social planning, or international cooperation, and for the mundane tasks of living a life are in the process of being worked out in practices (e.g., the Kaleidoscope Project, the Hill Center, Milan therapy, and interpretive/critical research) and by some of our most perceptive storytellers (including Rom Harré in *Personal Being, Social Being,* and *Varieties of Realism;* John Shotter, *Selfhood and Accountability;* Kenneth Gergen, *Toward a Transformation in Social Knowledge* and *The Social Construction of the Self;* and Richard Bernstein, *Beyond Objectivism and Relativism*). The work of these authors and their colleagues will, I hope, bring into being the stories of cosmopolitan communication.

10.
The Practicality of
Cosmopolitan Communication

The performance demands of cosmopolitan communication are relatively easy to state but far more difficult to put into practice. Or perhaps the gap between articulation and performance only seems great because there is no historical community in which cosmopolitan communication has been institutionalized as the "normal" practice. These performance demands seem daunting because they remain at the level of abstract statements rather than ingrained traditions; they seem academic achievements rather than intuitive, spontaneous responses to situations; even the examples that can be cited seem fragile, awkward, or unusual, far removed from the somehow "more real" world of rude power and untutored persons. Is it possible to institutionalize cosmopolitan communication as a "normal" part of society? If so, what kind of society would be created by it?

I write this final chapter with a sense of urgency. I believe that the social and material conditions of the contemporary world require an unprecedented increase in the sophisticated practices of communication. To continue to communicate with each other in the forms we inherited from other historical epochs is, I believe, ugly, ineffective, and dangerous. However, there is no inevitability in history; should we devolve into some horrid state of strident neo-traditionalisms, it would not be the first time that our species, poised on the brink of an important new way of being human, lost its collective nerve and determinedly strode backward.

The increased sophistication to which I allude begins with the "discovery" that communication is, and always has been, far more important than has been realized during most of human history.

This discovery quickly yields to the second, that there are important qualitative differences in forms of communication. We do not always do the same thing when we talk (or read or ignore each other). Depending on the manner in which we treat others like natives and put our resources at risk, we achieve coordination, coherence, and mystery in very different ways. Persons sitting beside each other in a theater may well be inhabiting fundamentally different worlds; persons talking to each other may be communicating across the barriers of different forms of communication that separate them far more than, for example, matters of ethnicity, gender, or national background.

Differences in forms of communication comprise different worlds in which we live, different notions of who "we" are, and different technologies for adapting to each other and to the world around us. There have been several distinct "ways of being human" in the past; I believe that the social dynamics that structure the contemporary world necessitate the continuing evolution of yet another.

Each form of communication has characteristics that make it better for some purposes than others. Patriotism and school spirit are best done in ethnocentric communication: Lt. Col. Oliver North's testimony before Congress in 1987 was rhetorically eloquent in the ethnocentric communication that he used; it sounded silly and rather frightening when heard in a cosmopolitan mode. The powerful impact that North made on the audience of the televised hearings resulted from his ability to create a context in which ethnocentric communication seemed appropriate. On the other hand, "progress" and "development" is done best in modernistic communication, where that which is old is always to be sacrificed to that which is new. This is the preferred mode of those with ambitious new plans. The Strategic Arms Limitations Talks (SALT) between the United States and the Soviet Union have been remarkably unsuccessful in achieving disarmament. Why? I suspect that they have persistently used ethnocentric communication for a task that requires cosmopolitan communication.

These observations raise the question of the "fit" between form and task of communication. In what form of communication should divorce decisions be reached, or disputes mediated, or classes taught? Should sermons be preached in neotraditional or in cosmopolitan communication? Can they? If so, how would they be different? In what form of communication should the annual presidential "state of the union" addresses mandated by the Constitution be performed? What differences would it make if parents used cosmopolitan rather than neotraditional communication to explain the "facts of life" to their children? Can advertising for beer, baseball, or political candidates be done in cosmopolitan communication? And, more basic than any of these, in what form of communication should answers be sought for questions like these?

I am not posing the questions of whether cosmopolitan communication *should* be practiced in contemporary society or even whether it *will* be. In my judgment, the social and material conditions of the contemporary world demand the practice of something very much like cosmopolitan communication, and there are an increasing number of individuals who engage in it. The more pressing questions are to what extent, by whom, and in what context cosmopolitan communication will be "privileged" over other forms of communication.

Society consists of a complex mixture of materials, stories, and skills in which not all voices are granted equal hearing, not all skills are equally appreciated, and not all practices are facilitated. The practicality of cosmopolitan communication depends on how its practices fit into this mixture.

It seems fitting to end this book with a meditation on some communication problems, a suggestion, and a comparison of several stories.

Some Problems

1. The performance demands of cosmopolitan communication require an unusual set of skills. To communicate in this manner involves: (1) "reading" one's own stories in

such a way as to be deeply enmeshed in a local culture while being enmeshed in the largest possible system comprised of all local systems; (2) being committed to the task of achieving coordination among incommensurate systems; and (3) being committed to the task of constructing the grounds for comparing what might seem to be incomparable systems. The first of these is a classic paradox; the latter two apparently require, at once, the wisdom of a sage, the patience of a saint, and the skills of a therapist. Such abilities are not in great supply; their combination in particular individuals rare. Is cosmopolitan communication a vision beyond human scale?

The question has teeth. Already there are suggestions that the level of complexity of contemporary society exceeds the ability of many to cope. Some cite the statistics of mental illness, the plight of the homeless, the persistence of a core of "unemployables," political apathy, psychosomatic symptoms, and so on, as results of an individual's inabilities to meet the performance demands of modern society. If those demands are increased in postmodern society, what will the less skilled communicators do? How large a percentage of our society can be counted as "casualities" of an overcomplex system before social institutions crumble?

2. Historically, those who have engaged in cosmopolitan communication have been aware of being abnormal. Whatever their differences (and they are vast!), shamans, sages, and visionaries saw themselves at the fringes of their local culture. If cosmopolitan communication is institutionalized as the "mainstream" of contemporary society—or even as the dominant pattern within a contemporary subculture—how will its practices and resources change? Can cosmopolitan communication be institutionalized as something other than an "alternative" to something else?

3. Many of the conflicts within and among the nations of the world cannot be solved by good intentions. How will cosmopolitan communication impact on these conflicts and problems? How, for example, can the inequitable growth in the world's population be controlled, or the resulting problems of starvation and inequitable standards of living be managed by institutions that practice cosmopolitan communication? Since the rise of stratified society—that is, since the agricultural revolution—ethnocentric communication has seemed "necessary." Is the communication revolution of sufficient magnitude to enable ethnocentric communication, whose limitations are by now all too well known, to be replaced by something else, whose limits and opportunities are only dimly glimpsed?

Cosmopolitan communication seems to depend on the willingness and abilities of all participants to eschew more direct means of achieving their ends, such as violence, coercion, and blackmail. How does a cosmopolitan communicator deal with an opponent who treats their conflict as if it were between incomparable social realities? Is there not some natural tendency to prefer the "easier" forms of communication in conflict in which one is absolved from the responsibility of understanding or caring for the others; in which one may be fully occupied by strategic decisions about how to "win" without looking beyond the particular conflict to issues about how victors and losers might subsequently live together with honor and dignity?

4. Although it originated in the West, modernity has become international. Will modernity produce the same kind of disillusionment in non-Western societies? Because modernity shares some aspects of the Western traditional culture, many disillusioned modernists find it impossible to be deeply enmeshed in Western neotraditional practices. Will non-Westerners be more or less likely to engage in neotraditional forms of communi-

cation? Will non-Westerners create an alternative to cosmopolitan communication as a response to modernity, or will their practices have much the same form as cosmopolitan communication in the contemporary United States?

A Suggestion: Substantive Irony

I suspect that it *is* too much to expect individuals to incorporate all the skills needed for cosmopolitan communication within their repertoire. Fortunately, it is not necessary. Rather, cosmopolitan communication is institutionalized when the material conditions of society are conducive, when the stories of the society facilitate coordination, coherence, and mystery in the cosmopolitan manner, and when the skills for cosmopolitan communication are privileged and disseminated throughout society.

If cosmopolitan communication is institutionalized, individuals will naturally learn the skills necessary to respond spontaneously in a cosmopolitan manner. This process is not a simple one of learning a few facts or techniques; it requires the development of a certain kind of experience.

Consider the paradox of enmeshment both within the local system and the largest possible system. Outside college classrooms, paradoxes must be lived with, treated as "friends" rather than queer oddities to be eliminated. The means of living on friendly terms with paradox is irony, and the development of irony apparently requires a staged sequence of development *within one's own local culture*. First, there is a deep (and exclusive) enmeshment in one's local culture. This enmeshment completes the extrasomatic gestation of the human being and transforms a neonate into a "person." Second, there is a rupture of enmeshment with the local system. This rupture may occur in many ways: alienation; migration from one culture to another; a traumatic personal or social event; or simply the accumulation of too much change. This opens the potential for further development of the person beyond the limits of the local culture. Third, there occurs a withdrawal. This withdrawal may take the form of shamanistic visions, graduate study, penance, vows, and so on. Wisdom and abilities are acquired that enable a qualitatively different encounter with those factors that initially ruptured local enmeshment. Finally, reentry or reenmeshment into the local system, in a way that transcends that system's stories and practices, concludes the process. (These stages, of course, parallel the shamanistic crises and the universal plot of the hero. See Campbell, 1949; 1959.)

Most of the stories humankind has told itself feature the importance of maintaining deep enmeshment in the local system. The ways of willing suspension of disbelief are well modeled and buttressed; "sincerity" and "loyalty" are much-lauded virtues. However, there is emerging a genre of institutions and literature that describes the ways of suspending belief, of reducing enmeshment in local systems. For example, the novels and essays of Hermann Hesse outline a three-stage progression to the goal of a morality that "will embrace all extremes of life in one unified vision":

> The child, he says, is born into a state of unity with all Being. It is only when the child is taught about good and evil that he advances to a second level of individuation characterized by despair and alienation; for he has been made aware of laws and moral codes, but feels incapable of adhering to the arbitrary standards established by conventional religions or moral systems since they exclude so much of what seems perfectly natural. A few men—like the hero of *Siddhartha* or those whom Hesse calls "the Immortals" in *Steppenwolf*—manage

to attain a third level of awareness where they are once again capable of accepting all being [Ziolkowski, 1969, p. xi].

The whole existentialist literature may be seen as training manuals for de-enmeshment. But the most powerful impetuses toward de-enmeshment are opportunities to engage in the practices of happy modernists: questioning assumptions, probing the meaning of things, celebrating change per se, and so on. Habermas' (1979) concept of the "ideal speech community" institutionalizes de-enmeshment by insisting that the assumptions behind all statements are open to question.

De-enmeshment from local systems is a transitory phase, a period in which something is learned preparatory to some other form of life. To be sure, many persons seem to get stuck outside the system, perpetually alienated in an interminable identity crisis. These experiences should serve as cautionary tales, however, rather than models to be emulated.

The story of withdrawal as a preparation for a qualitatively different enmeshment has been told over and again in human history, with different names, places, and events used to tell what is essentially the same story. Campbell (1949) calls it the "monomyth." Of course, the content of what the "hero" acquires in his withdrawal from normal society differs in each story in a way suspiciously fitting the nature of the threat to the local group and the local notion of what is admirable. Sometimes it is great wisdom, more often physical strength or magical power, and sometimes divine authorization. Think of Moses, the Buddha, and Ben Hur.

When the "problem" that produces de-enmeshment is modernity itself, then that which is learned is how to cope with the stories and practices of the strange loop described in Figure 7–2. At least part of that learning is a sensitivity to the longer range consequences of one's own actions. This sensitivity is more a perspective than a truth-claim and can best be said by contrasting three fictional characters: Faust, Gretchen, and Tyler.

Having made his deal with Mephistopheles, Faust fell in love with Gretchen, a traditional young woman deeply enmeshed in the culture of a small German village. He was unaware of the extent that his actions disrupted Gretchen's stories and practices. Events took their usual course and Faust moved on, his attention drawn elsewhere, leaving Gretchen pregnant without benefit of matrimony. Faust learned that Gretchen was to be executed for her immorality. With all the virtuous outrage of an efficacious "modern" person confronted with outmoded tradition, he broke into her cell the night before the execution to rescue her—and was dumbfounded when she refused his efforts to enable her escape.

In the film *Never Cry Wolf* (Amorak Productions, 1983), Tyler was a naturalist assigned to study the behavior of wolves in northern Canada. He described himself as a perpetual "watcher," never involved with life, always excluded from the "doers." While observing the wolves, he came to appreciate their ways and to be very protective of them. Originally terribly vulnerable, he became not only able to live by himself in close proximity to the wolves but to prefer it to the company of those humans who hunt wolves. However, his presence in the wilderness attracted other persons, some with powerful hunting rifles and none of his reverence. One of these shot his wolfly "neighbors." He raised the cubs until they were able to join the pack, then said:

In the end, there were no simple answers, no heroes, no villains—only silence. But it began the moment that I first saw the wolf. By the act of watching them, with the eyes of a man, I had pointed the way for those who followed. The pack returned for the cubs, as there are no orphans among the wolves. And eventually the losses of that autumn became a distant memory. I believe the wolves went off to a wild and distant place somewhere although I don't really know—because I turned away and didn't watch them go.

Gretchen, Faust, and Tyler acted and had an impact on that which they loved. Gretchen was violated and voluntarily submitted to the ministrations of her culture; Faust was puzzled and moved on to act yet again; Tyler was contemplative, seeking ways to preserve that which he loved, even if it meant turning away. Gretchen is a morality story for traditional society; Faust is a cautionary tale for happy modernists; Tyler is an example of cosmopolitan communication.

The least well-modeled aspect of cosmopolitan communication is that of reintegration with the local system and the larger system. No genre of literature gives examples of such integration except in the most fleeting or shadowy manners. Certainly none of the popular cultural heroes—Rambo, James Bond, J. R. Ewing—displays a deep enmeshment in both local and larger systems.

I suspect that some "local" stories are incompatible with cosmopolitan communication. Those deeply enmeshed in them cannot communicate in a cosmopolitan manner unless they go through some process of de-enmeshment, and even then they cannot re-enmesh in their local culture without substantially changing its stories and practices. Revolution or reformation of some local systems may be a minimal requirement for cosmopolitan communication.

The tension between the logics of particular local systems and the ability to be enmeshed in a metastory spanning many local systems is clear in an analysis of a recent event. On June 21, 1985, Shiite Muslims in Lebanon held fifty American citizens hostage. They had killed one hostage and released a number of others, but adamantly refused to free the rest. This event posed a provocation to which the American government had to respond. President Ronald Reagan had been elected in part because his predecessor, Jimmy Carter, was unsuccessful in securing the release of a group of Americans held hostage in Tehran for over a year. President Reagan's forte is political tough-talk. The logic of meaning and action in the president's local system was clear: a great power like the United States cannot allow a blatant provocation like this to occur without retaliation. If an appropriate target for retaliation is found, then the United States must act decisively (these phrases are standard government euphemisms for "kill people").

But even some American news media contained stories that presented the logic of the "other" local system. They noted that the Lebanese involved were in their early twenties and literally had known nothing but war all their lives. One of the pivotal events in their lives was an invasion by Israel that used American weapons and was widely perceived as "backed" by the United States. For a time, American forces were stationed in Lebanon, leaving only after a "patriot" exploded a truckful of bombs at the Marine barracks, killing hundreds of Americans. An American battleship—the New Jersey—shelled Lebanon, and many of the Muslim leaders believe that the American C.I.A. has tried to assassinate them. These young soldiers know they cannot successfully confront the United States in an open military battle, but they can gain national and international attention by taking hostages, and so they do.

Note the problem for Americans posed by understanding—however superficially—

these young, devout, Lebanese soldiers. As long as they could be dismissed as "not natives," different and inferior, they could be described to Americans in Americans' own terms ("fanatics," "terrorists," "irrational beasts"). If their behavior seemed irrational and immoral from an American vantage, the hostage-takers could be perceived as irrational and immoral. If the elaboration of the Muslim moral order sounded like foolish babble to Americans, the speakers could be perceived as foolish and the speech as babble to which no further attention need be paid. But what happens if these persons' worldview is understood as fundamentally different in *content* from the Americans' but essentially the same in that it is the result of a group of persons striving for coherence, coordination, and mystery, coping with the facts of life in a historically unfolding conversation? Now how do Americans respond?

The "modern" response is to determine which set of stories is "right." This consists of treating others as if they were not natives but in so doing placing one's own resources at risk. The result is to adjudicate among the claims and either support retaliation against terrorists or send clandestine support to them.

The cosmopolitan response is more complicated. It consists of finding a frame in which *both* sets of stories can be seen in their own terms and the interaction between them can be described. Translations of the moral orders of the Beirut Shiites and of the American government require a vocabulary that encompasses both. The terms in this vocabulary must be substantially ironic; not an attempt to find and express commonalties in both worldviews but a way of seeing both *as* historically evolving worldviews. "There is a kind of double-talk in irony where we say one thing, but really mean another" (Duncan, 1962, p. 384). Irony is not simply a form of "indirect speech," however, in which *one thing* is said but *another thing* is meant. Although substitution of one referent for another occurs, this is less important than an implied statement about the specificity of reference per se.

Above all, irony affirms antinomy. By indirect statement, it makes an assertion about what things are, but it does more than just that. By subtle mockery, it asserts that things are not only what they seem but something else beside. By combining mockery with indirect statement, it expresses an attitude of simultaneous complicity with and detachment from social conventions; simultaneous doubt and belief; simultaneous seriousness and play.

As a stylistic device, irony "works" by inducing multiple perspectives; by leading the participant through a variety of roles the adoption of which recasts the meaning of what is said:

> Irony holds belief, the tragic moment of truth, open to doubt. It exposes motives which the actors do not know or seek to hide. Roles shift and change. The audience is suddenly involved in the action through being addressed directly. The ironic actor withdraws from action to become an audience to other actors, and even to himself. He comments on the action in asides, or in soliloquy which audiences are allowed to overhear [Duncan, 1962, p. 381].

Cosmopolitan communication is less characterized by stylistic irony—the use of particular figures of speech—as by substantive irony. Where stylistic irony is a pattern of word usage, substantive irony is a form of life that has some of the same properties as the figure of speech. A "good reading" of the tragic intersection of stories in Beirut on June 21, 1985, must hold belief and enmeshment "open to doubt" and be filled with soliloquies and asides. The whole of this reading—simultaneously sympathetic and critical, accepting and interventionist, passionately involved and dramatically distanced—comprises the practice of cosmopolitan communication.

The institutionalization of cosmopolitan communication is a profoundly ironic concept. On one hand, cosmopolitan communication consists of a commitment to achieve comparability and coordination among fundamentally different social systems; on the other, it requires the revolution or reformations of some local systems. Deeply respecting the "otherness" of various cultures and persons, it nonetheless proposes an ironic combination of (tolerant, civil, benign) "social eloquence" and (intolerant, subversive, transformative) "intervention techniques." Like any modernist, cosmopolitan communicators encounter patterns of human socialization they deem as needing to be changed, invoke a powerful social technology, and celebrate the results; like ethnocentric communicators, they act upon but do not place their resources "at risk" to those who are "not natives."

But is this actually "irony"? Is it possible that the concept of cosmopolitan communication presented here is simply muddled, the result of my insufficient emancipation from ethnocentric or modernistic communication? Surely our collective understanding of cosmopolitan communication will increase as more research and more experience accumulate. I suspect, however, that the need to live on friendly terms with paradox and the utility of substantive irony will be major themes of any subsequent theory of communication, of society, and of the human condition.

Some Stories

I can wish for (but cannot envision) a society in which all individuals are socially eloquent, all have access to a powerful array of intervention techniques, and all are simultaneously enmeshed both in the local society and the whole of human culture. I do not know what such a society would talk about, how it would be achieved, what stories of honor and dignity it would tell. It is beyond my imagination.

I can envision a society in which rare individuals (and, more likely, small groups of like-minded individuals) possess the skills for cosmopolitan communication but only seldom find the opportunity to practice them. In fact, this seems a characterization of contemporary society, in which the practice of social eloquence is often taken as "weakness"; in which techniques designed to restructure the pattern of communication among disputants are seen as less effective than a punch in the nose (whether administered physically, verbally, or with an army); and in which ironic enmeshment is seen as a lack of sincerity or commitment.

And yet I can imagine the development of a society in which the requisites for cosmopolitan communication are institutionalized in the society as a whole, such that no single individual has to "possess" them but that they are easily accessible to all individuals. In this society, educational institutions facilitate not only deep enmeshment in the local culture but the staged sequence of rupture, withdrawal, and return. Various interventionist technologies are regularly employed by those embroiled in conflicts, and social eloquence is modeled by at least some of the leading characters in popular books, films, and television. It makes a good story.

Bibliography
Index

Bibliography

Asimov, Isaac. 1981. "The Blind Who Would Lead: God is an American Citizen and Voted for Ronald Reagan." *Macleans* 94 (Feb. 1981): 6.

Barrett, William. 1973. *Time of Need: Forms of Imagination in the Twentieth Century.* New York: Harper & Row.

Bateson, Gregory. 1972. *Steps to an Ecology of Mind.* New York: Ballantine.

Benedict, Ruth. 1934. *Patterns of Culture.* Cambridge: Riverside Press.

Berger, Peter. 1961. *The Precarious Vision.* Garden City, N.Y.: Doubleday.

———. 1979. *The Heretical Imperative.* Garden City, N.Y.: Doubleday.

———. 1982. "From the Crisis of Religion to the Crisis of Secularity." *Religion and America: Spiritual Life in a Secular Age.* Eds. Mary Douglas and Stephen Tipton. Boston: Beacon. 14–22.

———, and Thomas Luckmann. 1966. *The Social Construction of Reality.* Garden City, N.Y.: Doubleday.

Berman, Marshall. 1982. *All that Is Solid Melts into Air: The Experience of Modernity.* New York: Simon & Schuster.

Bernstein, Basil. 1972. "Social Class, Language, and Socialization." *Language and Social Context.* Ed. P. P. Giglioli. Middlesex: Penguin Books, 177–178.

Bernstein, Richard J. 1983. *Beyond Objectivism and Relativism: Science, Hermeneutics, and Praxis.* Philadelphia: University of Pennsylvania Press.

Bettelheim, Bruno. 1976. *The Uses of Enchantment: The Meaning and Importance of Fairy Tales.* New York: Random House.

Bigsby, C. E. 1972. *The Critical Idiom: Dada and Surrealism.* London: Methuen.

Bohannan, Laura. 1984. "Shakespeare in the Bush." *Annual Editions: Anthropology 84/85.* Ed. Elvio Angeloni. Guilford, Conn.: Dushkin Publishing Group, pp. 62–66.

Booth, Wayne C. 1974. *A Rhetoric of Irony.* Chicago: University of Chicago Press.

Branham, Robert J., and W. Barnett Pearce. 1987. "A Contract for Civility: Edward Kennedy's Lynchburg Address." *Quarterly Journal of Speech* 73: 424–43.

Briggs, Jean L. 1970. "Kapluna Daughter." Ed. Peggy Golde. *In Women in the Field.* Berkeley: University of California Press, 2nd ed., 19–44.

Brinton, Crane. 1963. *The Shaping of Modern Thought*. Englewood Cliffs, N.J.: Prentice-Hall, 2nd ed.

Bronowski, Jacob. 1973. *The Ascent of Man*. Boston: Little, Brown.

Burke, Kenneth. 1970. *The Rhetoric of Religion: Studies in Logology*. Berkeley: University of California Press.

Burtt, Edwin A. 1927. *The Metaphysical Foundations of Modern Physical Science*. New York: Harcourt, Brace, Jovanovich.

Calder, Nigel. 1976. *The Human Conspiracy*. New York: Viking.

Campbell, Joseph. 1949. *The Hero with a Thousand Faces*. Princeton: Princeton University Press.

———. 1959. *The Masks of God: Primitive Mythology*. New York: Viking.

———. 1962. *The Masks of God: Oriental Mythology*. New York: Viking.

———. 1964. *The Masks of God: Occidental Mythology*. New York: Viking.

———. 1968. *The Masks of God: Creative Mythology*. New York: Viking.

———. 1972. *Myths to Live By*. New York: Bantam.

Carbaugh, Donal. 1987 "Communication Rules in *Donohue* Discourse." *Research on Language in Social Interaction* 21: 31–62.

Chaffee, Stephen. 1978. "Communication Patterns in the Family: Implications for Adaptability and Change." Paper presented to the Speech Communication Association, Minneapolis, Minn.

Cheng, Chung-Ying. 1980. "Chinese Philosophy and Contemporary Human Communication Theory." Paper presented to the East-West Center, Honolulu.

Chomsky, Noam. 1986. *Knowledge of Language: Its Nature, Origin and Use*. New York: Praeger.

Clavell, James. 1975. *Shogun: A Novel of Japan*. New York: Atheneum.

Cole, John R. 1983. "Scopes and Beyond: Antievolutionism and American Cultures." Ed. Laurie Godfrey. *Scientists Confront Evolution*. New York: Norton, 13–32.

Conant, James B. 1962. "The Changing Scientific Scene 1900–1950." Ed. Walker Gibson. *The Limits of Language*. New York: Hill and Wang, 15–28.

Cox, Harvey. 1965. *The Secular City*. New York: Macmillan.

———. 1984. *Religion in the Secular City: Toward a Postmodern Theology*. New York: Simon & Schuster.

Cronen, Vernon E., and W. Barnett Pearce. 1985. "Toward an Explanation of How the Milan Model Works: An Invitation to a Systemic Epistemology and the Evolution of Family Systems." Eds. David Campbell and Rosalind Draper. *Applications of Systemic Family Therapy: The Milan Approach*. London: Grune and Stratton, Ltd., 69–84.

———, W. Barnett Pearce, and Lonna Snavely. 1979. "A Theory of Rule-Structure and Types of Episodes, and a Study of Perceived Enmeshment in Undesired Repetitive Patterns (URPs)." Ed. Dan Nimmo. *Communication Yearbook III*. New Brunswick, N.J.: Transaction Press, 225–40.

———, W. Barnett Pearce, and Karl Tomm. 1985. "A Dialectical View of Personal Change." Eds. K. J. Gergen and K. E. Davis. *The Social Construction of the Person*. New York: Springer-Verlag, 203–24.

Cushman, Donald P., and Dudley D. Cahn, Jr. 1985. *Communication in Interpersonal Relationships*. Albany: State University of New York Press.

Dance, Frank E. X. 1970. "The 'Concept' of Communication." *Journal of Communication* 20: 201–10.

———. 1982. *Human Communication Theory: Comparative Essays*. New York: Harper & Row.

Dizard, Wilson P. 1982. *The Coming Information Age: An Overview of Technology, Economics, and Politics*. New York: Longman.

Duncan, Hugh Dalziel. 1962. *Communication and Social Order*. New York: Oxford University Press.

Durant, Will, and Ariel Durant. 1965. *The Age of Voltaire*. New York: Simon & Schuster (vol. 9 of *The Story of Civilization*).

Eliade, Mircea. 1959. *Cosmos and History: The Myth of the Eternal Return*. New York: Harper.

———. 1961. *The Sacred and the Profane: The Nature of Religion*. New York: Harper & Row.

Farb, Peter. 1975. *Word Play*. New York: Bantam.

———. 1978. *Man's Rise to Civilization: The Cultural Ascent of the Indians of North America*. New York: Bantam, 2nd edition.

Fay, Brian. 1975. *Social Theory and Political Practice*. London: George Allen & Unwin.

Follett, Ken. 1985. *The Modigliani Scandal*. New York: Signet.

Foucault, Michel. 1970. *The Order of Things: An Archeology of the Human Sciences*. New York: Pantheon.

Fromm, Erich. 1962. *Beyond the Chains of Illusion: My Encounter with Marx and Freud*. New York: Simon & Schuster.

Frye, Northrop. 1982. *The Great Code: The Bible and Literature*. New York: Harcourt, Brace, Jovanovich.

Geertz, Clifford. 1973. *The Interpretation of Cultures*. New York: Basic Books.

———. 1980. Review of Donald Symon's, *The Evolution of Human Sexuality*. *New York Times Review of Books*, Jan. 24, 1980.

———. 1983. *Local Knowledge*. New York: Basic Books.

Gerbner, George. 1966. "On Defining Communication: Still Another View." *Journal of Communication* 16: 99–103.

Gergen, Kenneth J. 1982. *Toward Transformation in Social Knowledge*. New York: Springer-Verlag.

Gibson, Walker. Ed. 1962. *The Limits of Language*. New York: Hill and Wang.

Giddens, Anthony. 1979. *Central Problems in Social Theory*. Berkeley: University of California Press.

Gilligan, Carol. 1982. *In a Different Voice*. Cambridge: Harvard University Press.

Grene, Marjorie. 1974. *The Knower and the Known*. Berkeley: University of California Press.

Gribbon, John. 1984. *In Search of Schrodinger's Cat*. New York: Bantam.

Habermas, Jürgen. 1979. *Communication and the Evolution of Society*. Boston: Beacon.

Harré, Rom. 1984. *Personal Being*. Cambridge: Harvard University Press.

Harris, David. 1984. "Pete Rozell: The Man Who Made Football an American Obsession." *New York Times Magazine*, Jan. 15, pp. 12–14.

Harris, Linda M., Alison Alexander, Sheila McNamee, Marsha Stanback, and Kyung-Wha Kang. 1984. "Forced Cooperation: Violence as a Communicative Act." Ed.

Sari Thomas. *Communicaton Theory and Interpersonal Interaction*, vol. 2. Norwood, N.J.: Ablex. 20–32.

Harris, Marvin. 1979. *Cultural Materialism: The Struggle for a Science of Culture*. New York: Random House.

Hesse, Hermann. 1943/1969. *Magister Ludi: The Glass Bead Game*. New York: Bantam.

Hoffman, Daniel. 1965. "In the Beginning." Eds. Robert Wallace and James G. Taaffe. *Poems on Poetry: The Mirror's Garland*. New York: Dutton. 283–285.

Holton, Gerald. 1970. "The Roots of Complementarity." *Daedelus* 99: 1015–55.

Homans, George C. 1967. *The Nature of Social Science*. New York: Harcourt, Brace & World.

Huizinga, Johann. 1954. *The Waning of the Middle Ages*. Garden City, N.Y.: Doubleday.

Hunter, James D. 1981. "The New Religions: Demodernization and the Protest against Modernity." Ed. Bryan R. Wilson. *The Social Impact of New Religious Movements*. New York: The Rose of Sharon Press. 1–19.

Hymes, Dell. 1962. "The Ethnography of Speaking." Eds. T. Gladwin and W. T. Sturtevant. *Anthropology and Human Behavior*. Washington, D.C.: Anthropological Society of Washington. 13–53.

James, William. 1881. "Reflex Action and Theism." Ed. Walker Gibson. *The Limits of Language*. New York: Hill and Wang. 3–9.

Janik, Alan, and Stephen Toulmin. 1973. *Wittgenstein's Vienna*. New York: Simon & Schuster.

Jaspers, Karl. 1960. *The Way to Wisdom*. New Haven: Yale University Press.

Johnston, William M. 1972. *The Austrian Mind*. Berkeley: University of California Press.

Kang, Kyung-wha, and W. Barnett Pearce. 1984. "The Place of Transcultural Concepts in Communication Theory and Research, with a Case Study of Reticence." *Communication* 9: 79–96.

Kaplan, Abraham. 1964. *The Conduct of Inquiry*. San Francisco: Chandler.

Katriel, Tamar, and Gerry Philipsen. 1981. "What We Need Is Communication: 'Communication' as a Cultural Category in Some American Speech." *Communication Monographs* 48: 302–317.

Kaufmann, Walter. 1961. *Critique of Religion and Philosophy*. Garden City, N.Y.: Anchor/Doubleday.

———. 1980. *Discovering the Mind: Goethe, Kant, and Hegel*. New York: McGraw-Hill.

Kline, Morris. 1980. *Mathematics: The Loss of Certainty*. New York: Oxford University Press.

Koestler, Arthur. 1964. *The Act of Creation*. New York: Dell.

———. 1978. *Janus: A Summing-up*. New York: Random House.

Krauthammer, Charles. 1983. "Deep Down, We're All Alike, Right? Wrong." *Time*, Aug. 15, 1983.

Kuhn, Thomas S. 1970. *The Structure of Scientific Revolutions*. Chicago: University of Chicago Press, 2nd edition.

LaHay, Tim. 1981. Quoted by Curtis Lamont, "Answering the Moral Majority." *The Humanist* 19: 13.

Lannamann, John W. 1980. "An Explanation and Empirical Investigation of Relationship Development." Master's Thesis. Amherst: University of Massachusetts.

Le Corbeiller, Phillipe. 1966. "Introduction." *The Languages of Science: A Survey of Techniques of Communication*. Greenwich, Conn.: Fawcett.

Lee, Richard. 1984. "Eating Christmas in the Kalahari." Ed. Elvio Angeloni. *Annual Editions: Anthropology 84/85*. Guilford, Conn.: Dushkin Publishing Group. 18–24.

Le Guin, Ursula K. 1979. *The Language of the Night: Essays on Fantasy and Science Fiction*. New York: Putnam's.

Lévi-Strauss, Claude. 1964. *The Raw and the Cooked*. New York: Harper & Row.

Lewontin, Richard C. 1983. "Introduction." Ed. Laurie Godfrey. *Scientists Confront Creationism*. New York: Norton.

Lippy, Charles H. 1977. "Sympathy Cards and Death." *Theology Today* 34: 167–77.

Littlejohn, Stephen W. 1982. "An Overview of Contributions to Human Communication Theory from other Disciplines." Ed. Frank E. X. Dance. *Human Communication Theory*. New York: Harper & Row. 243–85.

Lyons, John O. 1978. *The Invention of the Self: The Hinge of Consciousness in the 18th Century*. Carbondale: Southern Illinois University Press.

MacDonell, Diane. 1986. *Theories of Discourse: An Introduction*. Oxford: Blackwell.

MacIntyre, Alisdair. 1981. *After Virtue: A Study in Moral Theory*. Notre Dame, Ind.: University of Notre Dame Press.

Macquarrie, John. 1974. "Creation and Environment." Eds. David and Eileen Spring. *Ecology and Religion in History*. New York: Harper & Row. 32–47.

Malinowski, Bronislaw. 1923. "The Problem of Meaning in Primitive Languages." Eds. C. K. Ogden and I. A. Richards. *The Meaning of Meaning*. New York: Harcourt, Brace and World. 296–336.

Marsden, George M. 1982. "Preachers of Paradox: The Religious New Right in Historical Perspective." Eds. Mary Douglas and Stephen Tipton. *Religion and America: Spiritual Life in a Secular Age*. Boston: Beacon. 150–68.

Marsh, Peter, Elizabeth Rosser, and Rom Harré. 1978. *The Rules of Disorder*. Boston: Routledge and Kegan Paul.

Maslow, Abraham H. 1964. *Religions, Values, and Peak-Experiences*. New York: Viking.

———. 1966. *The Psychology of Science*. South Bend, Ind.: Gateway.

Masuda, Yoneji. 1981. *The Information Society as Post-Industrial Society*. Tokyo: Institute for the Information Society.

Matson, Floyd, and Ashley Montagu. 1967. "Introduction." Eds. Floyd Matson and Ashley Montagu. *The Human Dialogue: Perspectives on Communication*. New York: The Free Press. 1–11.

Maturana, Humberto. 1978. "Biology of Language: The Epistemology of Reality." Eds. George A. Miller and Elizabeth Lenneberg. *Psychology and Biology of Language and Thought*. New York: Academic Press. 27–63.

McCarthy, Thomas. 1979. "Translator's Introduction." Jürgen Habermas. *Communication and the Evolution of Society*. Boston: Beacon. vii–xxiv.

McKeon, Richard. 1957. "Communication, Truth and Society." *Ethics* 67: 89–99.

McNeill, William H. 1982. "The Care and Repair of Public Myth." *Foreign Affairs* 61: 1–13.

Miller, George A. 1986. "What We Say and What We Mean." *New York Times Book Review*, Jan. 26, p. 37.

Miller, Gerald R. 1966. "On Defining Communication: Another Stab." *The Journal of Communication* 16:88–98.

Miller, Jonathan. 1983. *States of Mind*. New York: Pantheon.

Mills, C. Wright. 1959. *The Sociological Imagination*. London: Oxford University Press.

Morton, Kathryn. 1984. "The Story-Telling Animal." *New York Times Book Review*, Dec. 23, pp. 1–2.

Nagel, Ernest, and James R. Newman. 1958. *Gödel's Proof*. New York: New York University Press.

Narula, Uma, and W. Barnett Pearce. 1986. *Development as Communication: A Perspective on India*. Carbondale: Southern Illinois University Press.

Nisbet, Robert. 1980. *History of the Idea of Progress*. New York: Basic Books.

Nordstrom, Louis. 1980. "The Wayward Mysticism of Alan Watts." *Philosophy East and West* 30: 381–401.

Norris, Christopher. 1982. *Deconstruction: Theory and Practice*. London: Methuen.

Otto, Rudolf. 1923. *The Idea of the Holy; An Inquiry into the Non-Rational Factor in the Idea of the Divine and Its Relation to the Rational*. London: Oxford University Press, rev. ed.

Pearce, W. Barnett, Stephen W. Littlejohn, and Alison Alexander. 1987. "The New Christian Right and the Humanist Response: Reciprocated Diatribe." *Communication Quarterly* 35: 171–192.

―――, Stephen W. Littlejohn, and Alison Alexander. In press. "The Quixotic Quest for Civility: An Analysis of the Interaction Between the New Christian Right and Secular Humanists." Eds. Jeffrey Hadden and Anson Shupe. *Religion and Politics*. N.Y.: Paragon Press.

Peckham, Morse. 1962. *Beyond the Tragic Vision: The Quest for Identity in the Nineteenth Century*. New York: Braziller.

Pfeiffer, John E. 1977. *The Emergence of Society: A Prehistory of the Establishment*, New York: McGraw-Hill.

Philipsen, Gerry. 1975. "Speaking 'Like a Man' in Teamsterville: Culture Patterns of Role Enactment in an Urban Neighborhood." *Quarterly Journal of Speech* 61: 13–22.

Popper, Karl R. 1972. *Objective Knowledge: An Evolutionary Approach*. Oxford: Clarendon Press.

Raman, V. V. 1984. "Why It's So Important That Our Students Learn More About Science." *Chronicle of Higher Education*, April 4, p. 80.

Rapoport, Anatol. 1953. *Operational Philosophy*. New York: Harper & Row.

Redfield, Robert. 1953. *The Primitive World and Its Transformations*. Ithaca: Cornell University Press.

Reich, Robert. 1987. "Us vs. Them." *Common Cause Magazine* 13 (Jan./Feb.): 12–13.

Ricoeur, Paul. 1981. Ed. John B. Thompson. *Hermeneutics and the Human Sciences*. Cambridge: Cambridge University Press.

Roof, Wade Clark, and William McKinney. 1987. *American Mainline Religion: Its Changing Shape and Future*. New Brunswick, N.J.: Rutgers University Press.

Rorty, Richard. 1979. *Philosophy and the Mirror of Nature*. Princeton: Princeton University Press.

―――. Ed. 1967. "Introduction." *The Linguistic Turn: Recent Essays in Philosophical Method*. Chicago: University of Chicago Press. 1–39.

Rosenthal, Robert. 1976. *The Experimenter Effects in Behavioral Research*. New York: Irvington.

Ross, Ralph. 1957. *Symbols and Civilization: Science, Morals, Religion, Art*. New York: Harcourt, Brace and World.

Rossiter, Charles M., Jr., and W. Barnett Pearce. 1975. *Communicating Personally: A Theory of Interpersonal Communication and Human Relationships*. Indianapolis: Bobbs-Merrill.

Rubin, Lillian. 1976. *Worlds of Pain: Life in the Working Class Family*. New York: Basic Books.

Sagan, Carl. 1980. *Cosmos*. New York: Random House.

Sahlins, Marshall. 1976. *Culture and Practical Reason*. Chicago: University of Chicago Press.

Schaeffer, Franky. 1982. *A Time for Anger: The Myth of Neutrality*. Westchester, Ill.: Crossway Books.

Schank, Robert. 1975. *Conceptual Information Processing*. Amsterdam: North-Holland.

Schelling, Thomas C. 1978. *Micromotives and Macrobehavior*. New York: Norton.

Schiller, Herbert I. 1976. *Communication and Cultural Domination*. White Plains, N.Y.: International Arts and Science Press.

Schramm, Wilbur. 1954. Ed. "How Communication Works." *The Process and Effects of Mass Communication*. Urbana: University of Illinois Press. 3–26.

———. 1971. "The Nature of Communication Between Humans." Ed. Wilbur Schramm and D. F. Roberts. *The Process and Effects of Mass Communication*. Urbana: University of Illinois Press. 3–53. rev. ed.

Searle, John R. 1969. *Speech Acts: An Essay in the Philosophy of Language*. London: Cambridge University Press.

Selvini-Palazzoli, Mara, Luigi Boscolo, Gianfranco Cecchin, and Giuliana Prata. 1980. "Hypothesizing-Circularity-Neutrality: Three Guidelines for the Conductor of the Session," *Family Process* 19: 3–12.

Severin, Timothy. 1973. *Vanishing Primitive Man*. New York: American Heritage.

Shands, Harley Cecil. 1971. *The War with Words: Structure and Transcendence*. The Hague: Mouton.

Shank, Robert. 1975. "The Role of Memory in Language Processing." Ed. C. N. Cofer. *The Structure of Human Memory*. San Francisco: W. H. Freeman. 162–89.

Shannon, Claude, and Warren Weaver. 1949. *The Mathematical Theory of Communication*. Urbana: University of Illinois Press.

Shapiro, Michael J. 1984. *Language and Politics*. New York: New York University Press.

Shaw, George Bernard. 1956. *John Bull's Other Island*. As cited by Colin Wilson. *The Outsider*. New York: Delta.

Sheehan, George. 1984. "Marathons and the Human Race." *Time*, April 16, unpaginated advertising supplement.

Southern, R. W. 1953. *The Making of the Middle Ages*. New Haven: Yale University Press.

Stanback, Marsha, and W. Barnett Pearce. 1981. "Talking to 'the Man': Some Communication Strategies Used by Subordinants and Their Implications for Intergroup Relations." *Quarterly Journal of Speech* 67: 21–30.

Stapledon, William Olaf. 1939. *Philosophy and Living*. Harmondsworth: Penguin.

Steiner, George. 1967. *Language and Silence: Essays 1958–1966*. New York: Atheneum.

Tomm, Karl, M.D. 1987. "Interventive Interviewing: Part I. Strategizing as a Fourth Guideline for the Therapist." *Family Process* 26 (1): 3–13.

———. 1987. "Interventive Interviewing: Part II. Reflexive Questioning as a Means to Enable Self-Healing." *Family Process* 26 (2): 167–83.

Tuchman, Barbara W. 1966. *The Proud Tower*. New York: Macmillan.

———. 1978. *A Distant Mirror: The Calamitous 14th Century*. New York: Knopf.

———. 1984. *The March of Folly*. New York: Knopf.

Turnbull, Colin. 1961. *The Forest People: A Study of the Pygmies of the Congo*. New York: Simon & Schuster.

———. 1976. *Man in Africa*. Garden City, N.Y.: Doubleday.

Ury, William and Roger Fisher. 1983. *Getting to Yes: Negotiating an Agreement without Giving In*. New York: Penguin.

Voget, Fred W. 1975. *A History of Ethnology*. New York: Holt, Rinehart and Winston.

Von Vorys, Karl. 1975. *Democracy without Consensus*. Princeton: Princeton University Press.

Watzlawick, Paul. 1976. *How Real Is Real? Confusion, Disinformation, Communication*. New York: Vintage.

Wheelwright, Philip Ellis. 1962. *Metaphor and Reality*. Bloomington: Indiana University Press.

White, Lynn. Jr. 1967. "The Historical Roots of Our Ecological Crises." Eds. David and Eileen Spring. *Ecology and Religion in History*. New York: Harper. 15–31.

Whitehead, Alfred North. 1978. Cited by Ellen J. Langer, "Rethinking the Role of Thought in Social Interaction." Eds. John Harvey, William Ickes, and Robert Kidd. *New Directions in Attribution Research*. vol. 2, pp. 36–53. New York: Wiley.

Williams, Frederick. 1982. *The Communications Revolution*. Beverly Hills: Sage.

Wilson, Colin. 1956. *The Outsider*. New York: Delta.

Wittgenstein, Ludwig. 1921. *Tractatus Logico-philosophicus*. London: Routledge and Keegan Paul.

Ziolkowski, Theodore. 1969. "Foreword." Hermann Hesse, *Magister Ludi: The Glass Bead Game*. New York: Holt, Rinehart and Winston.

Index

Alcoholic's strange loop, 47–48
Anorexia nervosa, 21–22
Asimov, Isaac, 157
Austin, J. L., xix

Bacon, Francis: observations, 8; creed, 138
Bancroft, Hubert Howe, 58
Barrett, William, 164
Bateson, 54–57, 154
Benedict, Ruth, 74
Berelson, Bernard, xix
Berger, Peter, 157, 159, 177; and Luckman, 18
Berman, Marshall, 135, 150, 152–53, 155
Bernstein, Basil, 92
Bernstein, Richard, 151, 190, 191
Bettelheim, Bruno, 154
Bigsby, 164
Bohannan, Laura, 128–29
Bohr, Niels, 186, 192
Booth, Wayne, 67–68, 82
Branham, Robert: and Pearce, 62, 177
Briggs, Jean L., 110–11
Brinton, Crane, 29, 135, 138, 141–42
Bronowski, Jacob, 129–30, 160
Burke, Kenneth, 73
Burtt, Edwin, 12

Cahn, Dudley, 119
Calder, Nigel, 109, 139
Campbell, Joseph: *The Hero* (1949), 34, 182, 199–200; *Primitive Mythology* (1959), 34, 60, 71, 104–5, 107, 109, 154, 180; *Oriental Mythology* (1962), 127–28; *Occidental Mythology* (1964), 28; *Creative Mythology* (1968), 82, 84; *Myths to Live By* (1972), 112, 154
Carbaugh, Donal, 92; and son, 100
Chaffee, Stephen, 66
Cheng, Chung-Ying, xviii
Chomsky, Noam, 16
Christianity: as a culture, 136, 138–42. *See also* Modernity
Churchill, Winston, 51
Clavell, James, 114–15
Coevolution, xiv, xvii; of resources and practices, 24–25; of forms and ways, 91–95; historical, 192
Coherence, xx; definition of, 21–22, 67–76; in monocultural communication, 96; in ethnocentric communication, 119; in modernistic communication, 145; among "outsiders," 164; among relativists, 165; in cosmopolitan communication, 167, 170
Cole, John, 159
Communication: evaluation of, xiii-xiv, 112, 196; forms of, xiv-xvii, xx, 11, 29, 91–95, 195; as primary social process, xvi-xvii, 11; as poetic, xvi, 36; as constitutive, xvi-xvii, xxi, 9, 11, 15, 18–19, 31–32; discovery of, xvii, 3–10, 18, 25, 31–32; technology of, xvii-xviii, 4–5; discipline of, xviii, 7–10; economics and politics, xviii-xix, 4, 6–7; development as a profession, xix-xx;

revolution, xx, 3, 5–6, 10, 170; models of, 8–10, 19, 23–25; as a perspective, 23–25, 31, 36; cosmopolitan, 95, 167–71, 173; monocultural, 96–102, 112–17; ethnocentric, 118–123; modernistic, 142–47; neotraditional, 162–63

Conant, James, 82

Conflict: unnecessary, xiv; management, xiv; normal sequence of 186–88

Confucianism, 28–29

Context, xv, 46–48; change, 46–47; stable hierarchy, 47; strange loop, 47–48, 148–49; in monocultural communication 96–97; of modernity, 135–36, 145

Coordination, xx, 14, 32–66; definition of, 20, 32–33; conjoint, nonsummative, asymmetrical, 43–45; distinctively human features, 55–59; difficulties in, 59–66; in monocultural communication, 97, 168; in ethnocentric communication, 118–19, 129, 168; in modernistic communication, 145, 168; among neotraditionalists, 162; among "outsiders," 164; among relativists, 165; in cosmopolitan communication, 168–69

Cox, Harvey, 137, 157, 159–60

Creationism, 162–63

Cronen, Vernon: Pearce and Snavely, 20, 128; Pearce and Tomm, 182, 184

Culture(s): India, xvi, 7, 27, 29–31, 106–7; China, xvii; Greece, xviii-xix, 16; England, xix, 62–63, 75–76; Korea, 25, 27–29, 113; feudal Europe, 25–26, 125–26; Thai, 26–27; United States, 26–29, 121, 131–33, 144, 157; Titsany, 27; Shoshone, 58, 109; Malaysia, 70, 136; Inuit, 75, 110–11, 179; modern, 77–78; Bushmen, 111–12; Japan, 114–16; Australian (aborigine), 116–17; Kuwait, 121–22; Tiv, 128–29; Lebanon, 201–2

Cushman, Donald, 119

Dance, Frank E. X., 10

Darwin, Charles, 55; evolutionists, 162–63

Deconstruction, 80

Democratization, xviii, 169–70

Descartes, René: "*cogito.*" 8; self, 191

Dewey, John, xix, 16

Dizard, Wilson, 5

Domestic violence, 39

Donaldson, Samuel, 93

Duncan, Hugh Dalziel, 202

Durant: and Durant, 139

Eliade, Mircea, 107, 108, 126, 152

Eloquence, 167–68, 170–71, 178, 186, 188–89

Encyclopaedia Britannica, 5, 52

Enmeshment, 59, 71–72, 77, 83, 86, 105–7, 152–53, 199–203

Ethnocentric: definition of, 120. *See also* Communication

Farb, Peter, 51, 55–56, 58, 75, 109

Fay, Brian, 16, 171

Follett, Ken, 64–65

Foucault, Michel, 80

Foundationalism, 8–9, 21, 32, 36, 137–38, 145, 151

Freeman, Sally, 186–88

Fromm, Erich, 154

Frye, Northrop, 136

Functionalism, 20

Galileo, 77, 113, 129

Game theory, 63–64

Geertz, Clifford, 72, 74–75, 105–6, 178, 191–92, 194

Gerbner, George, 10

Gergen, Kenneth, 16

Giddens, Anthony, 66

Gilligan, Carol, 92

Gödel, Kurt, 9

Goethe, Johann Wolfgang von, 150, 152

Greek philosophers, xix, 123; Aristotle, 5, 55, 92; Archimedes, 8; Plato, 8; Parmenides, 16–17; Heraclitus, 16, 192

Grene, Marjorie, 12

Gribbon, John, 9, 186

Habermas, Jürgen, xxi, 23

Harré, Rom, 57–58, 99, 127, 194

Harris, David, 161

Harris, Linda, et al., 39

Harris, Marvin, 157

Hayakawa, S. I., xix

Hermeneutic, 49, 167. *See also* Interpretive social science

Hesse, Hermann, 165–66, 199–200

Heyerdahl, Thor, 36

Hill Adolescent Center, 182–84

Hoffman, Daniel G., 75

Holton, Gerald, 192

Homans, George, 16

Homosexuality, 34–36, 44–45

Hovland, Carl, xix
Huizinga, Johann, 125–26
Human condition: coordination, 49–59; coherence, 76; mystery, 86–87; definition of, 86–87; forms of, 94; in primitive society, 102–12; in traditional society, 124–28, 133; in modern society, 134–35, 147–55; neotraditionalism, 156–62; "outsiders," 163–64; relativists, 164–66; inherent tension in, 167–68
Hunter, James, 157
Hutchins, Robert M., 191
Hymes, Dell, 92

Incommensuribility, 62–63, 186
Ineffability, 80–82
Interpretive social science, 16, 171–78
Irony, xix, 199–203

Janik, Alan: and Toulmin, 15, 85
James, William, 16, 73–74
Jaspers, Karl, 191
Jennes, D., 110
Johnston, William, 94, 170

Kaleidoscope Project, 184–85
Kang, Kyung-wha: and Pearce, 28
Kaplan, Abraham, 12, 36
Katriel, Tamar: and Philipsen, 144
Katz, Elihu, xix
Kaufmann, Walter, 85, 165
Kepler, Johannes, 77, 142
Kline, Morris, 151
Koestler, Arthur, 12, 154
Korzybski, Alfred, xix, 67
Krauthammer, Charles, 132
Kuhn, Thomas, 11–14, 143, 151

LaHay, Tim, 158
Lang, Peter: and Little, 15
Language, 67–68, 72–73; snares of, 79–80; "second liberation," 82–83, 85
Lao Tze, 77
Lasswell, Harold, xix
Lazarsfield, Paul, xix
LeCorbeiller, Phillipe, 7
Lee, Richard, 111–12
LeGuin, Ursula, 85–86, 154
Lévi-Strauss, Claude, 16
Lewontin, Richard, 162
Liberation: from mere facticity, 72–76;

"second liberation," 82–86; modern technology for, 147; "liberation theology," 158; relativism, 165
"Linguistic turn," 15–18
Lippy, Charles, 80
Littlejohn, Stephen, 7–8
Logical force, 22–23, 39–40, 79; prefigurative force, 40, 96, 119, 122; contextual force, 40, 96, 119, 122, 159; reflexive force, 142, 181; practical force, 40, 181; implicative force, 40; logic of interaction, 41–43, 162–63
Lyons, John, 109

McCarthy, Thomas, xxi
MacDonell, Diane, 17
MacIntyre, Alisdair, 191
McKeon, Richard, 3, 23, 25
McNeill, William, 76
Macquarrie, John, 136
Malinowski, Bronslaw, 97–98, 106
Marines, 21
Marsden, George, 157
Marsh, Peter: and Rosser, and Harré, 63
Marx, Karl, xvii, 77, 139, 153, 147
Maslow, Abraham, 98, 101, 161–62
Masuda, Yoneji, 5
Matson, Floyd: and Montagu, 3, 191
Maturana, Humberto, 14–15
Mead, George Herbert, xix, 16
Meaning and action: interpretive (re)construction of, 16; as "resources and practices," 23; descriptions of, 172
Messages: mood-signs, 54, 56–57, 59, 103–4; simulated mood-signs, 54–55; metacommunication, 55
Milan method of family therapy, 180–82
Miller, George, 10, 19
Miller, Jonathan, 55–59
Mills, C. Wright, 143
Mindlessness, 96–97, 99, 102, 112–13, 117, 145–46, 185
Modernity, xviii, 94, 134–42; development of, 134–39; structure of, 139–42; disillusionment with, 142; happy modernists, 147
Monocultural, xviii, 96–97, 104–12. *See also* Communication
Moral order, xiii, xv, xx, 34, 55, 57–59, 62, 65, 79; monocultural, 104–5; ethnocentric,

126–28; modernistic, 148–55; relativism, 164–65
Morris, Desmond, 57–58
Morton, Kathryn, 69
Mystery, xx, 77–78; definition of, 22–23; "second liberation," 82–86; ironic tension, 83; in monocultural communication, 97; in ethnocentric communication, 120–21; in modernistic communication, 147; among "outsiders," 164; among neotraditionalists, 165; in cosmopolitan communication, 167, 170

Nagel, Ernest: and Newman, 9
Narula, Uma: and Pearce, 30
National development, 29–31
Neotraditional, 156–62. *See also* Coherence; Mystery
New Christian Right, 62, 158–60, 172, 178
Newton, Sir Isaac, 11–12, 16, 139
New York Times, 81, 106, 121, 132, 187
New York Times Magazine, 160
Nietzsche, Friedrich, 165
Nisbet, Robert, 152
Nordstrom, Louis, 160
Norris, Christopher, 80

Others treated as: natives, 113–17, 190; nonnatives, 129–33
Otto, Rudolph, 99
"Outsiders," 163–64
Oxford Times, 63

Paradigm(s), 11–14, 17–18. *See also* Kuhn, Thomas
Paradox, 85, 198; liar's paradox, 151. *See also* Irony
Pattern(s): self-sustaining scripts, xiv; of relationships in contemporary society, xv, xx, 20; of communication, xv, 3, 9, 11, 13, 19, 22, 32–34, 38, 92; of coordination, xx, 23, 28, 55, 57, 71, 95
Pearce, W. Barnett: and Littlejohn, and Alexander, 62, 177
Peckham, Morse, 73
Pfeiffer, John, 124
Philipsen, Gerry, 92
Philosophy of science, 11–13, 15; "scientific method," 11–12, 143; natural science, 137; as a threat, 161–63; model of interpretive/critical research, 171–78

Popper, Karl, 143
Postmodern society, xx, 94, 159–60
Poststructuralism, xx, 17, 80
Practices: definition of, 23–24; as expression, 39–45; as (re)constructive, 45; relationship with resources, 95, 105–12; monocultural, 97, 99, 104–5; ethnocentric, 119–20, 131; modernistic, 136, 146; cosmopolitan, 185–89
Professors, xvi
Progress, 142, 151

Raman, V. V., 162–63
Rapoport, Anatol, 11
Rasmussen, Knud, 180
Rationalism, 28–29
Rationality, 12–13, 23, 44, 151
(Re)construction: definition of, 24–25; applications, 25–31; of resources, 45, 92
Redding, Charles, xix
Redfield, Robert, 103–4
Reich, Robert, 120
Relativism, 164–66
Resources: definition of, 23–24, 39; expressed, 39–45; (re)constructed, 45; at risk, 92–94, 144, 147; monocultural, 97, 104–5; not at risk, 112–13, 128, 189; ethnocentric, 119–21; modernistic, 136, 146; cosmopolitan, 190–95. *See also* Practices
Rhetoric, xvii–xviii, xix, 9
Ricoeur, Paul, 17
Rockwell, Norman, 168
Roof, Clark Wade: and McKinney, 170
Rorty, Richard, 8, 15–17
Rosenthal, Robert, 16
Rubin, Lillian, 65
Russell, Bertrand, 15, 51

Sagan, Carl, 160
Sahlins, Marshall, 26
Saussure, Ferdinand de, 16
Schaeffer, Franky, 158–59
Schelling, Thomas, 60
Schiller, Herbert, 193
Schramm, Wilbur, xix, 19
Schutz, Alfred, 16
Searle, John, 74, 78, 80–81
Second-order cybernetics, 60–62, 68
Secular humanists, 62, 158, 172–78
Secularism, 157–58
Selvini-Palazzoli, Mara: et al., 181

Severin, Timothy, 120, 123
Shame, xv
Shands, Harley Cecil, 72, 83, 87
Shank, Robert, 119
Shannon, Claude, xix; and Weaver, 10, 51
Shapiro, Michael J., 17
Shaw, George Bernard, 163–64
Sheeham, George, 161
Smith, Jedediah, 58
Smith, William Robertson, 103
Social construction of reality, xvi, 17–19;
    fallibility of, 23
Sophists, xix, 10
Southern, R. W., 127
Stanback, Marsha: and Pearce, 170
Stapledon, William Olaf., 99
Steiner, George, 78, 82, 85
Story, 68–69; finished, xvii; storytellers, xvii,
    xx, 21, 49; related to practices, 21, 26;
    underdetermined by facts, 21, 84, 193;
    "good readings" of, 68–76, 78, 83, 92;
    institutionalization of, 69–70
Strange loops: definition of, 47. *See also*
    Context
Structuralism, 16–17

Theatre, 48–49, 177
Toles, Tom, 33
Tonnies, Ferdinand, 94

Translation, 178, 189
Truth, 137, 190. *See also* Foundationalism
Tuchman, Barbara, 51, 113, 126, 151
Turnbull, Colin, 110, 161
Twain, Mark, 58

Unintended consequences, 64–66
Unwanted repetitive patterns (URPs), 20–21,
    39, 128
Ury, William: and Fisher, 191

Verne, Jules, 5
Voget, Fred, 123
Von Vorys, Karl, 170

Wails, 164. *See also* "Outsiders"
Watson, J. B., 16
Watzlawick, Paul, 148
Wheelwright, Philip, 82, 85, 192
White, Lynn, Jr., 137–39
Whitehead, Alfred North, 96–97
Wichelns, Herbert, xix
Wiener, Norbert, xix
Williams, Frederick, 5
Willing suspension: of disbelief, 71–72, 79,
    81–82, 92, 182, 199; of belief, 83, 92, 177;
    irony of both, 202–3
Wilson, Colin, 146, 163
Wittgenstein, Ludwig, xiii, 15, 18, 67, 82, 99

W. Barnett Pearce received his Ph.D. in interpersonal communication from Ohio University in 1969. Chair of the Department of Communication, University of Massachusetts at Amherst, he has published widely on communication. His previous works include *Communicating Personally: A Theory of Interpersonal Communication*, with Charles Rossiter (1975); *Communication, Action, and Meaning: The Construction of Social Realities*, with Vernon E. Cronen (1980); and *Development as Communication: A Perspective on India*, with Uma Narula (1986).